Straight Face

For Trevor

Contents

List of Illustrations

Nigel with Elspeth Bryce in *Summer of the Seventeenth Doll*, Johannesburg 1957

Nigel as a reluctant Pantomime Dame, Hornchurch

Nigel in *Try for White* with Marjorie Gordon and Jane Fenn, Cape Town 1959

Page 6

Bruce Palmer at Northampton Repertory Theatre, 1954

Anthea Steed, 1997

Nigel in the homemade beard used to win a part in *Young Winston*

Page 7

As You Like It, with Gorden Kay, USA 1974

Nigel as Prince Albert in *Early Morning*, with Moira Redmond and Shirley Anne Field, 1969

Page 8

Nigel in Joan Littlewood's *Oh, What a Lovely War*, Germany 1964

Joan Littlewood

Nigel as Major Flack in *Privates of Parade*, with Joe Melia, 1977

Page 9

The Millionairess, with Penelope Keith, 1978

Nigel with Paul Eddington and Derek Fowlds for *Yes Prime Minister*

Page 10

Margaret Thatcher presents Nigel and Paul Eddington with an award, 1983

Nigel as C.S. Lewis in *Shadowlands*, with Jane Lapotaire

We Are Not Safe

I came across a peacock butterfly battering its wings against the sitting room window. They're always finding their way into the house and for some reason seem unable to get out again using the same route in reverse. I tried to catch it in my cupped hands but it kept avoiding me. Finally I snared it and, using words of encouragement which I was quite sure it understood, took it to an open window and released it. As it took off to freedom in the direction of the garden, a bird swooped down from nowhere and ate it.

If I've learned anything in life it is that it's never straight-forward. Nothing works out quite as it should or as you'd like it to. When it comes to career or relationships, because we're dealing not just with ourselves but with others, we don't expect things to be plain-sailing. We'd be very foolish if we did. But in matters of health we're very much on our own. When the Mighty Finger points down from above and from the tens of thousands of millions selects YOU, it is deeply shocking to us, and we can't avoid feeling just a little bit let down.

One of the lucky ones, I can boast of a virtually illness-free life. I had my tonsils and adenoids out along with everybody else when I was eight or nine and, after living on jelly for three days, found it not only soothing but addictive. Then, some forty years ago, I went in for treatment on my piles. The recovery period is something I shall never forget. But otherwise my only hospital experience had been as a visitor. Until, that is, the Mighty Finger determined that, at long last, it was my turn.

A year previously Trevor, my partner, and I had been to

the Virgin Islands in the Caribbean for a holiday. It was here that something odd happened to which the later extraordinary sequence of events surely must have been connected.

We'd gone snorkelling. It was one of those perfect days with the sea a bit choppier than we'd have liked for ideal conditions, but the sun and the salt air were making such inroads on the winter cold and persistent cough I'd brought with me from England that they were rapidly becoming a thing of the past. I was feeling healthy and invigorated and a good deal younger than my seventy years.

In an exuberant mood and wearing both mask and flippers, I jumped from the boat; there was a sound of tearing as my bathing costume caught on an unseen nail and, judging by the merriment of those left on the boat, my nakedness was for all to see. Trevor threw me a pair of shorts from the bag, but first I had to remove what was left of the bathing costume. Over the flippers. After a good deal of treading water, some of which I swallowed, and considerable fielding of banter, I managed to achieve this. The next thing was to get the shorts on – again over the flippers. This wasn't easy. Finally, feeling a bit worn out and in need of some privacy, I swam round to the prow of the boat and tried again. Eventually, there was nothing for it but to remove the flippers first, which I did, placing them neatly in the boat. I then slipped on the shorts with very little difficulty, replaced the flippers and, at long last, to the accompaniment of a rousing cheer from the boat, set off in pursuit of the other snorkellers.

The sea was rougher than I'd realised, but I have always been a strong swimmer and was enjoying myself. Ahead, amongst the boulders, I could see the white of the waves breaking on to the tiny beach. I struck out for the shore. It was at that precise moment that I thought I was going to drown. I – who had been brought up by the sea and who, all my life, had looked upon it as a friend rather than as something to fear. The truth was that, probably because of my exertions – I could think of no other reason – I had no air in my lungs. I didn't panic, but allowed the next big wave to take me in and dump me on the beach where, amidst a startled group of onlookers, I heaved and panted as though I was having a heart attack. And, for all I knew, I might have been.

That evening, I was taken to the immaculate island clinic where I was examined by a kindly nurse and doctor who put me on oxygen. The doctor then asked if I'd ever suffered from asthma. 'Many years ago,' I replied. 'When I was a student.' 'It never leaves the body,' he told me. When I got back to England, I saw an asthma specialist who gave me all sorts of tests and put me on antibiotics and an inhaler. In time the breathing improved.

This year, we chose to go again to the same place in the Virgin Islands. It is a sort of paradise on earth and I needed a complete break after seven months playing King Lear for the Royal Shakespeare Company. The holiday was idyllic and there was no recurrence of the breathing problem. On our return I got myself ready to work on a film starring Johnny Depp called *From Hell*. It was to be shot in Prague. The story concerned Jack the Ripper, who, in this version, led a double life as Queen Victoria's personal physician Sir William Gull. The part was a blend of the benign with Grand Guignol and I was greatly looking forward to it. It was the first big budget film I'd been involved with for some time. The twin directors, the Hughes brothers, were extremely likeable, had been over to the house, and even up to Stratford to see *King Lear*, staying until the small hours to have a drink with all the actors at the Dirty Duck. I'd been for costume fittings and had grown some appropriate sideburns.

A week before my departure, the asthmatic symptoms returned. I had to stop in the middle of a game of tennis as I had no breath. I went to my doctor who prescribed a similar treatment to the previous year and sent me for an X-ray.

I didn't seem to improve a great deal during the following

days, which was a bit worrying, but nevertheless, the evening before my flight, I began to pack. At just after six o'clock, I telephoned the surgery to see if the results of my X-ray had come through. Yes, they had, and they were normal. Would I like to speak to my doctor? They rang her extension but she couldn't be traced. 'Dr Watson's here. Would you like to speak to her?' Dr Watson's consulting room looks like a nursery. It is crammed with toys and books to amuse some of her younger patients while she is trying to examine them. She allowed me to speak no more than a couple of sentences on the phone before interrupting. 'Why are you sounding so short of breath? Get into the car at once and come down to the surgery.'

I did as I was told. 'There's no way you're going to Prague in the morning,' she announced after she'd examined me. 'I'm concerned that you might have a blood clot on your lungs. Flying could kill you. Another doctor might allow you to go, but, if he did, he'd be a fool.' My whole world had begun to turn topsy-turvy. I telephoned Trevor there and then, trying to keep the alarm out of my voice, and asked him to contact the Production Office in Prague and explain the situation. He then collected me and drove me to the hospital. The doctor wouldn't allow me to drive.

That evening, I was given all the tests including an ECG and a scan. As the scalpel-sharp Dr Watson had suspected, there was a thrombosis on the arteries leading to each lung. They'd found them in time, and things didn't look all that serious. At least they were treatable. 'Was it the long-haul flights?' I asked the consultant. 'Could easily have been. Sitting in one position for long periods without moving restricts the flow of blood. It's a common cause of thrombosis.' I weighed up the future. The Hughes brothers, Trevor told me, had reacted magnificently and had hastily rescheduled the shoot so that I should have six weeks to recover. That was a relief. Full of warmth and concern, they phoned the hospital from

Prague and reassured me about my continuing in the film at a later date.

The next day, the consultant came to see me. He told me that he'd been looking closer at the scan, trying to determine the cause of the thrombosis. There was an irregularity in my pancreas. It appeared to be a growth. He wanted me to see a specialist. Like all good medical people, he gave me the message loud and clear, straight between the eyes – then left me on my own for the implications to sink in and the imagination to get to work.

They found there was indeed a tumour and the urbane surgeon announced that he would have to remove it. It must have been there before I began work on *King Lear*, growing a bit, hanging around, biding its time. Before any of us could say 'knife', I was being wheeled down to the operating theatre, the anaesthetist was sinking a needle into a vein and, some six and a half hours later, the operation was over. I became dimly aware, as I lay propped against a hillside of pillows, that a large piece of blue sticking plaster which hadn't been there before now crossed my midriff, that there were banks of flowers all round the room, looking uncomfortably like a Mafia funeral, and that I was ravenously hungry. Both the surgeon and the pathologist believed that the 'lethargic' tumour had been removed without leaving a trace. To be sure, I would have to have some radiotherapy, 'Just to knock on the head anything that might be lurking,' said the surgeon with a reassuring grin. I pulled out of the film there and then. The future was too uncertain.

It is three weeks to the day since I had the operation. There is a mighty twelve-inch scar just below my waist which looks as if Jack the Ripper had embarked on personal vengeance at my absence. I'm feeling sore, housebound, impatient to be better but, above all, grateful that, unbeknownst to me, a guardian angel was hovering that evening in late June, guiding Dr Watson to make her incredibly perceptive diagnosis. She passes it off modestly as a 'wild guess'. But it saved my life. Of that I'm certain.

So that's what I mean when I talk about not taking anything for granted, especially as far as health is concerned. We never know what's around the corner. I've started to come to terms with it all now, even though the physical and emotional shock has been considerable. I swim every morning, though not with quite the vigour to which I'm accustomed; I'll work up to that. I walk twice a day – and sleep. Do I sleep! A lot of the rest of the time, in between the injections, blood tests and the intakes of pills, I thank my lucky stars. And I thank Dr Watson. My friends have been concerned and astonished by degrees. The house is bulging with flowers and get-well-soon cards. The rest is up to me.

I pick up a novel and put it down again. I listen to some music. I wander around the garden, conscious that pulling up weeds isn't the most sensible thing I can do. Seamus, our wonderful, exuberant dog, leaps around me totally oblivious of my predicament. We cuddle up together when we have our afternoon nap. Food is a bit of a problem. An awful lot of wind, but gradually it's getting better. At least my appetite is back. If anyone else tells me it's two steps forward and one step back I'll blip them. Someone said to me the other day, 'Now you've got all this leisure time, you should really take advantage of it, deadhead the roses, enjoy the summer, doze off in the sun (what sun?) – write a book . . .'

I

Best Love

'You ought to come if you can.' My mother's voice was clipped and un-English after so many years away. She wasn't sounding very agitated. I suppose it was because she didn't want to frighten me. My father had suffered two massive strokes in quick succession and I was being summoned to the death-bed.

I barely listened as she chuntered on about the family bits and pieces. I should be seeing them myself soon enough, though some I hardly knew, others I'd never met. 'I'll do my best,' I told her, wondering where on earth I was going to find the air fare. 'Oh good,' she said, as if I'd agreed to go to tea. 'We'll all come out to the airport to meet you so let us know when you'll be arriving. Oh, and don't forget to bring your bathing costume.' The line from Cape Town was as clear as if she'd been phoning from down the road. I replaced the receiver and stared bleakly at the wallpaper in front of me, not wanting to make a move.

Getting a flight wasn't easy. It was early summer over there and everything was booked solid. Luckily, the next afternoon I discovered a bucket-shop over a furrier's in Bond Street, of all places, and managed to get a cheap seat on a plane leaving the following day by telling them it was an emergency. That evening, I phoned home with the details, ironed half a dozen shirts, packed a hold-all and went to bed early.

The journey wasn't direct. It was 1968 and, apartheid being still very much in evidence, there were several countries over which we weren't allowed to fly. We zig-zagged across Africa, stopping only for interminable unloadings and refuellings.

The aircraft was bulging with humanity in all its forms. I was somewhere near the back with not nearly enough leg-room. There seemed to be a high proportion of children on board, and I had the misfortune to be sitting next to the most repugnant. Sleep was out of the question, nor could I settle to my book.

As we began the approach to Lourenço Marques, our penultimate stop, I could see through the port-hole that we were flying over a shanty town. The tin shacks were crammed together, giving no privacy. They were makeshift and rusted. We were flying low enough to see some of the people going about their daily lives, few taking notice of the gigantic plane skimming over their heads. I saw a child, naked as the day he was born, glance upwards at us, shielding his eyes from the early morning sun while a mongrel defecated in the sand at his feet. The picture haunts me still. It had been six years since I had last been in Africa. I suppose I'd forgotten what the poverty was like.

We were to spend the night in an hotel and carry on to Cape Town the following morning. The delay was unfortunate but I could do nothing about it. At the air terminal, I climbed on to the coach with the others, our luggage roped precariously to the roof, and off we set for the town.

Our first stop was the railway station, for some of the passengers were making their way by train to destinations in the Transvaal and Natal. Porters clambered over the roof to hurl precious suitcases on to the pavement below whilst the owners dismounted. To my alarm, I suddenly saw my hold-all flash by the window and rushed out to retrieve it.

As I was about to re-board the bus, a small, bare-footed boy of about six or seven, arms as thin as toothpicks, wearing a grubby shirt and a pair of ragged shorts which hung to just below his knees, held on by string braces, thrust a copy of the Johannesburg *Sunday Times* under my nose. It was an old friend. It would be fun sitting in the hotel leafing through the endless furniture advertisements in search of news. And there was the comic section, the Katzenjammer Kids and Blondie and Dagwood syndicated from the States in garish colour. I bought a copy and, keeping my hold-all beside me on the seat as the bus moved off, looked around me.

So this was Lourenço Marques. I'd never had the time nor the money to visit it in the past but, back in the Fifties, friends would holiday there and regale me with stories about how they'd met the young Aga Khan and his friends at a party, the fun they'd all had in fabulous 'L.M.' Nothing I could see through the window of the bus quite matched up to their descriptions of the town but then, to be fair, I wasn't in the mood.

Even when the windows look out on to papaya trees and exotic climbers, there can be something desolate about an hotel bedroom and this, with its insipid silk-screen prints and pastel curtains, was no exception. I whistled through the *Sunday Times* after lunch. Mostly local news. Had there been another war in Europe, I doubt you'd have known. The pages were dominated by 'MUST GO' offers of shoe polish and deodorants at slashed prices. I glanced idly at the social section in case I saw a face I recognised. It was then that I noticed the date. The paper was three weeks old.

I decided to have a wander round. I'd got no more than a few yards beyond the hotel entrance when, with half-a-dozen more copies draped over his arm, there was the same boy with the string braces. He had the nerve to try to sell me another so I gave him a piece of my mind. He lifted his huge, reproachful eyes like a chastened puppy. No sooner had he disappeared round the corner than I began to feel ashamed. After all, he was only trying to make a living, out there on the streets every day, in all weathers. Broke as I was, I could buy every one of the papers he had left and not notice the difference. I gave chase. The boy was nowhere to be seen. I ran to the crossroads and looked left and right but it was as though he had been swallowed up. I became obsessed with the need to find him.

All afternoon, I trudged the pavements barely noticing the town about me. I was a man with a mission: guilt, if you like. Rich white man, poor black child. Oh, my new English conscience, how it hurt. I gave myself a distant target, eleven p.m. If I hadn't found him by then I'd get myself something to eat, but not before. I must have walked for miles. The sun began to get low on the horizon. Soon the street lights would be coming on.

Conveniently, the deadline arrived as I was passing a café. I was reluctant to go in for that would have been to concede defeat but, through a gap in the curtains, I could see there were three or four couples inside and the food looked appetising. I went in. Half way through my meal, the door of the café opened and who should come in, still clutching most of the copies of the *Sunday Times* he'd had earlier, but String Braces. Without allowing him the opportunity of selling me yet another paper, I beckoned him over and, leaving only enough money to pay for my meal, emptied the contents of my pockets into his hands. He must have thought I was mad, and in a way I was. I was trembling and emotional, fully aware that people were looking at me oddly.

The South African Airways trip from Lourenço Marques to Cape Town was a great improvement on what had been on offer on the charter flight. No whining children and more leg-room, to begin with. The crew had that humourless, slightly vacant look I knew so well, while the passengers appeared bronzed and relaxed, toying with their complimentary cocktails and dipping into the in-flight magazine. Jaunty piano-accordion music was being piped through the cabin, reminding me of evenings in Pretoria with everybody round the *braaivleis* drinking Castle Beer and speaking in Afrikaans while I felt a total stranger. I felt a stranger again, my British passport tucked into an inside pocket, and my face a little grey from insufficient sleep and yet another disappointing English summer.

We were crossing the Karoo, mile after mile of nothing except the occasional *kopje* incongruously sticking up in the stark desert. It is said that once Africa gets into your bloodstream you can never get it out. You're hooked for life. When a landscape so barren and unwelcoming can make one ache to be down there amongst it revelling in its majesty and its silence, I know it to be true.

'You look older than your years,' pronounced my mother, bending forward and proffering a cheek for me to kiss. 'Thanks a lot, Mum.' I was disturbed to notice how badly she was limping. In 1957, an incompetently performed operation on her arthritic knee had left her semi-crippled. Her face was more lined now, the harsh sun doing her skin no favours. The rest of the family was there too. Jan and John, the twins, and Sheila. I think we'd all put on a bit of weight, John a bit thinner on top, Jan exuberant and dizzy, Sheila slow-moving, quieter and more reserved, the many children and grandchildren staring at me as if I had come from outer space.

John drove. My mother was in the front seat because she needed room, ducking in backside first, hauling in the offending leg afterwards, the pain showing in her face. 'Dad's just about the same, Nigel,' said John, driving more cautiously now than when he was younger. Then, with an upward inflection he said, 'I think you'll see quite a change in him, you know.' In those few moments I think I liked John better than at any other time since we were children. He seemed to understand what I was feeling.

The journey was unnerving. So much was familiar, quite a bit was changed. 'Robots' where there used to be a stop sign, buildings missing, new hotels – and the mountain, oh God, the mountain, how I loved it with a deep, deep passion. How often, in those early, poverty-stricken days when first I went back to England, did I dream of it or lie awake with the thyme-like perfume of the *fynbos* in my nostrils. And there it was in front of me. In my foolishness, I wanted to stop the car, jump out and throw my arms around it. John at the wheel was proudly ticking off the new improvements, my dear mother murmuring the names of the shops, street names, products on advertising hoardings, numbers of houses, anything that caught her eye.

Through Oranjezicht in the gardens and on upwards towards the low-lying saddle separating Table Mountain and Lion's Head, Kloof Nek, the steep road wider than before, the little houses with their tin roofs and verandahs, and, always in our sights, the mountain. I tried ducking down low in my seat to see whether I could catch a glimpse of the tiny cable car inching its way towards the summit, only half-listening to the overlapping fragments from my family, wanting to weep with joy at being home once more. 'Look, Nigel!' from my brother John.

There below was the breathtaking sweep of Camps Bay where I had spent my childhood, the sea an unreal blue, the breakers tickling the edge of the white sand, and, to our left, the majestic sprawl of mountain known as the Twelve Apostles dipping their robes into the ice-cold Atlantic. Down past the little cluster of shops, the palm trees lined up along the front like on the Riviera. So huge now. Could it really be possible that I had watched them being planted? One stormy winter, the great breakers burst across the front, half-drowning Mr Isaacs the chemist on the other side of the road and ruining his supplies of Sanatogen and suntan lotions. The following week, they had to replace the trees which had been swept away. Such excitement. Round the sharp corner into Victoria Road, and up past the police station. There it was. Our old house with its shingled roof and the pergola hung with Golden Shower. It hadn't changed.

Dad was propped up against a mountain of pillows. Despite the warnings, I was totally unprepared for what confronted me. To begin with, I barely recognised him. His teeth lay at some distance from his mouth in a mug on the bedside table.

He was paralysed down one side of his body. The bedroom was Dad's old consulting room, for he had been a GP. Now he was the patient and my mother the nurse. I kissed the top of his head and babbled something about how wonderful it was to be back, and to see the family again, how good he was looking, the weather, the rain I'd left behind me in London, my flat in Notting Hill Gate which he'd visited, anything I could think of. My mother and John stood in the doorway and listened. I held his strong hand in my own. Finally he spoke to me slowly, and out of the corner of his mouth.

'How are you getting on, Nigel?' Significantly he was asking not about me but about the progress I was making. 'Oh, fine, Dad, fine!' I lied. Though I had a small television job to return to so that my stay in Cape Town would be limited, this meant little to him for it was some years before television would be introduced into South Africa. Generally speaking, my career was at a low ebb and, though I'd kept it from my family, I had been doing domestic cleaning to raise a few bob for the rent.

'You're on the verandah,' my mother told me. I was grateful for the release as much as anything. 'See you later, Dad.' I left him with John who always had a special relationship with him. As I closed the door, I could hear John speaking to him gently, sure of his ground.

Alone at last while my mother went off to get the tea, I sat on the bed gazing out at the view I knew so well. Above, I could hear my sister Janette and her husband Dennis crashing about with cries of 'Andrea, I'm not going to tell you that again!' When we had all left home, the house had been divided in two, the main staircase blocked off and an independent one erected for access at the back. Jan and Dennis lived with their family where once our bedrooms had been, while my mother slept downstairs in the old dining room and my father in his consulting room.

The smell of the sea drifted upwards to where I was sitting. I wanted time to absorb it all, to catch up with what I'd chosen to eliminate from my life, to wallow a bit in the comforts of nostalgia, to escape down to the beach and be as I was when I was a child, watching my father going off for his early morning swim, my mother walking without a limp, the house one and not divided, with the terrible kids racing all over it as we had often done, Austin, the dog, in hot pursuit, barking his head off.

John went back to work, my mother brought the tea, a selection of Pyatt's No. 1 Assorted biscuits and sat with me. To our left, some half a mile out across the bay, was the rounded rock which looked like a baker's oven, giving the name Bakoven to the area. I'd never ventured close to it, but, as a child, John had investigated it countless times in his boat. To me it was just a landmark. The sun was at its height now, the light blindingly clear, the details sharp. Over the bay, the seagulls circled and settled, and I could see the shiny tips of brown seaweed as the tide withdrew.

My mother filled me in about my father's sudden decline. I was astonished that she was nursing him herself and suggested a day and night nurse but she was adamant that she could manage, so I dropped the subject.

Lena, our wonderful Cape coloured maid, came in to say hello. She'd been with the family off and on for nearly forty years and hardly looked a day older than when my mother first took her on at the age of nineteen. I gave her a hug and asked how her mother was. 'Fine, Master Nigel.' And her daughter, Rachel? 'Fine, Master Nigel.'

'She's a good girl, Lena,' announced my mother after she'd gone. 'Always very loyal.' We talked a bit about the family, how wonderfully supportive Janette had been, minding Dad when my mother had to go out. John too. Always happy to come over and see Dad, though he and his family lived some way off on the other side of the mountain. And Sheila and Ernie, her husband, over at weekends and on the phone most evenings.

I couldn't help feeling guilty that I hadn't been around over the crisis. 'Well, at least you're here now,' said my mother. In all the years I'd been away, she'd sent an air letter every week, scarcely ever missing, and never failed to jog my conscience when I forgot or had been too busy or too lazy to reply. It had been seventeen years since my farewell party in this selfsame house before I'd left for London to pursue a career in the theatre. Like Ulysses tempted by the sirens, I'd had to shut from my mind all thoughts of paradise – yet, now I was back, I could feel only detached as if I didn't belong.

The days dragged by with my father making little progress apart from the fact that he'd become incontinent. My mother worked round the clock to look after him and the strain was beginning to tell. She and I bickered. It came out of our anxiety, that I knew, but we had always been so close in the past and it was painful to find how far we had drifted apart.

One morning, I'd taken myself down to the little beach in front of Charlie Booth's house, not too far away so that I could be within calling distance. I'd handed my mother a blue towel and said that, if she needed me, she was to hang it over the wall by the front door and I would come running.

The day was clear, the sound of the sea lapping against the granite rocks was soporific and I found myself drifting into a blissful doze in the warm sunshine. Suddenly something woke me and made me look back at the house. Blue towel! I raced up the path towards the front door where my mother was waiting. 'Dad's had another stroke.' 'I'll phone for an ambulance,' I said. 'No.' I could hardly believe my ears. 'You can't cope any longer, Mum,' I insisted. She took my hand. 'He's a doctor, Nigel, and no fool. If he goes to hospital, he'll know he's going to die.' Dad had been a terrible patient. When his own doctor had prescribed pills – 'TAKE ONE WITH MEALS THREE TIMES A DAY' – Dad would gulp them all down at once. When I remonstrated with him he told me to mind my own business. Now there was no time for argument. I took the law into my own hands and phoned for an ambulance.

They carried him carefully down the precipitous front steps, wrapping a blanket around him so he shouldn't fall out. We started off. I held his hand the whole way to Groote Schuur Hospital as he struggled to get free of his bindings. It was hard for me not to remember him as a younger man with an eye for the girls. If John were to bring a girlfriend home, in a matter of seconds Dad would have managed to get her sitting on his knee. Not many years before, my mother had nearly divorced him, she said, when she found out that he'd been going out with his receptionist and had bought her a car. He was then in his mid-seventies. There was hope for us all.

The orderlies handled the stretcher roughly when we arrived at the hospital. 'Be careful with him. He's a very sick man!' I snapped, then, having no option but to leave him in their hands, went along to Reception to register him. By the time I'd found my way to the ward, it appeared that my father had undergone a miraculous recovery for as I turned the corner, there he was sitting up in bed, chuckling mischievously and holding the hand of an attractive nurse who was perched beside him on the white sheets. At eighty-six, Dad was incorrigible.

The days passed. Each evening I went with the family to visit him, though I was never alone with him long enough to say the things I wanted to say. I was half way through a cruel dream which, of necessity, had to be short-lived. My family, my old home, the mountain, the sea – Africa – none of it seemed real. I'd managed to catch up with a few friends, but had been in no mood for frivolous celebration, visited a few favourite haunts, but now, to my consternation, there wasn't much time left. Of one thing I was certain. Never again would I see my father alive. We'd not been close. I think I'd always been a disappointment to him. Choosing to leave University before I'd completed my course in order to become an actor was a bad move, something he never forgave. Through the years, his greetings to me had been squeezed on to the last eighth of the air letter sent by my mother. 'Dad wants to add a word, so I'll shut up.' They were brief, unrevealing words and always ended, 'No more space. Best Love, Dad.'

There were three large department stores in Cape Town in those days, Fletcher and Cartwrights, Garlicks and Stuttafords, which had a handsome restaurant with restrained decor, huge floral displays and comfortable chairs. I telephoned my old friend Sonny Cohen and asked whether I could take him to lunch. I should have known better. 'No. I'll take *you*.' Sonny had never married but had a string of beautiful young girls he liked to escort to concerts, art exhibitions or to the theatre. He and some gorgeous female went to every first night. He ran a mail order business from an office in Diamond House where my father used to have consulting rooms, so he knew him well. Sonny had a mane of flowing white hair which earned him the nickname 'Silver Fox', and a handshake which was both manly and painful. He was one of the kindest, most generous people I've ever met.

Sonny listened as I poured out my sad tale. I don't know how I would have coped had it not been for him. Each day, he'd arrive in his car to collect me. We'd go for a drive. My mother resented these constant visits and the fact that I was being snatched away when there was so very little time left before my return to England. I tried to explain that I was desperate for someone to talk to. It was tactless of me, of course, and she was hurt. Then, all of a sudden, it was time to pack.

Matron had my father up early as my flight left mid-morning, gave him clean pyjamas and put his teeth in. He was all ready for me when I arrived. He seemed a bit better, I thought, though the effects of the stroke were still very apparent. I sat on the edge of the bed, my eyes on the clock, and we spoke of this and that. The moment arrived. 'Well,

Dad, I have to go now,' I heard myself saying. 'Where are you going?' 'Back to England, Dad.' 'What are you going there for?' he wanted to know. 'I live there.' 'Do you?' He seemed genuinely interested. At that moment he gave a strange moan. I wondered if he might be having another stroke. He began to raise his arms, seeming to be staring right through me. 'Oh God!' I remember thinking. 'He's going to embrace me!' – not something I would ever have expected from my father. I leaned forward obligingly, but suddenly, summoning huge effort, he shoved me face downwards on to the bed.

When I picked myself up, I saw what had happened: he had been trying to catch a glimpse of a nurse who had been going through the ward and I'd been in the way. I got up and made my way to the door. I turned to wave, but he wasn't looking. His eyes were on the ankles of that young nurse with the ash-blonde hair as her heels tip-tapped down the long linoleum corridor.

On the way to the airport, I told my mother what had happened, saying it was a wonderful memory of my father to take away with me. But she snapped back, 'He wasn't himself. He didn't know what he was doing.'

On the plane back, mercifully flying directly to London for some reason I can no longer remember, I wrote a poem. I discovered it last year going through some papers in my desk:

HOME
To come home after years
and find
a childhood father cruelly changed
nursed day and night
a waiting family no longer young.

To come home after years
and find
the Cape I ached for in the twilight north

mountain blue and sea and sky
To look and feel a stranger
. . . a heavy heart.

To come home after years
and find
the morning beaches crammed with wives
eyes closed, minds blank, they bask content
the coloureds looking on.

To come home after years
and find
much changed yet not enough
an arrogance in the bleached white streets.
Home, home, home, home, home –
Just a word.

2

Spes Bona

One glorious summer afternoon at a tennis party, in the days when they still had such things, the shortish man with the bald head who would one day be my father gazed across the court at the girl with the soft dark eyes swinging her racquet and dashing about in an attempt to look as if she knew what she was doing, and made up his mind that she was for him. He discovered during the tea break that her name was Rosemary Rice, the daughter of a Coventry doctor, that her mother was an artist and that she was seventeen years his junior. Equally inquisitive, Rosemary had found out that her opponent, the red-faced man of forty whose attention seemed to be so little focused on tennis, was, like her father, a general practitioner, Charles Barnard Hawthorne by name. He hailed from Walsgrave on the outskirts of Coventry, one of four children – the others being girls – a public schoolboy educated at Epsom and Clare College, Cambridge, who had served in France during the First World War as a captain in the Royal Army Medical Corps.

His father having died when he was young, he had been brought up by his mother and three doting sisters, Mabel, Olive and Georgie. He grew into a sturdy young man who was used to being spoilt. Many years later, my mother admitted that she hadn't loved him but had been flattered by the intensity of his attentions. She was, she told me, used to having admirers – there'd been a Geoffrey, and a Leslie who smoked a pipe – yet the idea of this mature and stable man as the father of her children appealed to her. She made her choice. On her twenty-third birthday she walked down the aisle of Coventry Cathedral on his arm, wearing one of those hopelessly unbecoming dresses of the period – a sort of sack tied in the middle – the veil slung like a tennis net across her dark brown eyes.

It wasn't, to be sure, a marriage made in heaven, my father being used to having his own way, and my mother, having left school early to tend to her parents, knowing precious little of the big wide world around her. Eager to do the right thing lest she upset my father, she never achieved full independence until after his death many years later. For their honeymoon, they went motoring in the Welsh hills. In thick fog a car travelling in the opposite direction ran into them round a sharp bend. The driver was killed, my mother catapulted unhurt on to a grassy bank, my father losing some of his pride and the tip of a finger. For a good number of years after this, he dressed only with her assistance, while his piano playing was placed in abeyance until such time as he might recover sufficiently to continue.

The young couple moved into The Limes, a sturdy Edwardian house on the Binley Road, my father entered a practice not far away at Gosford Green and awaited the birth of his family. Sheila came first, I next and finally the twins, Janette and John. All within four years. My mother was going to have her hands full.

I never knew my father's parents for both had died before I was born, but at home their varnished portraits were on the walls above me, catching the light as I descended the staircase. Above me, Dad's mother Sarah, like a Gaiety Girl in her flamboyant hat, substantial bosom and reigned-in waist, to the right, my grandfather – less confrontational, more conservative – sitting formally posed and formally dressed at his desk. There were portraits, too, of their own parents, looking like something out of *Cranford* – she wizened in a frilly bonnet and he stern and forbidding with a starched shirtfront. Great-grandfather had been an itinerant parson who had ventured from the West Country selling God and elixirs to anyone who would have them, and wound up in the Midlands where the family had settled. I only wish that I could elaborate more on my father's history, but winkling information out of him was impossible. On the slightest suggestion of a probe the Hippocratic Oath barricades went up and anyone but a nincompoop would know that there was absolutely no point in persisting. Were you to bury him up to his chin in sand he would never divulge his secrets. My mother's side of the family was another kettle of fish.

Hers was a family of major social conscience. Elizabeth Garrett Anderson, one of the first women doctors in the country, was a second cousin, as indeed was Millicent Garrett Fawcett, President of the Women's Suffrage Society. Mother's aunt Amy married Jack Badley and together they founded Bedales co-educational school, an innovative and somewhat shocking concept in its day, which went on to become one of the most progressive teaching establishments in the country. Her mother Elsie, my grandmother, having graduated from the Royal Female School of Art, was taken on by her sister as the art mistress. Charles Rice, who taught mathematics, took a shine to the art mistress and they married. They had two children: a son killed in the Great War and my mother, Rosemary. Their marriage drifted over the years through various changes of circumstance, including Charles becoming a doctor, but sadly without a serious bond of affection Charles and Elsie separated in 1931, three years after I was born.

My mother's uncle, Edmund Garrett, was to eclipse all those strange and intriguing relatives. Consumptive, handsome and romantic, he was sent by the *Pall Mall Gazette*, where he worked as a reporter, to South Africa for his health. He became editor of the *Cape Times*, taking on all comers including his long-term friend and adversary, Cecil Rhodes. In a climate of jingoism, his was a refreshingly liberal presence, ambitious, courageous and humane. Eventually elected to the Cape Parliament, he used his influence wisely until consumption bested him and he returned to England to die.

Here at my home in Hertfordshire, in what we call the parlour, stands a highly polished bureau. At first glance it isn't particularly distinguished in any way. There are two pronounced cracks on the lid which don't seem to have worsened through the years and, to my mind at least, add to its charm, and the ornate brass handles, or what's left of them, seem to have been added at a later date and are not quite in keeping with the rest of it. The trim around the base is of a different wood from the top and recently has come adrift from its moorings. I keep meaning to stick it on again. It doesn't appear very English. There's a Dutch look to it. Its previous owners are reputed to have been Cecil John Rhodes and Rudyard Kipling, though as the latter was only a visitor to South Africa it seems unlikely that he would have encumbered himself with such a hefty piece of furniture. It had then passed to Edmund, my grandmother, and eventually to me. It stands there foursquare, somewhere between fond heritage and a rebuke, a testimony to a grander ambition than mine could ever be.

The home we had in the Binley Road was pleasant enough and there was a garden at the back where we children could play, but my father had become increasingly concerned about our proximity to the traffic. An academic friend of his, Gilbert Hutchinson, had been offered a University post – in Cape Town of all places – and managed to infect my father with some of the enthusiasm he himself felt about emigrating to the sunshine and fresh air of this land of promise. History was beginning to repeat itself. In those days, everybody went on the mail boat. In Great Uncle Edmund's day, the fare had been £56 – now it was a little more – and the journey took two weeks. Dad persuaded Hutchinson to let him tag along. Just to see what it was like.

My father was captivated by the place. He bought a house and a practice from a Dr Lester and came back to fetch us. It must have been galling for my despairing grandmother having to travel to Liverpool to wave goodbye to her beloved daughter Rosemary, particularly when her new hat blew off and went under a tram. Here we were emigrating to the same part of the world which her brother Edmund had so loved. It was a coincidence to which I don't suppose my father had given a second thought. He didn't have much time for Mrs Rice, as he would insist on calling her. In any case, he was a Hawthorne, his wife was now Mrs Hawthorne and all their children were Hawthornes. The Garretts were from the other side of the family.

As it turned out, the separation was not to be a long one, for, a year later, my grandmother was to join us in South Africa.

We sailed on the *Ceramic* in August 1932 with everything we possessed down in the hold: the grand piano, wardrobes, corner cupboards, a grandfather clock, a massive walnut sideboard, a dining table with adjustable leaves, my father's family portraits, my mother's collection of Crown Derby and Wedgwood, her crockery and cutlery, even the bedstead on which she and my father slept. On our arrival, in the unaccustomed glare of this brand new world, we paused briefly at the Hotel Cecil (after Cecil Rhodes, who else?) in Newlands while, several miles away in the centre of town, the furniture was being positioned and the portraits hung on the landing above the staircase, easily the best feature of 80, Queen Victoria Street, the house which was to be our home. It was a large and ugly pile, depressingly dark, with a rickety verandah in the colonial style and some steep steps leading up from the pocket handkerchief patches on either side of the path to a front door fitted with stained glass panels to let in some badly-needed light. Wrapped round the front like a mangy boa constrictor was a rampant and thorny bougainvillaea, coated with grime and eager for the sun. It never flowered because it never saw it – the house faced the wrong way. At the back, which paradoxically received the full blast of the sun, was a derelict conservatory containing wire hanging baskets with nothing in them and a few parched ferns in terracotta pots. Instead of glazing there were slats of whitewashed wood running from the house to the outside wall, ideal for young children to crawl across when their parents' attention was elsewhere.

Across the road were the public gardens. When the Dutch had settled at the Cape in 1652, a large vegetable patch had been planted to supply ships travelling to and from the East, the centre of the spice trade. The Cape was nicknamed 'The Tavern of the Seas'. Now the gardens were purely botanical. There were low ponds crammed with indolent goldfish and waterlilies, an equestrian statue to the heroes killed at Delville Wood, a clutch of steamy hot-houses where you could admire the tropical plants, an aviary, a museum and an art gallery with not a Rembrandt nor a Gaugin in sight, while further down was the public library, the cathedral and the House of Assembly where Great Uncle Edmund thirty years previously had spent so many hours in debate. With all these places of interest crammed into so picturesque a setting we could never fear boredom, and the generous spread of the gardens with their wide gravel paths proved an ideal location for Nurse Rodwell to exercise her young charges, the twins in a double pram, Sheila and I on reins to prevent our straying too near the water.

We'd arrived in the spring. The oak trees in Government Avenue were coming into leaf, the squirrels romped, the doves cooed and all over the mountain slopes the wild flowers blazed with glory. When the turbulent South-Easter descended on the town to slam doors and rattle roofs, it announced its arrival with a billowing 'tablecloth' which tumbled spectacularly down the face of Table Mountain. What a view we had from our bedroom window! Sheila was the lucky one. She was old enough to take in all the details. I was only three and a half and could hardly be expected to, while the twins would have been in another room gurgling away in their cots. As the months and years went by I would catch up and grow to appreciate the beauty all around me, discovering a place which would haunt me for the rest of my life.

Our family had come to Darkest Africa only to realise that it was, in fact, from Darkest England that we'd come. Here, as we were to learn, the air was clean and invigorating, the sun shone from a clear blue sky rather than playing peek-a-boo behind threatening rain clouds and, sleepy hollow though it was with its colonial affectations, its Victorian trellis-work, the hansom cabs and leisurely pace, the Mother City at the southernmost tip of the African continent seemed a bit like paradise. 'The fairest cape in all the circumference of the earth,' declared explorer Sir Francis Drake. With his experience of travel, he probably knew what he was talking about.

3
School

You're a wonderful fellah
Your legs are so yellah
You swim like a swallah
And dive like
a hake.

(Brother Quinlan)

I went to three schools in all. The first, St Cyprian's, was way up on the slopes of the mountain in Oranjezicht, with the bay somewhere down there, hidden by the trees and roofs. St Cyp's was for girls, unless you happened to be enrolled, as I was aged five, in the kindergarten, where a glorious time could be had spattering sheets of cartridge paper with poster paints and emptying the sand-pit all over the highly-polished parquet floor.

First thing, Miss Dushek would arrive in form-hugging tunic with black stockings to match to give us drill, with a staccato no-nonsense piano accompaniment. 'Astride, together, astride, together – step, hop, hop, hop – step, hop, hop – one, two, three, hop, – one, two, THREE!' Diminutive gymnasts flailed about doing their level best to keep up, not knowing quite what was expected. While it's over sixty-five years since I one, two, three-ed, Miss Dushek's jingles are as familiar to me now as if they had been international standards.

The school stood back in substantial grounds dotted with spindly pines, with the added attraction, just outside the main gates, of a neighbour's garden which boasted a loquat tree, the branches of which obligingly hung over the pavement well within the reach of agile *Kinder*. We'd guzzle the sweet fruit, caressing with our tongues the shiny, rather sensuous stones before spitting them out into the gutter. Deep in our heart of hearts we knew that we were stealing, and there was always the thrill of getting caught.

That summer, I was Michael, the youngest of the Darlings in Barrie's *Peter Pan* – my very first play, and what an adventure that was. Out there on the school lawn and in full view of the audience, we had to assemble Wendy's house from a collection of brightly-coloured stools borrowed from the classroom. I made rather a hash of it first time round and confused the issue, putting reds where there should have been yellows, greens instead of purples, sowing the seed in the minds of canny observers that a practical streak might never be my forte. I doubled as the crocodile, seeing my way with difficulty through my mask due to the rows of jagged teeth. Halves of tennis balls were my eyes, while my dyed green stockings afforded little or no protection against the pine needles, as I crawled by making menacing noises in my throat to instil fear. At a given moment, I had to remember to set off a large kitchen alarm clock concealed about my person which, at each of our two performances, earned a smattering of applause from the assembled parents which was oddly satisfying.

My sixth birthday arrived. I was encouraged to tune in to the wireless that afternoon. To my astonishment, I heard my name mentioned on the programme. Me? Was I dreaming? How on earth did they know that it was my birthday? My parents feigned innocence. I was instructed by the radio 'Uncle' to make my way to the airing cupboard where I would find something to 'surprise' me. When I opened the door, I couldn't see it at first, but then I did. Curled up on a pile of towels was a mountainous black cat. Seized by the emotion of the moment, I hugged her to me, which was probably a mistake as the wretched thing gave me ring-worm, and that, I'm very much afraid, was that. The cat was removed from the premises to an unknown destination. In spite of everything, though, I think it would be true to say that I was on a small cloud of happiness.

This was partly due to Miss Wood, my Form One teacher. I don't suppose she ever knew how hopelessly in love with her I was. On St Cyprian's Day every year there was a procession down Government Avenue involving the whole school dressed in white, for a service in St George's Cathedral. Two of the youngest were selected to march behind the head girl, who was carrying aloft a banner bearing the school emblem. We lucky ones clutched ribbons attached by small safety pins to the shoulders of her dress, which was considered a great honour.

After all the excitement had died down, Miss Wood took me on one side, said she'd watched me in the procession, and would I like to be her page boy as she was getting married? Try and stop me! Torn as I was between pride and jealousy, I could think of nothing else for weeks. Then I got mumps. Mumps! I was in isolation for the rest of the summer. Just about everything swelled up – under my arms, between my legs – I looked like Fatty Arbuckle. To me it was the end of the world. It certainly was the end as far as the wedding was concerned. One day a letter arrived signed Elizabeth Mitchell-Heggs with a photograph of the newly-weds, not at the ceremony – she was too tactful for that – but suntanned at the net in their tennis gear. There was never a happier looking couple.

Some twenty years later, after I'd become an actor and was on tour in what used to be Southern Rhodesia, I was at a reception where, quite by chance, I was once again to hear the name Mitchell-Heggs. I asked to be introduced to the dimly-familiar man nursing a drink. 'Are you by any chance related to Elizabeth who used to be my teacher?' 'She was my wife,' he replied. 'She died on Friday after a long illness. Cancer.' And he moved away.

For the Christmas holidays, the hottest time of the year, my parents had rented 'Verdun', a corrugated iron bungalow at Bakoven, which was beyond Camps Bay. A tiny beach supplied my father, even at low tide, with just sufficient water to immerse himself. The sea was icy. Three strokes out, three back, a gargle, some stretching exercises on the beach – touching the toes, or near enough – and ending up with a run between the rocks with Austin at his heels. It was a daily routine before breakfast. Austin wasn't ours. He was a friendly mongrel, most like a border collie. Dad called him a black and white 'Seldom', because you seldom saw another dog like him. We all grew to love him, and it soon became clear that he preferred being with us to going home to his rightful owner.

Already the little beach was casting its spell on the whole family. The smell of the sea air, the sound of the waves slapping against the rocks, the ebb and flow of the tides and, straight ahead, the magnificent view with Lion's Head thrusting up into the intense blue sky through the commotion of the surf at its feet, made us all long to be here permanently rather than in the stuffy confines of Queen Victoria Street.

St George's was next, the grammar school attached to the cathedral, that grimly forbidding pile at the foot of the avenue. Disappointingly, I was denied a place in the choir for it carried with it a stigma, a small reduction in fees. It would not have been appropriate had word got out that Dr Hawthorne's son was being educated at a cut rate.

Mrs Sohr was a dumpy little sadist known as 'Auntie' who had little or no patience with unruly boys. She looked cuddly and wasn't. Not in any way. In later years, cuts were things applied to salary or to scripts when they were over-long, but in those far-off days they were the swish of the cane, ruler or strap. Few things, in my opinion, can be quite so agonising or humiliating as bending over in front of your classmates to have your bottom whacked.

One day, 'Auntie' invited us to take part in a competition to test our ability to draw. We were to sketch whatever we wanted. 'Anything, Miss?' She flashed a rare smile. 'Anything.' Never someone who found it easy to make up his mind, I sneaked a glance at some of the other boys' efforts, mostly mundane things like sailing boats and aeroplanes, before choosing to divide my page very carefully into sections using my ruler, then, in what I hoped to be an original and imaginative way, illustrate in comic-script terms the story of Red Riding Hood. 'Auntie' beat me in front of the class. She was like that.

It was obligatory to learn the second language, Afrikaans. We learned it as children, because we had to. We read novels and poetry and wrote essays, but had little occasion to speak it. At St George's Grammar School Percy Piek did his utmost to steer its intricacies in our resistant direction. '*R-r-r-reenboogvlerties!*' he'd sing out. 'R-r-r-ainbow little wings!' And, suiting the action to the word, he would cavort around the classroom flapping his arms, looking in his black academic gown more like a bat than the butterfly he was attempting to emulate. That was one word at least that we'd never forget. As well as being no stranger to flamboyance, Piek had a filthy temper. Also, he could be very unpredictable. With the agility of an athlete, he would spring suddenly and for no apparent reason on to the lid of a desk at the rear of the class, then, hitching his gown about his knees, creep stealthily across the lids of the desks in front of him until, with a cry straight out of the primeval jungle, he'd pounce upon an unsuspecting unfortunate from behind, raining blow after blow upon him at random with demonic ferocity until he could go on no more and subsided with exhaustion. Shortly after I left St George's, I heard that they'd made him headmaster.

Camps Bay, in those days, was little more than a seaside village, a modest cluster of houses, three or four shops like Mrs Forbes's haberdashery, Sher's the greengrocers and Lambert's

Tearoom, where you could get scones plastered with quince jam and a dollop of cream. Along the road was the pavilion, a shabby, sun-bleached structure where the concentration of the sun had blistered away stretches of white paint to reveal beneath the naked wood surrounding the glass. The birds would make it worse, their beaks finding their way beneath the congealed paint as they searched for titbits. There was a tea-room at street level where we could buy cold drinks, and down below was a huge concrete swimming pool alive with small fish, for at high tide it was washed by the ice-cold Atlantic. It attracted few bathers for, in addition to the temperature, lurking in its depths were hazards such as slimy, slippery seaweed, razor-sharp shells, and concealed rocks, lethal with barnacles.

An added detraction was the seemingly limitless quantity of used French letters which the currents contrived to lure into secret pockets of rocks, a source of endless delight to small children accustomed to balloons at party time. Public-spirited grown-ups who passed by and saw us stretched full-length at the side of the pool trying to net these strange devices would frown disapprovingly, though the reason for their displeasure was never voiced. Perhaps it was too shocking. Their wagging fingers told us we were doing wrong. Far preferable were the heated public swimming baths just across the main road. I've never enjoyed swimming in fresh water as much as salt. Here, the pool was heated sea water, chlorinated, and there was a roof making swimming possible in all weathers.

Further up the Victoria Road, beyond the be-flagged police station, was another, and much smaller, bay. Bang in the centre of this idyllic spot was a vacant plot which my father decided to buy. The plans for our new home, carefully monitored by my mother, began to take shape. The two-storeyed building was to be set into the rocky cliffside and would rise above the main road, gazing down, over the tops of the trees, upon the glistening bay, so like a mill-pond in the summer yet so turbulent in winter. The land proved to be a snake-infested wilderness of wild mimosa and thorny *hakea*, the workmen having to drill deep into the bedrock to lay the foundations while avoiding the colonies of scorpions and ferocious-looking spiders whose own homes and lairs they were disrupting.

In the meantime, we moved into a house called Mersey Lodge on the windy ridge above our plot. Austin followed us from the beach one memorable day, took one look at the garden and decided to stay. We were all delighted, but his angry owner arrived with the police and we were accused of 'harbouring' her dog. Finally, seeing the odds were against her, she capitulated with what we all thought to be rather bad grace. Austin was now officially ours and the most precious addition to the family imaginable. His loyalty was total. When we arrived off the bus from school, he'd be in his favourite spot under the tree. Then, as we climbed the steps, he'd rise, contort his body into convulsions of squirming delight, wearing on his face what was quite clearly an idiotic grin, and we'd hug him and kiss the top of his head despite the fierce and repeated warnings from our father not to get too close.

The bus to school went from Victoria Road, so we had to race down the public steps to catch it. To the left of the steps, we could see our new house beginning to take shape and the retaining walls, built with rock dug out of the land, being pieced together under my mother's supervision as they were to dictate the outline of her garden. The site was out-of-bounds during weekdays, but over the weekends we'd walk the planks like so many pirates and push the wheelbarrows, drinking in the intoxicating smell of cement and new timber before pausing to view our domain. The road passing below was no problem, there being very little traffic in those pre-war days, while the house was perched some fifteen feet above it over a double garage. My mother had a teak pergola built over the flat roof of the garage and, for many years to come, it burst forth in summer with the vibrant orange bells of the

Golden Shower creeper. The land on the far side of the road was council property and nobody was allowed to build on it. Beyond was the glory of the sea. As the sun began to set, and the cars below began to straggle home, we'd sit on the half-finished walls watching the myriad changes in the sky conjured up by nature with never a danger of repeating herself.

Down to our right, as we looked towards Camps Bay, was a snaking path which led to a pocket-sized beach. I was soon to know every rock, every pool alive with its own private aquarium of *klip* fish, shyly-backing crayfish and exotic anemones sinuously waving their tendrils in the current like Salome's veils, and around it, like a protective blanket, quantities of sighing brown shiny seaweed which made its own particular symphony as the tides came out and in.

At school, one of the prefects who lived nearby was dragooned into keeping an eye on me when I went home, making sure I got on to the right bus and didn't jump off until the thing had come to a complete stop. One afternoon, without any warning, he suddenly rolled off the seat beside me and began thrashing about on the floor. The bus conductor and a burly passenger, showing great presence of mind, hurled themselves on top of him and forced what appeared to be a pencil between his teeth. It was later explained to me that he was an epileptic and that the pencil was to stop him swallowing his tongue. I couldn't help wondering, in my state of frozen horror, how anyone's tongue could be prevented from being swallowed – and particularly by a pencil – as one end of it was attached, but the image of this squirming prefect dribbling at the mouth was to haunt my dreams for many a year.

While the grammar school had been perfectly acceptable when we were living in town, the journeying to and fro obliged my parents to hunt around for somewhere a bit nearer. My brother and sisters were in the same boat, of course, and gradually we were all moved. For me, my parents' choice was the Christian Brothers – a name to strike fear into the stoutest of hearts. Deeply ill at ease, I stood in the quadrangle amongst the other new boys, each of us in vivid blue, green and gold striped blazers as Brother McEvoy, he of the hooded eyes, leapt athletically on to the slatted wooden bench to welcome us.

The school, or college as we were expected to call it, was in Green Point, only a mile or two from the centre of Cape Town, and built on the slopes of Signal Hill from which, at noon, a gun was fired each day, scattering the pigeons. Across Table Bay, we looked down on Robben Island, once a leper colony, then a penal settlement where Mandela was later imprisoned. The journey home from the new school, my parents' chief worry, proved to be even more difficult than previously, particularly at rush hour, when the buses would rattle past with the 'FULL' sign up, leaving a disconsolate group of small children in striped blazers with their hands outstretched knowing that they had a long wait ahead of them. Dominating the school was a huge brick clock tower, its hourly chimes provoking murderous thoughts amongst local residents. The property was quite narrow, sandwiched in amongst the single-storeyed houses, and ran from the High Level Road via a series of steep terraces and playing fields to the Main Road abutting Green Point Common where I got my bus. Somewhere down there, among the landscaped gardens and tennis courts, was the rather sinister rambling house where all the Brothers in their black gowns and rosary beads lived in seclusion, and to which we were not invited.

We new boys were soon to discover that teaching was by intimidation. Years later, I met one of the Brothers who had taught in a class junior to mine – no longer wearing the sweaty black robes held formally together by a wide sash, but in civvies. 'Oh, we were a terrible lot of frauds,' he giggled in a mock Barry Fitzgerald voice. 'Wearing those robes and back-to-front collars and all that piety. We'd no right at all. We weren't ordained, you know.' (Perhaps they weren't even Irish. They certainly weren't very good teachers.) This didn't stop them forswearing the company of women – with the solitary exception of Miss MacCormack who wore a built-up boot and provided, at a price, sustaining meals with pie-crusts and mashed sweet potato for those boys who couldn't manage to get home at lunchtime. In their deep pockets the Brothers carried a strap. It was composed of strips of black leather stitched together and soaked in brine. One end was tapered into a grip. It could be used with force on hands or behinds, depending on the mood of the Brother dispensing the punishment, and, being an Irish order, moods could be variable.

There was one Brother for each year of my schooling there. All good men and true, with reservations, though not exactly the seven pillars of wisdom. Much has been written about the Christian Brothers' approach to schooling at that time, their recourse to violence as a method of education, and questions have been frequently raised as to whether they paid more attention to results at exam times than to how, why and what they were teaching. Certainly, as far as the pupils were concerned, there was no room for individuals. Each day they followed the same curriculum, regardless of whether or not they showed an aptitude for the subjects, and there was a preponderance of mathematical classes, algebra, trigonometry and the like, which baffled me then as they baffle me now. When I think back on the agonising I went through learning about equations, decimal points, logarithms and what turns litmus paper blue, which from those days to this I've never once had occasion to use, I wonder whether the time might not have been better spent studying languages, art or music, which were not deemed to be an essential part of a young lad's education, but which might have been of some use as I made my way through life. So the misery of maths was drummed into me with the persuasive use of the strap, should my answers prove unacceptable. Oddly enough, my mental arithmetic isn't at all bad, even today. I can march into Tesco's and tot up the bill without a flicker, and sometimes in advance of the till. Perhaps the fear of the strap hasn't left me, and I can visualise one lying within easy reach of the check-out girl.

The Hail Mary is chanted by Roman Catholics the world over and, as schoolboys, we got to know it very well, though I have seldom had occasion to use it. When the hourly chimes from the school tower began to ring out, there'd be a clatter of desk seats as the whole class rose, the Jews and Protestants remaining respectfully silent while the Catholics began 'Hail Mary, full of grace, the Lord is with thee, Blessed art thou amongst women . . .' in a mechanical drone, which the rest of us suspected contained very little grain of thought. Should a boy be experiencing 'cuts' when the clock struck, the punishment would cease for the duration of the prayer, and as the last strokes of the clock faded and nail-bitten fingers flicked across blazers in the sign of the Cross, the strokes of the strap would be resumed.

So began my slow and often painful journey towards puberty. I remember my mother being very upset years later when she read an interview I'd given to the *Guardian*. I was quoted as saying that I'd had an 'unhappy' childhood. What I'd said, which was very different, was that I was an 'unhappy child'. How could any child, brought up in that paradise on earth, with everything he could ever want, away from the war, the bombs and the rationing, claim that his childhood was unhappy? She was hurt and puzzled. I couldn't tell her then, any more than I could have told her in those early days that the complexities I was encountering sexually were beginning to isolate me because there was no one to whom I could turn. I don't remember making many friends at school. The shyness which was to plague me later was already tightening its grip. I easily became tongue-tied and was inclined to keep my own counsel rather than risk making a fool of myself.

Where others boys gained in confidence, I began to diminish. As my legs got longer, my body bonier and my skin spottier, I became increasingly self-conscious, blushing to the roots of my hair when anyone spoke to me, taking to watching the world go by from the sidelines rather than get involved, doing things because they were expected of me rather than because I wanted to do them.

A stout man with patent-leather hair came to teach us to sing 'The Owl And The Pussycat'. We were to enter a competition at a hall in Greenmarket Square in the centre of Cape Town. We'd hit the big-time. Only one other entry was announced so we were convinced it would be a cinch because of the endless pains exerted by Mr McQuade to have us sing in a style which would put the Vienna Boys to shame. Many compliments to our prowess floated around the school. We were the nightingales of Green Point. Unhappily, the floor of the stage on to which we filed on the day had been polished until it shone like a mirror. The third boy in slipped and fell flat. The two following, unable to stop in time, joined him with a splay of arms. By the time they had dusted themselves down, the rest of us were in a helpless heap. The choir was presented at half-strength or slightly under. I don't remember singing a note. We came second.

Undeterred, the College announced a production of *The Pirates Of Penzance*. Herbie Heap, a stocky little chap from Standard V with oodles of confidence, was chosen as the Major General, and Ronnie Pinn, Titian-haired son of the Musical Director, was to play his mother's namesake, Mabel. Mr Capon, a floppy Italian artist with rather a lot of blackheads, was to design and paint the scenery and apply the make-up to the actors. I, to my horror, was to be one of the chorus girls who entered singing 'Climbing Over Rocky Mountain'. Naturally, all the grown-ups at rehearsal thought it wildly funny as we skipped in holding our skirts and flirted with pirates and policemen – who were lucky enough to have broken voices. The words and music of Gilbert and Sullivan have remained with me all these years. In fact, were the D'Oyly Carte Company to telephone tomorrow and announce a production, I could, despite my deep misgivings about having to wear a frock, go on and be word and note perfect.

The frock in question was peach-coloured satin, and there was a large picture-hat, reinforced with buckram, which was secured under my chin by a dainty peach bow. Before the dress rehearsal, we were ordered to take our costumes home to be ironed. The following day, clutching a very large cardboard box, I boarded the bus for school. When we got to the school stop, I tugged at the bell and, bearing my container as though it were a priceless treasure, inched my way from the front seat past the crowded seats of stern businessmen. Suddenly the bus swerved, the box flew from my grasp and the tell-tale frock, so lovingly pressed by my doting mother, flew out like a flag on a windy day, dainty slippers hit the windowpanes, while the whole upper deck erupted with laughter as I made frantic attempts to retrieve my items of female attire. Mercifully that ghastly hat which would sit on my head like a halo had remained in the box to spare my further blushes. Cramming the crumpled costume back into the box, I fled down the steps of the bus on to the pavement, painfully conscious that every eye was upon me.

The Pirates was a triumph. That shameful moment so many of us had dreaded, when we girls skipped on, surprised us all. It stopped the show. And how we all loved it from that moment on. Mr Capon's sets were magnificent. He was a scenic artist in the old style, but when his creations were erected on the school boxing-ring and subtly lit, those over-purple shadows and exaggerated perspectives worked like magic. He made us up in one of the classrooms. It was my introduction to a commodity on which I was to become dependent when I became a professional actor, Leichner's greasepaint. Each tube or stick had a number which was used to achieve different effects. There were colours for the base – Five and Nine for juveniles with a dash of Eight, Lake for shading, liners for lining, orange sticks for painting in wrinkles, powder to set it, a rabbit's foot to dust it, and Crowes Cream to take it all off at the end. The smell of the greasepaint was intoxicating to my young nostrils. It was rumoured that Madame Leichner, its inventor, used to take healthy bites out of sticks of it and greedily chew them to convince potential customers of the product's purity. It is something I've never felt obliged to try.

But what a night it was! And what cheering when we all trouped on to take our bows. On the way home in the car, I machine-gunned my parents with questions. Did they like this bit, did they like that? Wasn't the Major General good, and how about Ruth and the Pirate King? I don't believe they were all that impressed really, it was, after all, only a school show, but I think what did impress them was my enthusiasm. They'd never seen me quite so animated.

Then my voice broke. If only it could have changed overnight like most other boys I knew, all would have been fine. It took months. The more it cracked, the more my Dad insisted on mocking it with a yodel. It only seemed to add to my troubles. My moods started to blacken. I found it difficult to shake them off. I was beginning to despair. Was this growing up? Well, of course it was but no one had explained. While other boys were meeting behind the bike sheds, bravely chain-smoking in a grown-up way, I was going it alone. School was no help, just a punitive system where we were frightened into learning. I envied the Jewish boys preparing for their *bar mitzvas*. It gave them a focus to their lives which I sorely lacked. Like the Catholic boys chanting the Hail Mary, I was going along with it all without understanding why, only living because I happened to be alive. I suppose, in hindsight, I should have sought advice from my father. Yet, I was becoming aware that he didn't really have much time for me. I wasn't his sort of boy. When all the others were bringing girlfriends home, where were mine? I felt that I was a disappointment to him. He would have wanted me to box, captain the College Fifteen, be taller, cleverer, better-looking and have better prospects than any other boy in the school. I didn't fit the bill. There were two sons, that was true, but I was the elder and, besides, John was asthmatic which gave him preference. Also John liked cars which didn't interest me – in fact, I didn't learn to drive one until I was nearly fifty. In a way, I could see Dad's point. Yet, I didn't know what on earth I could do about it. And there had been the incident with 'The Gorilla'.

There was one Brother who was the absolute embodiment of a gorilla. Quite short and ruddy complexioned, he wore metal-framed spectacles and, when angry, which was fre-quently, the natural red of his face would become purple. He was a fearsome sight. He was also addicted to the strap. Yet, there was a softer side to him. Once, during exams, when I had mumps for a second time, he got on a bus and came over to the house to invigilate while I wrote my papers. My mother cooked him lunch and he smoked a cigarette in the garden. Exams, in those early days of the war, were an oddity. We answered papers prepared by the College of Preceptors in England. Each of our contributions had then to be mailed six thousand miles across the Atlantic, braving attacks by Heinkels and U-boats, and there wasn't a single boy in the class who, at the end of every year, didn't earnestly pray that the boat bearing them would be torpedoed. 'The Gorilla' had taken rather a shine to me. Now, we were all wise to grown-ups who got up to that sort of thing. We even angled to catch the A.1 bus with a certain conductor. When he did his rounds collecting fares, if you allowed this conductor to run his fingers up your short-trousered leg, you usually managed to get let off with a free ride.

When everyone had gone home from school one afternoon, I was rummaging through my desk for a book I'd forgotten when, to my astonishment, a stocky figure in black appeared from nowhere, and without a word of warning, hurled himself at me in a flying rugby tackle. For what seemed like hours, we wrestled on the floor of the classroom as 'The Gorilla', purpling by the minute, struggled to get his hand up my short trousers while I, practically wetting myself with laughter, tried to prise him off. We tired after a while and the incident went no further, though I shudder to think what might have happened had the beady-eyed Brother McEvoy made an appearance while we were rolling about. Neither 'The Gorilla' nor I referred to what had taken place again.

Being wartime, we were told that we were to be cadets, and one hot summer's day we were marched down to the armoury, which was at the back of where the Brothers lived, and handed a rifle. The school band, which comprised pipers, buglers and side-drummers, as well as one of the seniors draped in a leopard skin whacking the big drum, was formed up ahead of us, the command was given and we were marched round and round the asphalted cricket field until we dropped. This may sound like an exaggeration, but I remember it very clearly. Boys ahead of me keeled over in the heat of the day and gashed their heads on the hard surface. They lay where they fell. The cricket field looked as though we'd been setting the scene for the re-creation of the Battle of the Somme. It was barbaric. I refused to succumb, marching doggedly round and round again, the rifle digging into my bony shoulder. They weren't going to get me to faint.

My elder sister Sheila was even more severely afflicted with introspection than I was. She had been an enchantingly pretty little girl, but when adolescence struck she began to lose all her self-confidence. Her hair became straight and mousy, so she parted it in the middle and yanked it back over her ears like one of the Brontë sisters, catching it behind the nape of her neck with an elastic band. Her body language mirrored her despondency. It became painful for her to walk into a crowded room so she edged in crab-wise. She found it hard to smile; it was as though she was forcing her lips to part across her teeth. She shut herself away and wrote poetry, going into long periods of silence and deep, dark moods. Even today, despite having had a happy marriage with six children and an increasing number of grandchildren, she is still desperately shy. What was it about the Hawthornes that brought this about? The twins were shy, too, but far more outgoing than Sheila and I. As a result, my elder sister and I became very close. I was the intermediary when fights broke out between John and Sheila. He'd tease her mercilessly and she'd give chase. My mother came to know that I could sort things out and effect a temporary truce. One winter, Sheila began sending her poems to the Squirrel Club, a children's section in the weekend *Cape Times*, and they were published. It must have given her a good deal of gratification to see her name in print, but any good which might have been done was shortly to be undermined by a series of poison-pen letters she was sent which featured her poetry in a derogatory way. It was cruel and scary. Each letter had been cut from a newspaper the way gangsters do, and pasted on a blank sheet to form a sentence. We thought we knew who was responsible – a sister of a friend, even the friend himself – but nothing was ever proved. We concluded it was born out of envy. It didn't stop her writing, nor the poison-pen letters from arriving.

None of us seemed to be maturing happily despite all the physical beauty we had around us, the fresh air, the freedom. We just couldn't seem to get going. John, my brother, was shunted around from school to school, never able to settle. Nowadays, he would have been identified as dyslexic, but then he was thought lazy or backward or both, so Dad moved him on, desperately hoping that he would settle down. My sister Janette went to a convent school. She was no intellectual, but met things head on in a cheerful and carefree way, looking forward to the time that she could catch the bus from school and be with her beloved horses. Then there was Sheila. And there was me.

4

Bioscope

In many ways, South Africa was, and probably still is, lagging behind the times, and being in Cape Town was like living somewhere that hadn't caught up. There was a great determination to be sophisticated and in touch, but six thousand miles separated us from what was going on, and we were doomed to be colonial. The war distanced us even further. When I was at school there was almost no live theatre, and the little there was was usually amateur. This doesn't mean to say that sometimes it wasn't rather good and performed with affection; the word amateur, after all, stems from the Latin verb 'to love'.

Occasionally the big syndicate, African Consolidated Theatres, which owned the lion's share of the cinemas, would use those with acceptable proportions for stage plays, often performed by local semi-professional companies with an imported English star above the title. I remember seeing pantomimes with Lucan and McShane, Tommy Trinder and Ivor Novello in an approximation of a pantomime, *Perchance To Dream*. Gwen Ffrangcon-Davies, who became a close friend many years later, toured with her partner, the stocky Marda Vanne, in both Shakespeare and contemporary successes such as Emlyn Williams's *The Wind Of Heaven*, Noël Coward's *Blithe Spirit* and J. M. Barrie's *What Every Woman Knows*. Both women were firmly established actresses in the London theatre. Another touring group was the Munro/Inglis Company, run by Nan Munro and Margaret Inglis, two highly accomplished and successful actresses, both South African. Mostly, however, our tastes were directed towards the bioscope as it was still called – rather proving my point about lagging behind.

The three main cinemas in town in those days were the Coliseum, the Plaza and a fantastical 'Spanish' auditorium, the Alhambra, with fake cypress trees, Moorish architecture, and a night sky with twinkling stars. Occasionally the Alhambra was the chosen venue for theatrical presentations. It was large, so productions were generally on a grand scale, and, after the final curtain had fallen, the audience would trickle across the road in their finery to dine at the Del Monico. I remember seeing a passion play at the Alhambra in which Christ was represented by a follow-spot for, in those days, He wasn't permitted to be portrayed by an actor. It must have been very difficult for the Disciples to play the more intimate scenes with a glorified Tinker Bell (the voice was disembodied as well). The actors were obliged to stare devoutly into space while it was their nightly fate to be dominated by the unfairly amplified and sonorous boom of the Son of Man.

For the bioscope, audiences would dress up as though for the theatre. It was an event. There was no slopping around in any old thing, unless, of course, you were visiting one of the bio-cafés which were usually off the beaten track, distinctly seedy, and where they slammed a tray on the ledge in front of you so that you could tuck into a meal while watching the film. You had to be fairly undiscriminating about your diet on these occasions as the food was served in the dark, and you had no way of checking what might be on your plate or in your cup. Generally speaking, it was wiser to leave it to one side and give your full attention to the film.

Brother Nelson was an Australian. He walked with a pronounced limp, which was generally assumed by my schoolmates to have been the result of having a ball and chain attached to his ankle while serving as a convict. He decided that he was sufficiently handy with a projector to introduce a film evening once a week. He selected a Friday night so that it shouldn't conflict with homework. We began seeing films first of all in one of the upstairs classrooms, but popularity soon obliged him to move down to the hall in the quadrangle. There was invariably a Popeye, Oswald Rabbit or Felix the Cat, but the quality of a great deal of the more light-hearted American short items was distinctly variable. Rarely were we shown feature films of any merit, a missed opportunity typical of the Brothers; they were usually about gangsters or cowboys like Hopalong Cassidy. I think we must have seen almost every film William Boyd ever made, and got to know every rock in the Hollywood Hills like an old friend. If you had been lucky enough to win a Merit Card for achievement in the classroom that week, you got in for nothing, and as there was always pressure on pupils to 'support the College', a full house was practically guaranteed.

The film would break down repeatedly for various technical reasons or just plain incompetence, and Brother Nelson wasted a good deal of time as he painstakingly rethreaded the tangle of celluloid. Despite all this, so began my love of the cinema, indicating, I like to think, the emergence of a child of some imagination.

I was eleven and a bit when the Germans bombed Coventry, and I can still see my father's face as he weighed the news in disbelief. On a balmy Cape evening in November, so very far away from it all, it was difficult for us to imagine the grey, densely-packed city we'd left only eight years previously now so cruelly devastated, its inhabitants distraught and its Cathedral, where we'd all been baptised and my parents married, a smouldering shell. Our own contribution to the war had been strangely tepid – as if we were playing a game of Let's Pretend. Dad, well beyond the age of conscription, was head of the St John's Ambulance on our side of the mountain, so, as children, we would act as guinea-pigs while he and the volunteer nurses put our arms and legs in splints, bandaged our heads, and submitted to being carried around on stretchers. There was a small shelter in Camps Bay – just the one, as far as I remember – so heaven help us had there been an air raid.

We children dug one of our own on the vacant plot next door. We managed to get it quite deep and it might even have been serviceable, watched over as it was by a protective photograph of Mr Churchill cut from *The Outspan* magazine.

Being on the coast, we were obliged to observe blackouts, for there was a remote possibility that we might have been spied by a passing U-boat which had lost its way. So up went the blackout curtains, while the headlamps on the car – a German DKW (illustrating yet again my father's disregard for convention) – had part of the glass painted out so that only the minimum of light would show. Early on there was no rationing, though there was a shortage of certain foodstuffs. Scotch was expensive as it was imported but, if you needed to drink claret by the gallon – and there were those that did – it would cost you as little as five shillings. Butter was one and eightpence a pound, the same price as bacon, while a pound of tea was two and eleven. You could get fifty cigarettes for a shilling, and a brand-new Studebaker would cost under three hundred pounds.

When, at the beginning of hostilities, Chamberlain had made his doomladen speech, 'I have to tell you now that no such undertaking has been received,' we all sat around the radio-cum-record-player scarcely daring to breathe, yet there were many South Africans who were in two minds as to whether we should join in, it being Europe's war. Most people suspected that many Afrikaners had no intention of siding with the British whatever the enemy when the treatment we meted out in the Boer War concentration camps still rankled, as indeed did all the indignities of imperialism, and a large number were actively pro-Nazi. But in Parliament the old soldier Smuts won the day by thirteen votes and, only three days after Britain and France had declared war, South Africa had taken up the gauntlet on behalf of the Allies.

We became very used to seeing men in khaki, particularly when the Mediterranean became a no-go area for the Allies and troopships would find their way to the East, as they did in Vasco da Gama's day, via the Cape. A journalist called Lucy Bean, who my father said 'Liked the sound of her own voice', elevated herself to celebrity status by inaugurating a campaign of hospitality for visiting troops, and the kindness and generosity meted out to them by the citizens of Cape Town became legendary. Often we would see groups of Tommies strolling by the front of our house, puffing away at their Woodbines and taking in the view, so we'd leap upon them, invite them in, take their names and addresses and write to their families back home (not mentioning the name of their ship for security reasons) just to say that they'd been round for tea and were well and in good spirits. I remember the time the Aussies landed – going the other way, that is to say clockwise – and how badly they behaved, smashing the plate glass windows of big department stores, taking over the buses and trams and generally roughing up the town. All was forgiven because of the war, and there was perhaps a smug satisfaction in seeing others behave rather worse than we did.

I should have been brighter at school than I was. I had shown promise earlier, but, as time went by and I became more and more self-conscious, I began to lose confidence. When exams came round, I'd stare in panic at the questions, unable to find a way of responding. I could hear the seconds ticking by on the clock over the door, the squeak of the invigilator's shoes as he patrolled the aisles, the dipping of pens in porcelain inkwells, the scratch of nibs, a sneeze, a cough, the traffic going by outside. Sometimes, it was almost as though I wasn't really present – as though it were part of a dream. It wasn't lack of preparation, for I was always conscientious to a fault. The preponderance of scientific and mathematical subjects in the curriculum hampered me, it was true, but I should have done better than I did in the manageable subjects – English, History and Geography. Outside examination periods were

I to be asked a question in class, quite often I would stand for what seemed hours, my mind a total blank, feeling that every eye in the room was upon me. I seemed to have no armour which would protect me, no bluff which might turn disadvantage into advantage. I feared rejection far more than the strap, so that, instead of stepping forward confidently into manhood, I was retreating, without knowing why.

Nowadays, when there's a problem child, the parents are called in to discuss matters with the teachers, though I don't think that people recognised that I had a problem – least of all my parents. And perhaps I hadn't. It was all in my head. Whatever the pains I might have been experiencing as a growing boy, they didn't seem important enough to discuss. In my last year I was summoned to a private pep-talk with Brother McEvoy, as was each boy in the class. He didn't ask me to sit down, just gazed at me, his eyes only half open, as if torn between his position as head of the school who was responsible for both my education and my future, and an even more pressing need to fall asleep. Some minutes went by before he spoke and I was beginning to feel very ill at ease. At last he made up his mind as to what it was that he needed to say. 'Hawthorne,' he began, 'what will become of you?' That was it. No more.

Perhaps my parents might have helped me, for surely, surely, they must have been aware of my dilemma. It was my own fault for not having gone to them with my problems. I have always been independent – the Aries in me – and felt that I should find my own way in life without enlisting the help of others. I've kept to this policy, with only a handful of lapses when I was really desperate. I'm grateful to my parents for many things. My presence on this earth to start with. The happy and healthy environment in which I was brought up. The way they gave me moral support despite having disapproved of my choices. Of course my Dad was angry when I walked away from University to join a professional company as an actor. I can appreciate how such a seemingly irresponsible act must have infuriated him, yet it's a decision I have never for a moment regretted.

There were other lessons they taught me, and it is for these that I owe them the most thanks. We were brought up to do as we were told, to speak when we were spoken to and not to answer back, to behave at table, to stand erect and without fidgeting when the National Anthem was played, to respect our elders, not to lie and not to cheat. These principles have guided me through life. Dad was a man of honour. All right, he was the most terrible flirt, and there were times when he led my mother the most awful dance. But, given that he was culpable of masculine frailties, he was honest. It was a quality I much admired in him and one which I have done my utmost to emulate. Conscious of his gullibility, people less scrupulous than he would try to take advantage of him, as they have done – and do – with me, but his strength was his honesty and they couldn't touch that.

We were coming to the end of our schooling. The Gilbert and Sullivan fad had slowed down a bit. I hadn't been in *The Mikado*, as my harassed parents thought the time might be better employed with my nose in my books. Then the school decided to revive that old favourite, *The Pirates Of Penzance*. Once again, I took no part. Until, that is, I was summoned to Brother McEvoy's office early one morning – a rare privilege – where he solemnly informed me, 'Bernard Culhane has been taken ill. Can you go on tonight as the Pirate King?' It was the mixture of heaven and hell at one go. But, yes of course I could!

I was thrown into the arms of the latest producer, an elocutionist by the name of Sybil Marks. All day long she coached me. It had been six years since I'd climbed over rocky mountains as one of the girls, but a lot of the words and the tunes had remained with me. That night I went on to a packed house. I got to the Pirate King's song, my solo, 'Oh better far to live and die, under the brave black flag I fly'. I was going great guns until I couldn't remember how the second verse began. Instead of panicking, I just sang the first verse twice. With the piano thundering away below I don't suppose many could hear the words anyway. The evening was a triumph and, the following morning, Brother McEvoy of all people came up to me and, placing a suspiciously friendly hand upon my shoulder, solemnly announced, 'Hawthorne. You saved the college!' Nobody had ever given me such praise before. Suddenly, after years in the background, I was the centre of attention. Everybody wanted to shake me by the hand. It was the equivalent of my having flattened the school boxing champion, bowled out Len Hutton first ball, or scored the winning try in the last thirty seconds. But there was no time for success to go to my head. My parents quite rightly insisted that I should set all that aside and concentrate on finishing my studies.

In any case, the following evening Bernard Culhane returned to his role, rather ungratefully complaining that I'd ripped one of the cardboard tops that folded over the Wellington boots he wore in the show – something I might well have done in the heat of the moment – but I thought the least he could have done was to thank me for covering for him. Secretly, though, I was relieved it was all over and that I'd got through it without having made a hash of things. I couldn't help being intrigued by how nervous I'd been when I'd heard the audience taking their seats before the performance, yet how that had evaporated once the curtains had parted and the stage lights were up. I'd enjoyed myself, felt an exhilaration, a freedom – even a pride at having been part of the show. I'd dared to improvise when I couldn't remember the right words, knowing the audience to be completely on my side.

I had grown tall and leggy, outstripping my father – a source of great pride to him. I was determined to reach six foot. I knew how thrilled he would be. On the strip of wall alongside the dividing doors between our dining and sitting rooms, our respective heights were noted regularly in pencil. Being the tallest in the family seemed to be my greatest claim to fame. It was certainly my best chance of continuing in my father's good books. Also, it was around this time that I suspected that I might be Jesus Christ.

This had nothing to do with my height, naturally, indeed very little to do with anything other than the confusion going on within my changing mind and body. I knew that I was different from other boys. I looked the same, yet I thought in a different way, at least I presumed I did; I had no way of knowing for sure. There was a boy called Tony whom just about everybody in the class admired. He seemed so handsome, so confident and so at ease with himself that it was hard not to envy him. He wasn't particularly bright or good at sports, but the warmth of his personality made us vie for his attention. I know this to be true because several of the boys I spoke to in later years admitted it to me. He had a magnetism which made us want to set him on a pedestal. When it came to carrying a torch for Tony I was no exception, though I very much doubt whether we exchanged more than half a dozen words the whole time we were at school. I was far too paralysed with shyness. Of course it wasn't only the boys who found him personable – the girls did too. In their droves. He seemed to be surrounded by admirers. So why, if other boys besides myself found him so attractive, did I imagine myself to be so different? The answer was simple in its complexity. I'd come to realise that I felt more deeply about him. I didn't even know what I meant. He wasn't just someone I could glance at and think, 'I wish I looked like that.' There was an uncomfortable disturbance deep within me which I couldn't for the life of me understand. As boys around me began to boast of their conquests with girls, how they'd chatted them up at the bus stop, how they'd snogged in the back row of the bioscope, I had to keep silent. I'd had none of these experiences. Nor had I wanted them. Indeed, girls whose company I shared most days of the week – like pretty Marjorie Hustwick – must have wondered why; what they could have done to offend me. I'd turned into a loner. Then the mists began to clear. There was a reason for my being different. I had been sent to earth on a mission. I was the new Messiah.

The obvious place, therefore, towards which I should gravitate would seem to be the Church. Here I would learn about myself and my various connections both national and international. I became passionately involved. I went to confirmation classes in addition to choir practice, was confirmed by the Bishop, served at Holy Communion – in fact, it was almost as though the parish church of St Peter's in Camps Bay had become my second home. I read not just the Bible (well, not all of it) but every religious book on which I could lay my hands and, when I found out that my own mother had been neither baptised nor confirmed, I telephoned the Bishop to ask for his advice, talked my dear, patient mother into attending instruction and, in due course, would be present as a witness at both her baptism and her confirmation. My sanctimony didn't end there. I set up a makeshift altar in my bedroom and invited my sister Sheila to attend services. Rather surprisingly, she went along with it. I look back on my behaviour now with horror. I must have been a real little prig, a major pain in the neck. There was, however, a redeeming feature which was to end my compulsive swallow-dive towards the priesthood as suddenly as it had begun.

Mr Fenton, the vicar at Camps Bay, having no pulpit, would position himself in the aisle separating the front pews and the altar to deliver his sermons. An explosive speaker, he would accompany his sermon with flamboyant gestures, a good deal of coughing and sniffing, while the nearest surface – usually the pew – would be thumped repeatedly for emphasis. A welcome irreverence was beginning to seep into my church attendances. It hadn't escaped my notice that Mr Fenton enjoyed his tipple and that, at Holy Communion, he would fill the chalice with rather more wine than was strictly necessary for so sparse a congregation. Later on in the service, one of my duties as a server was to replenish the chalice with wine and water, enabling the priest to rinse the cup and imbibe the contents. I used to allow rather more water than wine. He never referred to the matter but I will always remember the dangerous look he would flash me as he raised the chalice to his lips. And there was worse to come.

Sermons appeared to be sacrosanct. It wasn't fair. You couldn't put up your hand as you would at school and say, 'I didn't understand that bit.' The vicar would seal the end of his weekly sermon by turning to the altar, making the sign of the Cross and muttering, 'In the name of the Father and of the Son and of the Holy Ghost. Amen.' In other words, that was that. Nobody had the chance of arguing a point. One evensong, I took in a notebook and, over a period of weeks, wrote down things I didn't understand and needed explaining. Finally, I bearded him in the sacristy. He looked at me in alarm as I reeled off my questions and then, by way of humouring me, gave a few rather vague replies. These I wouldn't accept. Fenton showed his impatience, obviously anxious to get over to the rectory to greet his parishioners, and here was this wretched boy trying to catch him out while he was struggling to remove his vestments. The situation worsened. I wasn't taking prisoners. If he couldn't give me satisfactory answers to what I wanted to know, then I couldn't possibly attend church again. And I said so. The poor man floundered under my onslaught but we both knew that my mind was made up. For months he used to roar up on his motorbike trying to persuade me to return, but I never did. I was following in my grandmother's footsteps, finding my faith in the world around me rather than being persuaded by ritual and ceremony.

I may have cast the poor vicar into outer darkness, but his wife Mary still held my esteem. Being a keen amateur actress herself, she had frequently put on shows in our parish hall. One day she encountered a tempestuous young sailor with a London accent and a beaky nose. She'd seen him strolling about Camps Bay on his own, assumed he was lonely and had offered him a lift. I have since suspected that he sought company of a different persuasion. He let slip that he was a West End actor and had appeared opposite John Gielgud in Gordon Daviot's *Richard Of Bordeaux*, although there was no mention of his name in the cast list at the front of the published play. But he did seem to know what he was talking about. He took our tiny stage and transformed it with a series of ingeniously improvised paraffin-tin lamps and dimmers into a really efficient unit, he taught us make-up and put on a production of an Emlyn Williams play called *The Late Christopher Bean* in which Mary Fenton played Gwenny, the leading role. It was a great success and people came from miles around to see us. The following year we did several one-act plays, and I was in a rather preposterous drama called *The Astonished Heart* by Noël Coward, after which I was ticked off by my mother for gulping down 'martinis' with undue haste. She advised me that even a seasoned drinker would have been flat on his back within minutes at the rate I'd consumed them. The productions were purely amateur, of course, but I was getting a taste for the theatre and the people in it which must have worried my parents, for I was in the throes of Matriculation – my final exams at school.

With the family rapidly growing up, the demands made on my father's limited purse strings were proving uncomfortable. It was perfectly true that, during the war, he'd had the area very much to himself. So many of his medical rivals were in khaki. But Dad was, by now, in his sixties and any prospects of slowing down, which I'm sure he would have liked to do, seemed pretty remote. My poor dear mother had no money of her own and her own mother was living on the smell of a paint rag. No, my father was the sole source of income. Dad didn't believe in spending money unless he had to. When market day arrived, my mother had to beg him to let her have some cash to buy provisions. Each week, the most terrible row would ensue. 'I'm not made of money. Where's it all going to come from? I can't afford to be paying out all the time!' It would have been far simpler to have allowed my mother a certain amount each week for household expenses, but my father had no intention of changing the habit of a lifetime. If we, as children, wanted money to go to the bioscope, get a season ticket for the bus, buy birthday or Christmas presents – it was a battle royal. Dad was obsessed with waste. At mealtimes, we had to finish every crumb. 'If you didn't want it you shouldn't have asked for it.' Presents qualified as a waste. Our own presents were very modest, though I remember once receiving a bicycle which I was told was American. Its tyres were very wide, and it was extremely heavy. It took all my strength to budge it more than a few feet. Eventually, it lay neglected at the back of the garage, grist to my father's mill – 'and when I buy him something he doesn't use it' – when money matters were being argued.

At school I became very conscious that I was just about the only senior boy who didn't own a sports jacket. Our blazers had such vivid stripes that they seemed rather extravagant garments on semi-formal occasions like going into town or going by train to visit my grandmother. I explained to my Dad that it would be very nice if I could get out of my school uniform occasionally, but I got the familiar response. One day he took pity on me and asked me up to his bedroom. Dad had long before moved out of the double bed he and my mother had shared, and slept on the verandah. There were canvas blinds which could be let down during the winter, when he would smother his bed with rugs and everything waterproof he could lay his hands on. He seemed to sleep impervious to the gales which threatened to wrench the blinds from their moorings, his vigorous snores, as the rain bucketed over him, reverberating around the house and keeping the rest of us awake. In their bedroom, my mother and he had a wardrobe each, my Dad's being twice the size of my mother's. It was a magnificent mahogany piece we'd brought from England, with racks for his black ties, rails for his black shoes, hanging space for his collection of black jackets and striped trousers and special cubicles for his stiff collars. From the back of this cumbersome piece of furniture he pulled a brown woollen suit. Opening up the jacket, he pointed to the label inside which proclaimed 'Harris Tweed' and invited me to sniff the cloth. It had a musty smell with which I was familiar as he would occasionally wear the suit when he was off-duty. The material was thick and coarse, hot to wear and ginger-brown in colour. 'We'll go down to my tailor in Long Street,' he told me. 'He'll make you something.'

I hadn't quite taken on board that my Dad's intention was to have a sports jacket made from the jacket of the suit. His Cape Malay tailor took time to make his decision. 'I'm afraid, Doctor,' he concluded as I stood there, swathed in tweed, 'there's no way this jacket is going to fit this boy. However much I take it in, you see, it will always be too big.' My father found it hard to conceal his disappointment. Finally, he had a brainwave. 'Make it out of the trousers!'

In due course and after several fittings, I was allowed to bring my sports jacket back home. By then it had turned into a loathsome thing. In his effort to make the rest of the jacket look as good as possible, the tailor had concealed the large assortment of irregular bits and pieces underneath the sleeve so that when I lifted my arm there was a sort of jigsaw puzzle on the underside. Determining to keep my arms by my sides at all costs, I wore it to the school bioscope that Friday. Someone dubbed me 'Sackcloth and Ashes' and the name stuck.

My father was increasingly out in the evenings. He had become a prominent Freemason, being Grandmaster of this Lodge and that, and was also a member of the M.O.T.H.S. (Memorable Order Of Tin Hats), the Owl Club, the Rotary

Club and a founder member of the Oxford and Cambridge Society, which would meet for a dinner on Boat Race night. My mother, who, in common with the other wives, would not normally be expected to attend many of these functions, compensated by going to whist drives and beetle drives and sometimes the bridge or gin rummy equivalent. They had both joined the Camps Bay Bowling Club, but it was my mother who revealed an unexpected talent. She entered the Western Province Novice Cup – and won. The following year, she won the Open Cup. I don't think it had been done before. It was a thrill for us all to see our mother the centre of attention. Her role, for far too long, had been to look after the household, do the cooking and the shopping, tend to my father, bring up the children and drop everything to answer the phone which always seemed to ring at mealtimes. 'Three, nine, eight, double one, five, Dr Hawthorne's house?' Then, after a pause, 'Charlie, it's Mrs Absolom. Can you pop in and see her this evening?' And, from the dining room, 'No, I damn well can't. Tell her I'm out.' Now it was her moment. She was photographed for the papers, and in the house the trophies were given pride of place for a whole year. Dad was never very good at bowls and didn't particularly enjoy it. He couldn't see what all the fuss was about. He hadn't the patience. Added to which, the club blazer with its vivid stripes didn't go with his ruddy complexion. He stuck to team events and avoided singles until finally he got bored and gave it up.

The war was entering its most dramatic phase, the invasion. We all had charts and marked the progress of the Allies on a daily basis. As we listened to the news on the wireless, at last, here was something to which we could relate. Not just a series of bombing attacks but a concerted advance into enemy lines. It was enormously exciting. In celebration, I made a model Spitfire out of balsa wood and tissue paper from a kit. On its maiden flight it fell to the ground, shattered beyond repair. It was just about my only contribution to the war effort.

Secretly, I was considerably relieved as, had it continued, I should have had to join up. Now, with the smell of victory in the air, with any luck, I'd be let off the hook. I don't suppose even then we realised how lucky we'd been to have escaped it all. There had been little or no privations, we'd come through unscathed, though sons and daughters of friends inevitably were killed in action or posted missing. The family hadn't been separated, we'd had all the food we needed, vegetables, fruit and chocolate. Our limbs had grown sturdy in the sunshine and sea air, and our lungs had benefited from regular climbs and horse rides up the mountain.

As I prepared to take my first faltering steps into the great, wide world, and we, the Hawthorne family, proudly swung our Christmas lights across the front of the house in the shape of a 'V' for victory, the bewilderment with which puberty had plagued me showed no sign of disappearing. I assumed it would go when it was time for it to go. I proudly measured my height on the wall and clocked six foot exactly if I stood very straight and held my breath. School at long last was behind me. No more Brother this and Brother that. No more strap. I was a young man. I used my father's razor to shave, and, haunted though I was by Brother McEvoy's discouraging lament, 'Hawthorne, what will become of you?', I felt that something would. Something. I didn't know what.

5

Now What?

One of the most enduring lessons we learned at Christian Brothers' College was guilt. Never could it be levelled at our Roman Catholic teachers that they tried to make converts of us. It was as though there was a pact. Indeed all religious instruction doled out to the Protestant and Jewish boys was of a fairly innocuous nature, with one glaring exception which stands out in my memory like a beacon. We were told about Oscar Wilde and his wickedness. Reading from a tract, the Brother responsible told us that Wilde was one of the wickedest men that had ever lived, that he had been sent to prison for his wickedness, where the weight of his crimes was so great that his body had exploded and his entrails had run down the walls of the cell. For those boys who had read Frank Harris and others, this was snigger-worthy, and word of the blatant misrepresentation spread round the school like the bush fires which, on a regular basis in the summer, would sweep across the mountainside. It was, I suppose, an oblique warning to us of the perils of homosexuality. We never found out whether a similar warning had been given to the Catholic boys who probably needed it as much as the rest of us. Insidiously, a feeling of guilt was encouraged, so that we came to question our every action. It has remained with me all my life – as indeed have the 'perils' of homosexuality.

Early on, we were introduced to a system of torture known as 'self-denial'. It was supposed to be character-forming. If, for example, I was expecting an important letter, I would have to bypass the letterbox without opening it, or, if this temptation proved irresistible, or on the spur of the moment I'd forgotten,

I would be expected to leave the letter I was anticipating where it lay in the letterbox while removing the others. If it remained there for several days, so much the better, my character would be the stronger for having resisted the temptation. Were I to throw caution to the winds, do the unthinkable and open the letterbox hoping that I hadn't been observed, immediately I would be aware that I had sinned. Guilt, the accompanying torture, would haunt me. The test was applicable to almost anything enjoyable, and there was even the danger of feeling guilty about feeling guilty.

Generally speaking, white South Africans are notoriously selfish people used to being waited on and, even though I had been born in England and couldn't be classed as a true South African, I grew up as selfish as the rest. Compared with other families, even with our limited resources, we had spent the war in the lap of luxury. There were, of course, boys at school whose lives had been more affected than ours, with fathers and brothers fighting in North Africa and Italy, but for the majority of us, I think, the war wasn't an immediate threat and therefore something of an unreality. When news of what had happened in the concentration camps was released, it shocked us to the core – the Jewish boys, in particular, being made horribly aware of how lucky they had been to have spent the war so out of reach. The selfishness came as a direct result of our having been pampered in our homes. We didn't have to lift a finger. All the dirty work was done for us.

Katie, Marie, Suzie, Esther, Rachel, Becky, Dolly, Lettie, Queenie, Hattie, Helen and Bessie in their caps and aprons were at hand to scrub, brush and clean up after us. Not all at once, but a succession of them trundling their Hoovers and flicking their feather dusters at the cobwebs. Some maids lasted longer than others who stole or drank or sneaked in boyfriends. Some were lazy, didn't turn up, couldn't or wouldn't manage the work, were hopeless at taking telephone messages, had problems getting on with the children, were abusive, aggressive, or both, which usually resulted in the police having to be summoned or – horror of horrors – brought bugs. The fumigators would have to be contacted, the room evacuated while they installed their deadly smoke-bombs, the doors and windows hermetically sealed until it was deemed safe to go in, and everyone giving the offending maid's room a wide berth as though it were the isolation ward in a fever hospital. Dangling from the doorhandle would be a cardboard sign bearing the skull and crossbones with 'DANGER! KEEP OUT!' written in red in both official languages.

Lena Goliath was an exception. To begin with, we knew her surname. She had a very close relationship with my mother. They could sit down over a cup of tea and discuss their respective families, exchange cooking tips and generally gossip to their hearts' content. Lena, being warm-hearted, garrulous yet industrious, fitted in extraordinarily well. We met her first in Queen Victoria Street when she came to work for us in her late teens. She had a naughty streak and was more than a match for the four children. She gave as good as she got and we loved her. On birthdays, a multi-tiered cake would be baked, the lucky one getting to lick the bowl. Often as not, it was a layered sponge covered with icings all the colours of the rainbow and scattered with 'hundreds and thousands', little multi-coloured pellets of sugar, the name of the child spelt out in wobbly writing with chocolate. Though she worked with the family, on and off, for something like forty years, we knew very little about her or even where she lived. The servants' quarters in those early days were above the kitchen and pantry, reached by a winding staircase. In our new home, there was a room specially built on to the back of the house which was hers. It was small and stuffy, no different from 'girls" rooms up and down the country. She held a position similar to a maid in England in the Victorian or Edwardian eras, and we knew no more of her circumstances, nor those of the others who worked for us, than families did then.

The Cape coloured people infiltrated the sluggishness which characterised the personality of the Western Cape, helping to shake it out of its ditch-water dullness with their energy and humour. This was a segment of the country which bore little relationship to the rest. With its sweeping mountain ranges, its vineyards and rocky coastline, it resembled Europe rather than Africa in feeling as well as appearance though, unlike the north, the majority of the ethnic people were of mixed blood. Even though tribal Africans were present, they were not in as great profusion as they are today. For many generations prior to apartheid, the Cape coloured people chose to keep to their own part of town. Their homes were painfully modest when set beside the often lavish mansions of the whites, sometimes little more than shacks, but they clung together as a community, dependent upon the 'European' – by which was meant the white – for their livelihood. By and large, the relationship wasn't a bad one and, although the economic difference between the races was often considerable, there was harmony and, generally speaking, they were fairly treated.

Slaves brought from West Africa, the island of Madagascar and from the East, where Holland ruled the spice trade after the new way through had snatched the monopoly from Venice, bred with the early Dutch and later the Huguenot settlers. Their progeny were the ancestors of the present Cape coloured people, their features as varied as their faiths, their skins offering no conformity of pigmentation, and many passing as white. In Cape Town, they celebrate each New Year with a carnival like a Mardi Gras. It used to be called the Coon Carnival, though I suspect that has been politically corrected. Each troupe would take the whole year to prepare. The finest silks and satins were found and they would dress as minstrels in tailcoats and top hats, incongruously blacking their faces to be sure they looked the part. On 2 January, known as the second New Year, a competition would be held at the Rosebank Showground, and the winners would dance the night away in the side streets of town and the length and breadth of District Six, strumming their ukuleles, getting drunker by the minute, the stragglers serenading the world at large with traditional songs like '*Daar kom die* Alabama' – the *Alabama* being one of the old merchant ships which travelled to Batavia in the spice trade days – and '*Sukerbossie*', which Eve Boswell later turned into a popular hit. We used to love these carnivals and look forward to them each year, but if we thought that the exuberance demonstrated in those two shorts days and nights was the norm we were misguided. The reality was that poverty and inequality governed their lives.

As I grew up in Cape Town, I began to be aware of some of the injustices: the way the police behaved towards them, the way some whites expected them to step to one side when they met on the pavement, the way they always sat at the back, on the buses or at church. Although our lives were intertwined, we kept our distance. In those days, it was accepted that the housewife telephoned the local grocery shop with her order and the goods would be delivered later the same day. With difficulty, a young Cape coloured lad would pedal his bicycle with its outsized wicker basket crammed with provisions along the Victoria Road and carry them up the front steps and to the back door where my mother would check the items against her list. It was customary to take certain goods on approval – items of clothing, for example – so that, if they didn't suit, or didn't fit, they could be returned and the money refunded. It was equally possible for my mother to complain to the butcher that last week's leg of lamb was tough and expect an apology and a complimentary leg of lamb sent as a gesture of good will. Fruit and vegetables were available either at the market or from horse-drawn carts which patrolled the area on certain days of the week. The driver of these carts, whatever his name, was always known as 'Sammy'. One of these drivers, a handsome Cape coloured lad, took a shine to my sister Janette, then in her mid teens. Someone reported to my father that they'd been seen sitting together on a patch of grass under a tree sharing a joke. Janette was given a stern talking to and that particular 'Sammy' came round no more.

I still see Lena when I go back to Cape Town. She's now in her eighties and finds work difficult because of her arthritis, so we take care of her, making sure that there is no need for her to continue scrubbing and polishing other people's houses unless she wants to. She's a gracious old lady with a wonderful spirit and pride, though I can't rid her of the habit of calling me 'Master Nigel' however hard I try – and she invariably asks me when I'm going to get married. When I think of the loyalty she has shown to my family through the years, the journeys she has had to take to get to and from our various homes on her days off, the sense of humour that she has maintained throughout in the face of the tribulations life has imposed upon her, I can only marvel. She is a very special lady.

Dad suggested that I went to see Neville Shute, who was a director of Southern Insurance, the firm which had its offices on the ground floor of the building where he had his consulting rooms. I had yet to make up my mind in which direction my future lay and he thought that insurance might appeal, as well as bringing me in some money. Mr Shute was a debonaire gentleman with public school manners who offered me the job of junior clerk in the Motor Department. It seemed to matter little that I knew nothing about cars and couldn't drive. I had an important-looking desk behind the counter so that, when a customer came in, I could leap to my feet and attend to his or her needs. I used to pray they wouldn't ask me a question I didn't understand, though, despite my shyness, I rather enjoyed having this contact with members of the public. It was also my duty to deal with third party motor insurance and issue declarations and tokens when required. Some of these requests came from out of town and there was a drawer in my desk reserved for them which, one day, I hoped to get round to answering. When I was off sick with a tummy bug, they went through my desk and discovered rather a lot of these letters, so, on my return, being confronted with my misdemeanour, I fully expected to be given the sack though, for some reason, they decided to keep me on. As I wasn't enjoying the job at all I think I might have welcomed the push, though the resultant confrontation with my father might have been awkward.

The head of the Motor Department was Lewis Lewis, a breezy, middle-aged man with a large moustache, who enjoyed his food and seemed to be thoroughly at ease with the world in which he lived. One of the reasons for this must surely have been that he spent as little time as possible at his desk. Around the periphery of the high-ceilinged office where we all worked was a partition which comprised units occupied by senior members of the department. There was a frosted glass door which bore the incumbent's name. That named for Lewis Lewis was invariably closed and no discernible movement could be detected within.

It was 1947, the year of the royal visit. We were given special dispensation to shut up the office on the day the King and Queen and the princesses drove from the docks up Adderley Street, and we stood shoulder to shoulder amongst the heaving throng waving our flags and cheering ourselves hoarse. Several of the more diehard Afrikaans clerks gave the procession a miss to take advantage of the deserted beaches, but for the rest of us, it was with a tremendous feeling of pride that we welcomed the royal visitors and, when we saw how uncomfortable by comparison the Governor General and his wife looked in all their finery – for they were the Van Zyls, Afrikaners to their fingertips – there was more than a feeling of smug satisfaction.

Mr Lewis was a film-maker. It was this hobby which so frequently dominated his working day. Early one afternoon, he shut up shop, pulled down the blinds and we were each invited to find a seat in one of the larger booth partitions located at the rear of the office. A projector had been set up and, in glorious technicolor, we watched his film of a trip from St Helena in a two-masted schooner, rigged fore and aft with topgallant sails on the foremast, the boat pitching and tossing in the turbulent sea. I sat enthralled. Mr Lewis knew what he was doing after all. His feeling for film – even with the minimal experience I possessed – was remarkable. Here was no amateur but an artist to his fingertips, with each frame demonstrating his flair. He was not unaware of my enthusiasm – Eisenstein with his acolyte. He promised another film the following week, and once again we sat round on the floor of the little back room to watch. No such romantic excursion this time round. It was a heart operation in grisly detail. I don't remember too much about it as I keeled over early on and had to be revived by Miss Knowles, the cashier who had befriended me. Neither of us being married helped and I could go to her with my woes – well, some of them. My unmanly behaviour during the screening of Mr Lewis's film didn't exactly enhance my standing in the Motor Department, but watching it that afternoon began to stimulate an interest in me outside the tedious realms of motor insurance – and it had very little to do with running away to sea.

It was Mr Van Heerden, I remember, an Afrikaner working as an agent for the company, who pointed the way. In idle moments, I had taken to doodling on the back of my notebook. My early efforts were never very good, but I had a certain flair and drew with enjoyment. One day, I became aware that I was being observed. I swung round in Christian Brothers guilt. 'What the fuck are you doing wasting your time in a place like this? Get out and do something useful with your life!' His tone was brusque – almost impatient. He strode off through the swing doors. As I waited for them to settle, I began to consider what he had said. I had taken a year out of my life to please my Dad, but it must have been clear to everybody from Mr Lewis down that motor insurance was not something which would obsess me till my dying day. I asked my father whether he would let me go to University and, to my surprise, he agreed. Perhaps Mr Shute had had a word with him.

The only trouble was that I had no idea what to do with my degree, should I be lucky enough to get one. A friend mentioned that you could take a BA with a diploma in broadcasting, of all things. If I intended to make a career in that medium, I would need to specialise in appropriate subjects, the chief of these being English and Afrikaans. While welcoming the former, I dreaded the latter, particularly with the experience of school so fresh in my mind. It was suggested that, with the University on the far side of the mountain, I might go over to Rondebosch and stay with my grandmother, who had a spare room in her flat. It was a fair old hike from there to the campus but the exercise would do me good. I gave in my notice at the insurance company and, while there wasn't a person who didn't wish me well in my academic future, nobody seemed at all taken aback at my going, the surprise being that I'd lasted as long as I had.

When Dr Rice, my maternal grandfather, decided to retire I was two years old. He sold both the house in Coventry and his practice and he and my grandmother agreed to separate, though they never divorced. A year after we had arrived in Cape Town, she decided to join us. She was sixty-four and becoming increasingly deaf. Unhappily, my father and she didn't get on. Whether or not he was jealous of the attention my mother gave her it's hard to say, but when she visited he communicated by bellowing at her, calling her 'Mrs Rice' rather than a pet name, and never conversing for longer than he thought he could get away with without appearing rude. Consequently, she found it even harder to adjust to the new country and, having been discouraged from being too near us, moved several times in quick succession. The enforced separation from my mother must have been particularly wounding, and while it was true that they could be in touch by telephone, a visit to one another would take the best part of a day. Another bombshell came when Dr Rice stopped sending her money. However, in 1935 her cousin Agnes Garrett died leaving her an annuity of £200 a year which, to the end of her days, gave her precarious financial independence. By the end of the decade she had exhibited, with great success, a collection of floral studies of wild flowers of the area which would lead to the commissioning of a book with a foreword by the prime minister, General Smuts.

The origins of the book were in the world-renowned Kirstenbosch Gardens set on the eastern slopes of Table Mountain on land bequeathed to the nation by Cecil Rhodes on his death in 1902. The small area of the south-western Cape is acknowledged by botanists to be one of the richest in the world, there being more than 2,500 species indigenous to the Cape Peninsula alone. Just after the First World War, an Englishman, Robert Compton, took over as director of the gardens and, slowly but surely, a representative collection of all the country's indigenous plants was established which meant simulating the arid conditions of the Karoo, where many of the succulents thrive, on a mountainside where rainfall, particularly during the winter months, was abundant. Professor Compton remained director of Kirstenbosch for thirty-five years. His meeting with my grandmother was the beginning of a partnership which was to occupy fifteen years of their lives.

For each painting my grandmother received something in the region of £2. Today, this sounds a pittance, especially as I know to what lengths she went to ensure accuracy. On many occasions I was with her as she sat painting in silence, not daring even to remove either her hat or coat lest the flower in the glass of water in front of her should wilt. With her intimate knowledge of botany, which she had taught at Bedales as well as art, the detailed work she produced in water colour would have satisfied even the most critical of experts as well as enchanting those looking at the picture as a work of art. Most of the specimens were chosen by Professor Compton or by those in charge of the herbarium attached to the gardens, but occasionally I accompanied my Gran, now well into her seventies, up the slopes of the mountain in search of material. She carried a walking stick made of cherry-wood, her fine white hair catching the wind, her frail hand with its high, purple veins stretching forth to pluck the bloom of her choice, confident that, if challenged by a busybody, the permit in her pocket would dispel any argument.

Her flat in Rondebosch was on the first floor. It was a plain, modern building divided into two flats, the lower having the advantage of the garden. Gran had surrounded herself with her books and her flower paintings. There were several examples of her 'mosaic' work, a style she had evolved whereby each petal and each leaf of each flower would be painstakingly scissored from the finished sketch and then glued, piece by piece, one on top of the other, on to black paper. To complete the oriental look, her signature was added vertically, with a small pagoda symbolising the 'Garrett'. It was all done with gentle humour and more than a touch of self-mockery. Unnecessary doors in the flat were blocked off and converted into cupboards crammed with household items or painting materials, the curtain which concealed them a treasured, hand-printed cotton from West Africa. In the kitchen, she had spliced together with her own hands some broomsticks which could be taken, by means of a pulley, up to the ceiling to dry the washing. It was a gadget such as this which would earn the distinction of being labelled a 'Rice Device'. She had a lodger, a nurse by the name of Miss Chowles, who adored her and looked after her, did her shopping for her when she was busy and sat with her when she felt she might be lonely. As in my father's case, Miss Chowles believed that the best way of getting my Gran to hear was to bellow at her, little knowing that if you spoke quietly but enunciated you had far more chance of getting through. 'I do wish they wouldn't shout,' my grandmother would complain. 'I can never hear what they're saying.' In the flat below lived a jazz pianist who would drive her to distraction when he practised because she could hear only the bass notes, which were more or less the same for every tune he played. She had a diminutive appetite, existing largely on Bemax and prunes for breakfast, something light for lunch and a boiled egg, sometimes two, or something on toast in the evening. Special teaspoons were set aside for the eggs which, as a result, were stained almost black. She drank China tea. When I came to stay, she realised she'd have to buck up her ideas a bit, and constantly asked me what I would like to eat. Being far too polite to make demands, especially knowing how cautious she had to be with money, I usually settled for what she was eating, though I was sparing with the prunes, and made up for it when I traipsed up the steep hill for lectures at the University.

My first few months as a student were a revelation. I met up with old school friends like Jobie Stewart and, for the very first time in my life, felt liberated, for no longer did I have to learn what I was told to but was free to study as I chose, to exchange ideas and opinions with my peers. Jobie was a year ahead of me and had embarked upon drama as a subject for his BA degree. He was the sort of person everybody liked. I had known him since he was twelve when he had a mop of golden curls, for we were in the same class at the Christian Brothers. Now he was a slim young man in his late teens with a huge grin and a sense of the ridiculous. He was the first person I'd met who thought dogs were human beings and treated them accordingly, an original who encouraged a select few to join him in his irresponsible world of make-believe. He was to become my great friend. From having more or less ignored one another at school, we became inseparable. Through him, I was introduced to the humorous writings of James Thurber, S. J. Perelman and the novels of Caryl Brahms and S.J. Simon, and while he, having taken Drama as a subject, was clowning his way through *Gammer Gurton's Needle*, I was trudging through the Anglo-Saxon Chronicles in the English Department as well as trying to survive the indignity, in Afrikaans lectures, of having to stand up in front of everybody and read aloud from novels or poems as an example of how not to speak the language.

The English Department announced that it was to present *Twelfth Night* and, not knowing the play, I, in an impetuous moment, agreed to accept the role of Curio. It's one of the smallest parts Shakespeare wrote and not even remotely interesting to play, but the production introduced me to the finest Malvolio I have seen on any stage. The student's name was Gerald Bester. He was extremely tall and beaky – wonderfully funny – yet tragic at the same time. He never became a professional actor, and it has been many decades since I last saw him but, to this day, I remember every inflection of the 'letter' scene and studied him with a terrible envy as he rehearsed. Gerald by his very appearance was an outsider. You noticed him because he was different. It is what helped make him an exceptional Malvolio. The University boasted a tiny but compact theatre known as The Little at the top of Government Avenue. In the years I spent at Varsity, it was a place I came to know rather better than my text books. Jobie persuaded me to attend drama classes. There were lessons in movement, mime, improvisation, voice and verse-speaking which, although not strictly essential to a future broadcaster, or in some cases even welcomed, were in the same sort of area. In a building next to the theatre was a fully equipped broadcasting studio where I was to learn microphone technique, how to present a classical music programme, write a radio documentary, read the news and direct drama. While Jobie encouraged his friends to appear with him on the stage, I did my best to entice them into my radio programmes. Peter Lamsden, Meryl O'Keeffe, Tony Holbery and Cecil Jubber were the only other students taking the broadcasting diploma. This small band of enthusiasts became firm friends. No professor, no lecturer, no pompous student escaped our merciless impressions. It was at University that I learned to laugh.

My parents, naturally, were rather hoping that I would learn to be a scholar, but academic I wasn't and never would be. I was too anxious not to say or do anything wrong or out of place, and even though I had an appetite for research, my tendency to panic during examinations remained. For two years, I struggled to keep up, though the Little Theatre in the Avenue was claiming my attention more and more. What was it about the place with its stage flats stinking of the size, its creaking uncomfortable seats, its dark and chilly atmosphere which made it so captivating?

We got wind of the fact that a producer was returning to Cape Town with the script of Tennessee Williams's play *The Glass Menagerie* under his arm. It was to be presented at the Little Theatre and, needless to say, we all wanted to be in it. As we didn't know the man, nor he us, we decided to rehearse a programme of one-act plays, get sponsorship and a suitable venue, and invite him to the opening in the hope of being considered. All through the vacation, we rehearsed our project. It worked. He came and, as a reward for our enterprise, we were invited to audition for him. But, it was Jobie with his wide grin who got the coveted role of Tom. I was hopelessly disappointed and asked the producer why he had made the choice. He told me that I was a character actor and that it would be many years before I would make my mark. Many years. I couldn't understand what he was saying. An actor's an actor. What had my appearance to do with it? I was as right for the part as Jobie. The producer shook his head sadly and, in compensation, offered me the job of stage manager which, swallowing my pride, I accepted.

Having been obliged to admit to myself on a number of occasions in the past that I lacked a practical streak, I approached my new job with trepidation. Fortunately, there were others around me to take over if I seemed puzzled, but I learnt to cleat a flat and how to put up a set from a ground plan, though I would invariably have a problem hanging doors or putting up curtains and pelmets. Far more fascinating to me was the world of magic which was being created around me. Williams's story involved a domineering mother whose crippled daughter nursed a collection of glass animals, a gentleman caller lured in as a possible spouse, and the rebellious Tom who had escaped to sea, a part which I came to acknowledge fitted Jobie like a glove. He had a great success and it was clear that the theatre was something he enjoyed and for which he had a talent. It had happened so suddenly for him, and I tried not to be envious that his future had been so easily determined. Perhaps our producer, Leonard Schach, had been right after all. It was going to take me a long time to get anywhere.

It was a play by Bridget Boland called *Cockpit* which helped to point the way. Set in Eastern Europe at the end of the war, it involved a group of displaced persons herded together in a disused theatre. When there is a rumour of a plague epidemic, panic sets in, and to quell the disturbance an opera singer, in the group by a streak of good luck, is persuaded to come forward and sing. The old theatre swings back into life as the stage manager lowers an ancient backcloth, the rusty dimmers lower the lights, a carbonised follow-spot picks out the singer who is draped in bits and pieces unearthed in the wardrobe, and the aria begins. Needless to say, it does the trick. It sounds corny but, in fact, the play was extremely moving and had an extraordinary effect on the audiences who packed the theatre each evening. The actors played together as the perfect ensemble; indeed, there was a working atmosphere which I can't remember having been equalled in my fifty years in the theatre. Jobie played the British officer in charge, I, wearing a moustache, was his sergeant. As two young actors on the threshold of their careers, though we didn't know it at the time, we got the feeling that everyone wanted us to succeed.

Jobie's parents ran the Arthur's Seat Hotel in Sea Point. I remember the day that he came in to school very late looking woebegone, and how we were all told to be especially kind to him as his father had just died. It was heart disease, which was to claim Jobie's own life in his sixties. Mr Stewart, the hotelier, met Jobie's mother when she was a chorus girl at the old Tivoli Theatre in Cape Town. He'd gone backstage without an invitation and took her on one side to whisper, 'From now on, I'm going to be the only man who sees those legs.' Far from seeming a heavy-handed approach to Dot, it did the trick. In the years following his death, she grew into a formidable matriarch, stern of visage and dangerous if crossed – as when she found out that her son Jobie was 'a queer'. Many were the times when I spent the night at their home overlooking the sea at St James's, the tiny beach with its brightly painted bathing huts to the right, and the little railway line, running parallel to the main road, which carried the electric trains to and from Cape Town and seemed to dip in and out of the very waves themselves. 'Granny Dot', as she liked to be called, would receive me from her bed, having already breakfasted, her tray delivered by either Doreen or May, two maiden sisters who had ministered to her every need for years and, well-prepared for visitors, leaning at ease against the pillows, would greet me in a baritone voice and an infectious laugh, ending in a fit of coughing whenever I said something which amused her.

I would reciprocate by inviting Jobie to stay over at our home in Camps Bay. He didn't particularly relish mealtimes and once referred to my mother as 'arguably the worst cook in Africa'. Besides, my father could be very awkward with guests and invariably there would be an ugly scene if they neglected to leave a clean plate. After meals, Dad would commandeer the sitting room and blast away at the grand piano, threatening, it seemed, to bring down the ceiling. He frequently chose 'Rustle of Spring' by Sinding or one of Chopin's works, usually one of the more difficult pieces, a mazurka or a polonaise with which he couldn't quite keep up. The 'Minute' waltz was a particular favourite, though not of ours. He'd stop and start again repeatedly in his determination to achieve the perfection which somehow always managed to elude him. His persistence, though admirable in some respects, could be trying as, in a smallish house, there was no escape. Dad was happiest at the organ where he could thunder away to his heart's content, and one day, though dismissive of their beliefs which he found rather quaint, he undertook the post of organist at the Unitarian Church because they had a fine instrument with all the pipes and it gave him a chance to practise. It was at one of these weekend visits to our house that I introduced Jobie to the Cambrian Society.

My mother had been invited to one of their musical evenings and had dragged me along, an extremely unwilling companion. Madam Myfanwy-Mayer, clearly in the driving seat as far as the society was concerned, made her entrance to rapturous applause. She inclined her head graciously to left and right, a stout figurehead of a woman with silver hair and the sort of contralto voice that might warn ships off rocks. Her songs on this particular occasion had been chosen to reflect not her dramatic intensity, which could be considerable, but rather her naughty sense of humour. They had been selected from an Edwardian musical called *The Arcadians*. As her partner, she had selected Mr Rosser-Dummer, who looked the stereotypical Dickensian undertaker. Together they sang 'Oh, what very charming weather', finishing up with a little dance of such oddity, with such flashing of smiles and flirting of eyes, that I was captivated. Mrs Rosser-Dummer glided on next. She was a diminutive lady with a fine mezzo, and always wore a long evening dress which totally obscured her feet so that, her entrance being unruffled and serene, she gave the impression of being on wheels. Her performance, good though it was, bore no challenge whatsoever to the gracious lady who followed her. Gladys Coleman, who had sung so splendidly at our house-warming, now, on the stage of the little hall, launched into 'What is life without thee?' from Gluck's opera *Orfeo ed Euridice* with magnificent aplomb, and the audience thundered their applause. The programme seemed constructed to go husband, wife, husband, wife and so on, so it was Mr Coleman's turn next on the flute, distinguished by his managing to produce no sound whatsoever from the instrument itself. All that the audience was privileged to see was his frenzied fingerwork, and all we could hear was his staccato breath across the holes of the flute. In a break with convention, it was Mr Rosser-Dummer's turn next in a solo. It came as no surprise that he should sing of Death, his voice deep and lugubrious, his mournful eyes lifted heavenward, his hands clasped before him as if in prayer. The programme ended when the entire cast raised the roof with the Welsh National Anthem for which we all stood. I begged my mother to ask them all over for a similar evening at the house, and invited Jobie without telling him what he had in store.

Nobody who had even the smallest ability was let off lightly. My father was persuaded to play the piano, I found a comic item to recite, my sister Sheila sang 'Trees' and Ernie, her new boyfriend, paid tribute to 'The Dying Swan', performing with ferocious concentration on the cello. The evening was declared to have been an enormous success and even my mother's contribution of 'light snacks' – prunes stuffed with cream cheese, known for some reason as 'angels on horseback', and fish paste on savoury biscuits – attracted not a breath of criticism.

That night, after they had all gone, Jobie and I lay in our beds, going over and over the joys of the concert. It was astonishing how close I felt to him. We thought so much alike it was as though we were brothers. I knew that I felt for him deeply and that he was someone with whom I wanted to spend the rest of my life. My voice faltered every so often as I spoke in my nervousness. I'd never divulged my emotions to anyone before and hardly knew how to say what I wanted him to know. I couldn't believe he wouldn't be sympathetic at the very least. I knew him well enough for that. He, above anyone. I spoke in a low whisper lest anyone in the sleeping house might stir and overhear my confession. When finally I came to a stop, there was a long silence. Then he said, 'I couldn't possibly, Nige. You make me laugh too much.' And that was that. I'm not sure our relationship ever recovered from that evening when the Cambrian Society came and I decided to unburden my soul. A distance grew between Jobie and me. Not a great chasm, but a wariness on his part. Perhaps understandably. We still continued much as before, spoke on the telephone for hours, laughed at the same things – but when it came to holidays, he'd take other friends. I was never invited. Slowly but surely our paths were beginning to drift apart.

By the end of my second year at University, my progress was arousing concern. There was no doubt at all that my activities in the theatre had been getting in the way. I wasn't applying myself to my books as I should, and professors were looking at me over their half-moon spectacles as if silently to echo Brother McEvoy's dire pronouncement, 'Hawthorne, what will become of you?' In addition, I had persuaded myself that I was pretty hopeless at broadcasting and lacked the commitment. In short, I was dithering around at a loss to know in which area I wanted to focus my life.

At the height of this uncertain period matters were taken out of my hands. Leonard Schach, the producer who had cautioned me that I might have a long wait before being successful, announced a production of Arthur Laurent's wartime American play, *Home Of The Brave*. Jobie and I and Tony Holbery were offered excellent parts though, this time, with a surprising innovation. We were to be paid. Not much, of course, but enough to say in a tentative way that we had 'turned professional'. There was only one truly professional management in town, which was run by actor/manager Brian Brooke, who one evening came to see the play and, on the strength of what he saw, wrote inviting me to join the company. Jobie and Tony had offers from the newly-formed National Theatre which was doing *Hassan*, the dramatic verse-play by James Elroy Flecker, to be directed by the famous British director Basil Dean who, during the war, had run ENSA. The difference between the two companies was considerable. They did 'Art'. The Brian Brooke Company was 'commercial'; we did pot-boilers and 'West End successes' like farces and frothy comedies with French windows. Having been selected by the latter, perhaps this was the line my future career would be taking?

I had been to the cramped Hofmeyr Theatre on many occasions to see their productions. One needed a fair bit of imagination to describe the building as a theatre, for it was totally encased in an extremely ugly yellow brick office block hard up against the mid-nineteenth-century Dutch Reformed Church which owned it. In fact, the two buildings were so close they gave the impression of holding one another up. Well, I suppose they were in spirit. The Hofmeyr Hall, for that was how it was known in those days, had no raked auditorium, only two dressing rooms, no wing space or flying space and one side of the audience was entirely taken up by high, curtained windows looking out on to the church clock tower – which mercifully didn't chime, though the glass rattled distractingly whenever the South-Easter blew.

These qualifications apart, the hall had a surprising amount of atmosphere, and when I had gone there as a member of the audience I'd generally been enthralled by the experience, if not by the play itself. Students are inclined to be dismissive of conventional material performed in a conventional way, and I was no exception. The standard was variable as the company was small and stretched, yet the leading lady was exceptional, and her performance as Catherine Sloper in *The Heiress*, which Leonard had directed, had been subtle and deeply moving. I might now have the chance of acting with the great Petrina Fry, for that was her name. Not even her best friend would have described her as a beauty; she was minute and had a snub nose like a Pekinese, but her range was enormous, her energy colossal and her talent invariably dwarfed the performances of those around her. It was time for a decision to be made. But first, there was the venerable parent to confront.

Oddly enough, when important moments such as this arise, the memory of what happened and who said what to whom is so much less clear than with silly, trivial things. Perhaps it's because the memory is so painful that one subconsciously erases it. Suffice to say that a stunned silence greeted the news that, not only was I going to pull out of University before completing my degree, but the reason was that I meant to become a professional actor. I know that my father was bitterly angry, feeling that the money he had scraped together for my education had been squandered and, even though he himself had dabbled in the theatre while at Cambridge, he had lost all interest in it by this time, looking on it as mere 'dressing up and pulling faces' and not in any way to be taken seriously – certainly not to be considered as a way of making a living. My decision must have been a massive disappointment to him and I don't believe he ever forgave me. I tried to explain that, at long last, I'd stumbled on something I really wanted to do and felt that, given wind in the right direction, I might even succeed. He didn't believe a word of it. I'd let him down. My mother was encouraging, but then she was optimistic by nature, believing that only good would come out of something about which I'd made up my mind. Besides, she knew me well enough to realise that I'd go to the ends of the earth to prove to her and my father that I'd made the right choice, for I had inherited his pride, and wouldn't shirk the commitment.

It was customary in South Africa for a twenty-first birthday to be celebrated with a huge party. There was no time for such indulgence in my case as, that very morning, I reported for work at the Hofmeyr Theatre. 'My dear chap,' said Brian Brooke across the desk. 'You couldn't have joined us at a worse time. I've just come from a meeting of the auditors and, without boring you with all the details, can offer you only three pounds a week.' My suntan must have paled a little at the news, but I'd burned my boats and had no option but to accept. The job offered to me was to be an assistant stage manager and to play small parts 'when required', which meant that they didn't have to give them to me if they didn't want to. There was a new production every three weeks or so, depending on the success of the previous one. An English actor, Gabriel Toyne, had joined the company with a certain amount of trumpeting to play Descius Heiss in *The Shop At Sly Corner*, a creaking thriller about an antique dealer who specialised in Japanese netsuki. As you can imagine, there weren't a great many of these lurking in the antique shops of Cape Town, but nevertheless, as one of my duties, I was despatched to borrow any I could find. In this sort of company, a great deal depended on good will. Most of the furniture used on the stage came either from our own homes or those of friends, while if we were attempting a period play, it had to be hired or, if we could get away with it, borrowed from collectors. In addition, I had to mark up the prompt book to be sure that all the cues were clearly and correctly annotated – 'Stand by door bell. Go, door bell' and so on – which I believe I did with reasonable if not immaculate efficiency, and sat 'on the book' to prompt the actors when necessary in rehearsals, which were already well advanced by the time I joined.

Gabriel Toyne was a stout man who liked his drink, a bully with a filthy temper, sharply critical of those opposite whom he was playing. One of these unfortunates was in the role of the crook Archie Fellowes. Gabriel fired him a couple of days before the opening night and a small deputation descended on me to persuade me to take over. It was a good part with a lot of sneering and blackmailing so, of course, I agreed, despite the fact that there didn't seem to be any extra financial consideration. My first professional job and I was playing one of the leads – whether by default or not didn't come into it. The programmes were hastily reprinted with the rearranged cast, amongst whom was a brilliant actress, Hilda Kriseman, later to be a stalwart on the BBC Rep, and Tony Wright, who became a Rank star a few years later and who had offered his services to the Brookes by sending them a photograph of himself in a G-string. He was hired on the spot.

My success as Archie was to lead to other things. Toyne was to direct *Edward My Son*, Robert Morley's excellent play co-written with Noel Langley, about a ruthless man and his alcoholic wife. I had the small, unlikely role of Mr Waxman, the Viennese foot specialist attending the young Edward. Toyne, having cast me well against type for this mature individual, insisted that I play the role with a pronounced limp and leaning on the silver knobbed walking stick I had managed to prise from a friend of the family. On the opening night, my stage-managerial duties having occupied me right up to the moment immediately before the rise of the curtain, I realised that there was only a short scene before I had to make my appearance. I raced to the dressing room, threw aside my working clothes and pulled on my formal suit, then embarked on a hasty make-up of how I considered a fifty-five-year-old man might look – rather like someone out of *Shangri La*, as it turned out. As I grabbed my walking stick from the prop table, someone whispered urgently, 'Your hair!' I raced back to the dressing room, seized the Johnson's Baby Powder and coated my light-brown locks as effectively as I could before limping on to the stage, having made my entrance by the skin of my teeth. Afterwards, my father commented, 'Interesting stuff, giving a foot specialist a deformed foot, but need he have had quite so much dandruff?'

Toyne tinkered about rather a lot during the production with what he called 'tonal' lighting. The play comprised a number of scenes in different locations. The idea was to paint each of the stage flats in two different colours so that, when cleverly lit, it would look like different rooms. He never achieved this distinction. However hard he tried, however many times he experimented, it always looked like the same room. He arrived one evening for the performance – in which he played the headmaster – distinctly the worse for drink. We left him nursing a cup of black coffee, but a couple of minutes before he was due to appear, he was nowhere to be found. We searched everywhere – up and down the fire escape, every nook and cranny. Eventually one of the actors had no option but to step forward to announce that the part would be read by another actor that evening as Mr Toyne had become suddenly indisposed. Barely had the words left his mouth than there was an eruption from the back of the theatre: 'Who's fucking indisposed?' The startled audience swivelled round to see Gabriel Toyne, who had been dead to the world, struggling to his feet, and watched mesmerised as he lurched down the aisle and through the pass door, slamming it with a mighty crash. He insisted on going on. 'You're pissed, old chap, pissed as a newt!' Brian told him. 'I'm not allowing you on my stage.' Toyne was a big and powerfully built man but, between us, we managed to hold him down and lock him in the Gents where, until he passed out cold, his beating on the door and persistent return to the four-letter word was to punctuate what was left of the first act.

It was around this time that I was given a rise in salary. The company had need of a publicity manager and, on my acceptance of this exalted position, I was given another pound a week. Four pounds a week! I was rich. Somehow, I had to fit in this new position with my duties as a stage manager, as well as the increasing demands being made on my services as an actor. Each day, I had to be up at the crack to prepare and hand in the advertisement which was to appear in the *Cape Times* the following morning. The same with the evening *Argus*. It was company policy that it was more eye-catching if the wording differed from day to day. I had to come up with crowd-pullers every morning before rehearsals, which proved so much of a strain I began to look upon it as an imposition. I'd moved from home into town by this stage, as the travelling would have been impossible. In Bree Street, on the edge of the Malay Quarter, John and Madeleine Farley had a rambling mid-Victorian house which, being artists themselves, they let out to those with a similar persuasion. John's paintings hung on every wall of my room, in the hall, up the stairs, in the bathrooms – in fact the whole place reeked of linseed oil. The late Forties was a fascinating period for art in the Cape. There was a wealth of talent about and I always wished that I'd been able to afford to buy one of John's pictures. Freda Lock was another artist whose works I coveted, but it was not to be. I had a very good reason for wanting to save my pennies.

I had become friendly with Ba and Shaun Sutton, two other English actors who had joined the company, and asked them over to Camps Bay to meet my family. Over lunch, I had broached the subject of a stage career in England. Did they think I'd stand a chance? They were tactful enough to make encouraging noises. It wasn't as though I was unhappy as a member of the Brian Brooke Company, but I felt that, in many ways, it was the end of the line. It was either them or the National Theatre, there was no other, and the National was already favouring Afrikaans plays and actors. I knew that Jobie wanted to try his luck overseas too, which was an added incentive. In fact, we had discussed the idea when his tour of *Hassan* played Cape Town. It was a huge decision to make. Preposterous, reckless, absurd – not even to be contemplated by the cold light of day. Neither of us had any money, nor the prospect of making a large sum in a short space of time. Also, we were totally ignorant of what hardships we might face when we got there. We had no delusions about the streets being paved with gold, we knew that we would be entering a new world of austerity and rationing, but equally had no real concept of how much unemployment there might be in the acting profession, how hard it would be to get started.

Over the next few months, the idea began to crystallise. It was time to count our pennies, and save up for the boat trip. Our enthusiasm for adventure proved infectious. In two short weeks, seven hopefuls including Tony Holbery and Hilda Kriseman were to leave the shores of Table Bay, hoping to make their names in Shaftesbury Avenue. The press got hold of the story. 'The tragedy is that, to make their careers on the lines they themselves have chosen, South Africa is no use to them except as a training ground . . . they will all be missed,' wrote the critic of the *Argus*. The other English-speaking critic, Ivor Jones of the *Cape Times*, had been especially kind to me both as an amateur and after I'd turned professional. I decided to seek him out to say goodbye. He wasn't in his office, but I was told I could find him at his favourite haunt, the Café Royal which had an upstairs bar. Though it was only mid-morning he was well on the way. 'And what can I do for you, young man?' I told him that I was off to try my luck on the London stage. He extended a limp hand. 'See you back in six months, dear boy,' he said. I could feel the blood rushing to my face in anger as I leapt to my feet. 'No you bloody well won't!' The words came through gritted teeth.

With just about everything I possessed in the hold of the *Arundel Castle* and a two-week voyage on the open sea ahead of me, I would find plenty of time to ruminate on what I had let myself in for. Foremost in my mind was my madness in going to London with only twelve months' experience in the theatre, no training to speak of, no financial back-up – for my father had shaken his head sadly, 'I can't help you, I'm afraid' – and no contacts. What was I thinking of? It was far too late to turn back. I waved at my disappearing family until I could see them no more, and with one last look at the mountain I loved almost as much as I did them, flicked the stub of my cigarette into the churning waters and went below. At least when we got there I'd be able to see Ba and Shaun, for they had sent my father a telegram the week before: 'Will meet boat train Waterloo.' There was plenty to celebrate. It was the day following my twenty-second birthday and Festival of Britain year in England, the place of my birth. I had six months to prove myself.

6

Home

To come from the blue, white, yellow and green, the iridescent colours of the Cape, to the dull, grey overcrowding of England was a major shock. Back there was space, tall mountains, clear skies, here were endless and, to my young eyes, ugly buildings jammed up on each other in such dark, smoky profusion that my heart sank into misery and fear as the boat train rattled into London.

They were there at the barrier to meet me, Ba and Shaun, as good as their word. 'I've got you an interview,' Shaun told me as we humped my luggage in the direction of the taxi rank. I was to go to the Embassy Theatre in Swiss Cottage to meet Anthony Hawtrey, who was putting together a company for the summer season in Buxton, Derbyshire. I could hardly believe my ears. It was so unexpected. On the boat train, I had counted my pennies to find that all I possessed in the world was twelve pounds and a few coppers. It wasn't going to take me very far, so with any luck . . .

Hawtrey was a solidly built man with the aquiline profile of a well-to-do Roman. One of the last of the actor-managers, he settled behind what seemed an unnecessarily large desk to tell me that he'd been given a good report of me by Shaun and would I be interested in the job of assistant stage manager and playing small parts? He leaned across the desk to proffer a silver cigarette case, but I beat him to it. An almost full carton of fifty Senior Service I'd bought on the boat was under his nose in a trice, and he had no option but to capitulate. Then, with the supreme agility of youth, I sprang to my feet lighter at the ready before he had a chance to fumble for the matches.

Eyeing me steadily, he eased back in his armchair, effortlessly blowing out the smoke through his nostrils, the epitome of sophistication. 'Are you prepared to take off your coat and roll up your sleeves?' he asked in his urbane drawl. Barely had the words left his mouth than I had tossed my jacket nonchalantly on to the nearest chair and was in the process of unbuttoning my cuffs when he raised his hand to stop me. 'I didn't mean now,' he said wearily.

In only three short days I'd got myself a job, and some digs in South Kensington. Salary of seven pounds a week. And I was to act. The gods were smiling on me at last. And while on the subject of 'the gods', with the security of a summer season at hand, I went on a theatre spree with the little money I had left and, for the next two weeks before leaving for Buxton, saw a play every day – sometimes two if there was a matinée, going without a meal rather than be late for the gallery queue. In those days you could get in for half a crown or even less and, although the view of the stage was hardly perfect, there was an excitement about going which has never quite been replaced by booking through a ticket agency.

In the time I had left, I wandered around London, trying to come to terms with its vastness, yet being astonished at how small the buildings were after the skyscrapers to which I'd been accustomed, feeling particular disappointment with the set pieces like Piccadilly Circus and Trafalgar Square which I had imagined to be on a far grander scale than the reality. I found myself star-spotting around St Martin's Lane and Charing Cross Road, frequented pubs like the Salisbury, known to be popular with theatre folk, and became a regular at the self-service restaurant in Lyon's Corner House, Leicester Square, where you could eat as much as you liked for surprisingly little. Jobie had cautioned me to eat as many vegetables as I could so that, despite the rationing, I would be getting the maximum amount of nutrition. He had left for Warrington in Lancashire where, like me, he'd got a job in weekly rep. Tony was in Felixstowe and Hilda Kriseman in Chesterfield, the others visiting relatives or friends. So I was on my own in London in those two eventful weeks, yet somehow managed to fill my days with enough adventures to stave off the feelings of home-sickness that were already beginning to manifest themselves.

The shows I was seeing were proof conclusive that I'd come to the right place. The standard, with a few exceptions, was astonishing and the theatres themselves glorious shrines of great architectural beauty. When I got the opportunity of landing a seat in the front row, I'd hang over the gallery rail gazing down upon the multi-tiered chandeliers – reminding me of Lena's birthday cakes – finding the horse-shoe shapes, the ornate ashtray boxes, the velvet curtains with their swags and tassels, the whole Edwardian elaboration unbelievably cluttered and romantic. I was being privileged to watch my heroes and heroines from these dizzy heights – Robertson Hare, that star of the Ralph Lynn – Tom Walls farces with his shining bald head and cries of 'Oh calamity!' was in a terrible piece of hokum called *Will Any Gentleman . . . ?*, yet he was the actor I chose to see on my first night in London. I loved farce, though forced to admit that it was rather more fun to perform than to watch. Mr Hare didn't let me down and his appearance of bewildered outrage, his muffled bleats of 'Thing upon thing!' are with me still. I fell under the spell of Anouilh, seeing Margaret Rutherford, Paul Scofield and Claire Bloom in the haunting *Ring Round The Moon* with a stunning set by Oliver Messel. Laurence Olivier (the actor who at that time most inspired me) had brought over from America *The Consul*, an opera by Menotti, and I was lucky enough to catch one of the last performances. The story concerned displaced persons, the very group of people we had encountered only eighteen months earlier in our production of *Cockpit*. The press had been scathing about it, but I remember a packed house jumping to its feet, myself included, to cheer to the echo at the curtain call. In Cape Town, theatre audiences were accustomed to applauding politely, seldom giving way to their feelings. I had never been in the midst of such an emotional response, and it made me prouder than ever before that I too was a member of so glorious a profession.

Yet, far from diminishing in my mind, I was being reminded, almost on an hourly basis, of what I had left behind. I had only to glance upward at the watery London skies to be taken straight back in my mind to the Cape Town equivalent. I had only to reach for my ration book, ride on the crowded Underground, go past a bombsite, gaze across the river at the Festival of Britain's Dome of Discovery which I couldn't afford to visit, to realise how out of place I was in this strange, exhilarating new world. Would I ever belong? I took consolation from the fact that I was to be working in a short while – yet it was only a brief summer season. What, I wondered, would happen when it was over?

From my new digs, I wrote my first letter home. Earlier that evening I'd had an altercation with the landlady, who had rapped on the bathroom door demanding to know whether I knew what time it was. I'd called out helpfully that I thought it was just after eleven, and got a terrible earful about taking a bath at such an ungodly hour. Unnerved and puzzled by this fierce attack, I finally pushed it from my mind as an example of eccentric English behaviour, then sat up in bed to compose a letter to my mother in which I tried to put into words some of my reactions to this chilly country and its curiously chilly people. The young are quick to make judgments. I went on to tell her some of my feelings about leaving her and the family – with all the packing and rushing about prior to my sailing, there hadn't really been time. One of the saddest farewells had been to my beloved grandmother, Mrs Rice. It was as though we knew, as we embraced on the quayside, that our paths were separating for ever. I had posed for a photograph with her and Sheila and her husband, Ernie, whose bonny child Sally, my god-daughter, I held in my arms. As usual, my Gran faced away from the camera as if fearful that it might launch an attack upon her. To the casual observer it might have appeared that she was indifferent to the occasion, though this I knew to have been very far from the case.

I determined to write regularly to my grandmother giving her all the news, and to my mother, who I knew had been hurt and puzzled by my decision to break up the family. For my parents and for my grandmother, England was home and always would be. However much they loved the new country in which they'd settled, their hearts would be in that home across the seas, yet, the furniture we'd brought with us excepted, the house we had built bore little relationship to the country of our origin. It was a thoroughly South African home with its verandahs, its stone-walled terraces, and whitewashed interior. The outside of the house was white too, yet with a dash of pink which, in a practical moment, my mother had suggested might soften the glare. Other expatriates would often try to simulate what they remembered of the old country, but no such duplication would have been to my parents' taste.

That said, the Cape with its fresh air and uncluttered streets suited my father down to the ground, though he feared the heat of its sun because of his fair complexion. His skin would redden and blister alarmingly and he would resort to the extreme measure of sprinkling his raw scalp with methylated spirits in an attempt to alleviate the pain, crying out several times as he did so, 'Oh, my poor head! Oh, my poor head!' Though he wrote seldom, in his own way he'd keep in touch with members of his family back in England, receiving letters from his sisters, Mabel, Olive and Georgie, from their homes in Surrey and Leamington Spa on occasions such as Christmas – as we did on our birthdays, for the aunts had been enlisted as god-parents, each of us benefiting throughout the war from an annual half crown postal order. 'Have you written to thank

Auntie Georgie for the postal order?' 'Not yet, Mum.' 'Well, will you please do so.' Yet, as far as I knew, my parents had no plans to return to the other home – the home they would always know as home. To begin with, they couldn't have afforded to do so but also because, in their own way, despite the frictions, they were content.

That feeling of contentment was very far from my own restlessness. With my sexuality a growing concern I had been desperate to get away. At twenty-two, unattached and uninvolved, I was lonely. I needed to find a partner with whom I could spend my days without constantly having to justify his presence to baffled and possibly hostile parents. And surely I had chosen the right profession? The theatre was supposed to be rife with homosexuals, yet the ones I'd met so far had not appealed to me, being too camp and obvious, not the sort with whom one could be seen without people staring and tongues wagging. Some day I would find someone discreet, gentle and warm-hearted who would share my likes and dislikes, someone with the same sense of humour who would put up with my foibles. Little did I know how long it would take me.

On the train to Buxton, I watched the English countryside flash by through the carriage window. It was a trip into the unknown. I found myself apprehensive that my limited acting experience should count against me. The job was vital to me, it was imperative that I hold it down. My suntan mercifully had begun to fade, yet I couldn't help but be conscious that I was a foreigner in this grey land with its smoking chimneys and joined-together houses. I suppose I must have sported a South African accent despite the Englishness of my upbringing and couldn't imagine there would be too many South African plays in which I could shine in the Buxton repertoire. If regional accents were required I'd just have to bluff it out – acting was all pretend, anyway. In those days, we had to provide most of our own clothes unless it was a period play, and my cheap suits and sports jacket were in the suitcase on the rack above. There was a dinner jacket, too, and plenty of ties, cravats and scarves to ring the changes. My precious workman's lunch box which held my Leichner make-up, without which no actor worth his salt would travel, was stuffed into a corner, but pride of place was given to the two ten-by-eight professional portraits I'd splashed out on in London just in case they'd need them for the display frames outside the theatre. They were by Landseer – not the Victorian artist of 'Monarch of the Glen' fame, but a theatrical photographer who somehow managed to make everybody look identical. Behind each head was a nimbus and the face was in every case methodically wiped of wrinkles and blemishes – and consequently of personality. I was, I told myself, all things considered, equipped – but only just.

It should have been an exciting journey, that train trip taking me to my first job in England, yet I felt strangely flat. My upbringing may have left me bewildered but it had been both civilised and comfortable. Although we had never been wealthy, we had always had enough on which to live and, by and large, I had been surrounded with the minimum of torment. But now I was doing what I'd wanted to do. It was too late for indecisive silliness, the train had just passed Chapel en le Frith and we'd soon be in Buxton.

The Opera House was a splendid piece of Victoriana with an imposing entrance, ideally placed for a theatre, its architecture splendidly in keeping with the handsome stone buildings which comprised the attractive spa town. We weren't playing there though, we were in the Playhouse up the road. By contrast this was an unprepossessing building, though it adjoined the splendid Spring Gardens with their high, glazed windows like a gothic conservatory. The dressing rooms were under the stage, dusty and airless. A few years ago, I went back there just to see what it was like. They were playing Bingo in the stalls and the dress circle had been sealed off. Pretending I was there in an official capacity, I strode purposefully in the direction of the pass door which, as I well remembered though it had been nearly fifty years earlier, led to the part of the building inhabited by the actors. The door ahead of me said 'No Entry' but, as nobody seemed to be looking, I tried the handle and it yielded. There was just enough light for me to see that I was standing on what used to be the stage. Here we had performed plays like *The Ghost Train* and *George And Margaret*, the farce *Charley's Aunt* and a thriller set in a convent, *Bonaventure*. I turned in the direction of the staircase which used to lead to the prop room and the dressing rooms, but it looked rickety so I decided not to risk it. It's always sad to see a theatre being used for other purposes, sad to see it emasculated, but they can't rob it of its memories. For two seasons I'd cut my teeth on that stage and beyond the fire curtain, where now someone was calling out 'Lucky for some – number 13', had sat an audience.

Brian Whittle was married to the set designer, Mamie Purvis. Brian was the small, dark-haired, constantly-scratching stage manager whom I grew to loathe. He was my immediate boss. It was my own fault, I suppose, wanting to be an actor first and foremost and not, like him, a stage manager. He didn't like actors and he certainly didn't like me. I suppose that seeing me he must have felt let down by Hawtrey, who had lumbered him with someone who wasn't a master carpenter or in any way committed to the technical world of stage management. I was introduced to my first get-in when, early on a Sunday morning, we began to assemble the set for the four-handed comedy, *Castle In The Air*. 'The library of Locharne Castle in Aberdeenshire', announced the programme, followed by a list of the people from whom I'd begged, borrowed or stolen the furniture and properties. My first job was to help carry the stage flats from the lorry parked outside the dock doors and help cleat them together to form the set. Cleating was a knack. You had to flick your wrist in such a way that the rope ended up over the hook at the top of the high flat. I got rather good at cleating. But there my accomplishments ended. My aptitude for putting up pelmets and curtains hadn't improved, and I was even worse at hanging doors. Brian saw my weakness in a flash and, each week, those were my allotted tasks and the bane of my life – as well he knew.

Shaun was the producer, or what we now term as the director, and his wife Ba was in most of the plays. She was an appalling giggler, something to which in those days I too was prone, so I used to dread being cast opposite her. Sooner or later we would both be rendered helpless and speechless, locked in joyful agony. But it was to be another month before I would be given my first role, the curate in *Murder At The Vicarage* by Agatha Christie in which, as part of my duties, I had to prepare a three-course meal complete with dumplings and, worse still, sit at the table with the rest of the cast and eat it with them. In addition to having inherited my mother's lack of expertise in the kitchen, I seldom found time to prepare the food with any thoroughness, and the murderous looks of the members of the company as they struggled to remember the lines while downing my personal interpretation of beef stew are with me to this day.

Weekly rep no longer exists, but it was a good training ground for the actor. It was in the days before democracy had made its equalising entrance through the stage door, and actors did as they were instructed and weren't invited to make suggestions. Shaun Sutton was perfect for the job of director, a warm and friendly man who did his homework. We diligently scribbled his instructions into the margin of our scripts – in pencil as they had to be returned – 'cross down right to French windows, light cigarette and exhale before sitting armchair. Sip sherry before speaking' – all written in actors' shorthand. We all did a great deal of smoking. It was very useful if you weren't very sure of your lines, and few of us were. Rehearsals began first thing on Tuesday morning, the previous production having opened the evening before. In the afternoon we learnt the first act, coming to the theatre in the evening to perform the other play. After a quick drink at the pub when it was all over, we went back to our digs to learn lines, for the next morning we were expected to know Act 2. And so on through the week. Sundays were free, unless you were unlucky enough to be a member of the stage management, as I was, when it was always your busiest day.

'What are you doing on Sunday?' asked Jobie, phoning from Warrington. I explained that I had a get-in. 'So have I.' We agreed to meet early afternoon in Manchester, which was sort of half way. I arrived in good time and sat around on a bench reading the Sunday papers. He kept me waiting for seven hours. Eventually, I had no option but to grab a sandwich and catch the last train back to Buxton. As it pulled out of the station, Jobie came racing down the platform waving frantically. 'We'll have to make it another time!' I mouthed through the closed window. I wasn't angry. Jobie always made me laugh. Two weekends later, rather than risk a recurrence and knowing from experience his appalling track record for punctuality, I decided to go to Warrington after I'd finished work on Sunday morning. Brian, rather reluctantly, let me go before lunch in order to catch my train. Sunday trains took for ever and there was a good deal of shunting and going backwards. I thought we'd never get there. When at long last we did arrive, I took a cab to the stage door of the theatre where Jobie worked. As we greeted one another, I noticed that he'd asked the cab driver to wait. 'You'll have to rush if you want to catch the last train,' Jobie explained, pushing me back into the seat.

There was also the matter of relatives and friends of the family. I had been getting letters and postcards as they dutifully tried to make contact. Marjory Gibbs had been at Bedales when my grandmother had been teaching art and they had remained in touch, so I'd been given strict instructions to look her up. She lived in Kingston-upon-Thames and I was invited to lunch one Sunday to meet her. Because I was expected to work, Sundays were always a tricky proposition but, because we had a fairly easy set for Emlyn Williams's truly terrible play, *A Murder Has Been Arranged* – the empty stage of the St James's Theatre in London – I was allowed to go on condition that I was back by the evening to give a hand with the lighting.

Marjory turned out to be a delight. Her only son had been killed in the war and she had separated from her husband, so I was particularly welcome as someone to mother. She knew that in those days I smoked, and asked in her precisely enunciated way whether I would like my cigarette before or after lunch. Alarmed that my intake was to be rationed, I changed tack. 'I wonder whether it would be possible for me to wash my hair?' I asked. To clarify, I explained that the previous evening I had been in a play called *Travellers' Joy* and, as I was playing the manager of the hotel who was a man of mature years, had used some shoe whitening on my hair to help with the age, and hadn't had time to wash it out. Without batting an eyelid, she handed me a jug for rinsing and led the way upstairs to her bathroom which was a-gleam with white porcelain. She passed me a clean towel before leaving me alone so she could get on with the preparation of lunch. As I raised the jug over my head to rinse away the shampoo, the handle snapped, the jug crashed through the porcelain basin and, in seconds, there was broken china everywhere and the carpeted bathroom was awash with soapy water. I stood aghast at what had happened, then heard her call from below, every consonant in place, 'Everything all right, dear?' Her face was a study as she surveyed the devastation, but she was wonderful about it, taking full responsibility and mercifully refusing point blank to accept my offer to replace things and repair the damage. It was an inauspicious start to a friendship, but somehow we managed to survive it and would remain close until her death in 1970.

A Murder Has Been Arranged lived up to our expectation as a real stinker, though the audience loved it and later voted it as

Play of the Season. The fact that we all had to dress up as ghosts of history somehow made it worse. 'Perhaps you are – Henry of Navarre,' someone had to say to me, which never failed to set me off into a fit of giggling. I really would have to do something about these irresponsible lapses. I had been warned that Mr Hawtrey couldn't abide gigglers and that, should he make one of his unscheduled visits, I'd be out on my neck. A few weeks later, he was to be given that opportunity.

The play was *Charley's Aunt.* I had played Charley in Cape Town, finding it one of the most boring parts ever written – a lot of hard work for very little reward – but, to my acute disappointment, when the castlist went up on the board, I was allotted that same character. When I'd done it previously, I'd had a bout of giggles one night when, in the Third Act where we were all in evening dress, the actress playing Kitty had moved over to me from her seat by the fire without realising that the fire-irons were caught up in her lace skirt. The clatter they made must have wakened the dead. In the Buxton production, whenever I got to that same moment, I'd begin to laugh. Why I should have done so baffled everybody in the company including me. In this production, Kitty was placed nowhere near the fireplace. One Friday night, I was told that Hawtrey was out there and that I'd better watch myself. However, when the moment arrived, nervousness made me giggle more than ever, so much so that I had to leave the stage. After the show there was a stern knock at my door. 'What happened?' Hawtrey demanded to know. I thought on my feet! 'It was terrifying!' I told him. 'I totally forgot what I was supposed to say next, so I thought the best thing I could do was – well, to leave the stage as quickly as possible.' There followed an ominous silence broken finally when Hawtrey inclined his head in a debonair way as if to indicate his acceptance of my story, then promptly invited me to join his company at the Embassy Theatre in London at the end of the season. London!

The winter of 1951 was my first in England as an adult and one of the coldest on record. The theatre was situated in Swiss Cottage, which proved a drab and unfriendly place after Buxton. There was a constant stream of traffic, it was dark, grimy and crowded. I found a room with a gas fire in nearby Winchester Road and assessed my situation. I may have been offered a London season, but nobody had mentioned anything about acting. It was clear that I was expected to continue in my least favourite role, that of assistant stage manager. But, I was getting £7 a week so had no real cause for complaint. The Embassy no longer exists as a commercial theatre, having been taken over by the Central School of Speech and Drama, but was at that time fairly flourishing. The opening production of that 1951 season had been *Women Of Twilight*, written by Sylvia Rayman, a local waitress, which had proved a great success.

On my first evening, having settled into my digs, I went along to see the show which was a bit melodramatic but great fun. As the cast took their curtain calls, the batten holding the red velvet front curtain snapped in half, the severed pieces plunging dangerously to each side, narrowly missing the actors. Correctly sensing an emergency, the stage manager called out, 'Bring in the fire curtain!' A hand, which I'm very grateful was not mine, reached out, pulled a lever – the wrong one – and triggered off the sprinkler system. Chaos ensued. I've never seen actors move so fast. Screaming members of the public gathered their belongings and raced for the exits as the nozzles in the ceiling drenched them and all which lay in their path. As an experience, it was rather more dramatic than the play.

The next morning, I was called early. The set had to be dismantled and dried out in the wintry sun which had, for a few precious moments, settled on the vacant plot next door. There was another performance that evening. In addition, the front curtain had to be wrung out and repaired, my old sparring partner Brian Whittle, the stage director, himself perilously going up in a bosun's chair to secure the new batten. Miraculously, the curtain rose again that evening as though nothing untoward had happened, though, as it did so, there was a strong whiff of damp in the air.

There being a strong middle-European flavour to the locality the policy of the Embassy Theatre was to include a handful of plays each season which might appeal specifically to the Jewish community. The first of these, in which I walked on, was based on Louis Golding's famous novel *Magnolia Street*, and featured a radiantly beautiful June Brown, now Dot in *East-Enders*, Alfie Bass and Irene Handl. In the lead was Lily Kann, a stout, temperamental actress with a severe astigmatism. She may have been good at her job but, to put it mildly, she could be demanding. One evening she hauled me over the coals for giving her a bad throat. There was far too much dust in the building, she told me, it was a disgrace, the whole acting area should be sprayed with water before she made her appearance. For a while I toyed with the idea of activating the sprinkler system again, but eventually made do with a small hand spray which I used just before each performance, and on the last night, with enormous satisfaction, left a small puddle on the Windsor chair upon which she spent a good deal of the first act.

The months went by, I was wretchedly cold and homesick, and there was no improvement in my status in the company. Added to which, a number of visiting companies were given slots in the season and they were bringing their own stage management. One of these provided an evening of Grand Guignol starring Ellen Pollock and Griffith Jones. I was co-opted to help with the stage management, though it wouldn't be long before they wished they'd kept their mouths shut. In *The Mask*, the first of the playlets, Griffith Jones played a coal miner whose face had been horribly scarred in an accident, obliging him to wear a discreet cloth across the offending part. The masked miner, we learn, discovers that his wife is having an affair with a fellow miner and, in a stormy scene, confronts her. Later, the lovers plot to murder the poor man and dispose of the body by tossing it down the mineshaft. The boyfriend would then don the mask for public appearances and nobody would be the wiser. That was the theory. During the action of the play, while they were in the middle of a reckless clinch, the door was supposed to be flung open to reveal the jealous husband. On the first night, for some reason the handle, a small, ordinary brass handle such as might be found in a coal miner's cottage which I'd put on with my own fair hands, refused to budge. It was the only door on the set and it wouldn't open. Griffith Jones, understandably eager to make his dramatic entry, looked to me in desperation. When I couldn't manage to turn the handle either, I proffered my advice: 'Climb through the window!' Now, it should be borne in mind that, for the purposes of the play, the window was supposed to be directly over the mineshaft. The first night audience was treated to the spectacle of the extremely lanky Mr Jones squeezing with great difficulty through a rather small cottage window in order to interrupt the lovers who, by this time, having been snogging for some while, were becoming increasingly aware that, because of the time factor, something extra might reasonably be expected of them in the interests of authenticity.

The next day I came in early, having paid a visit to the hardware store and changed the lock on the door – quite a feat considering my limited technical expertise. Despite my hard work, despite the brand new lock, the same thing happened that evening, and the following – and, in fact, each evening of the week. 'It's jinxed!' I declared defensively to the furious and disbelieving actors.

My spell of bad luck didn't end there. Pollock and Jones were performing some of the more grisly bits of Shakespeare's *Titus Andronicus*. There was a scene in a forest for which the theatre had come up with an old-fashioned bit of scene painting. Tree trunks framed the sides of the stage, while the verdant branches above swayed and rippled in the breeze. Immediately following the forest scene came the banquet where it is revealed that Tamora has eaten her sons in a pie which had been baked for her in revenge. On the first night, I gave the cue for the leafy border to be hauled up into the flies to make way for the banqueting table groaning with make-believe food. However, my signal was misinterpreted and, together with the trees, the foliage began to make its way downwards rather than upwards. Frantically, I flicked the cue light to the man in the flies but to no effect. The trunks of the trees, being made of canvas, began to fold into a neat heap on either side of the stage, while the batten holding the canvas, continuing its descent, revealed the crudely tied ropes which were supporting it from above. Down and down came the batten until, at long last and to my infinite relief, it stopped – roughly at head height. Ellen Pollock swept in majestically – clearly a determined effort on her part to quell the audience's gathering hysteria – but she didn't quite gauge the height of her headgear so that when it connected with the batten it was knocked askew at a rakish angle over one eye, pushing her off balance and adding to the growing impression at the inquest that she was inebriated. Neither she nor the rest of the evening ever fully recovered. Naturally I was held responsible though, peculiarly enough, I wasn't dismissed. How long would my luck hold?

I had been asked by an old friend of my father's, Laurence Hedley-Prole, whether I would care to come over for Christmas dinner. I wrote back to thank him, saying that alas I wouldn't be able to as I'd already had an invitation from my cousins, the Percivals. I then wrote to my cousins warning them that, as the play was opening on Boxing Day, I hadn't been told whether or not I would be expected to work on Christmas Day – anything was possible in our business – but would let them know as soon as I myself knew. On 23 December I was told that I wouldn't be working on Christmas Day, so I rang the first number on my list, apologised for the confusion and said that I would be free and delighted to join them, noticing at the same time that they sounded a little surprised.

During the meal, I excused myself to go to the lavatory. I stood for a while washing and drying my hands while I tried to work out the situation. All was not well. My worst suspicions, which had started to nag at me during the turkey, now were confirmed. Beryl, who had been next to me, was a Hedley-Prole. She wasn't a Percival. I was in the wrong house. I made up my mind to keep quiet about it when I returned to the table, though I knew I should have phoned the Percivals at once to explain the mistake as they were probably, at that very moment, sitting around wondering whether or not to begin their meal without me. But I didn't. Hoping it would all go away, I tucked into my Christmas pud and bluffed it out. What was it about me? Whatever I attempted seemed to go wrong. There were no two ways about it, I was disaster-prone.

The cold winter dug its merciless way deep into my bones, and I wasn't enjoying myself much at work either. After *You Can't Take It With You* in which, probably because of my African connections, I was cast as a black man, I was given very little to do in the way of acting. I began to get restless. In desperation, I made an appointment to see the manager of the Embassy Theatre, Oscar Lewenstein, later to make his name as a producer. I remember telling him that, with all the visiting companies bringing their own staff, I couldn't help feeling redundant. He must have listened to me in disbelief. No one, surely, talks his way out of a job? He asked whether my reason for coming to see him was because I wanted to leave. I said that I thought that it was. Could he perhaps help me with a few introductions, or at least point me in the right direction, as I knew nobody in London. 'My dear boy, I don't know anyone in London myself,' he told me. And that was it. I was out on the streets. It was my own doing, of course, and I realised that I was being either incredibly brave or incredibly stupid.

It was the beginning of February, London was grey and we were all longing for the spring and a bit of good news. We didn't get it. The nation was thrown into further gloom by the death in his sleep of the King. I stayed up all night opposite the Cenotaph to watch the funeral procession for I had much respected the King's integrity and had been moved whenever he spoke in public, aware of how painful it must have been to struggle with an awkward stammer.

For week after week, I had been walking the streets in search of work. In those days, theatrical agents tended to have their offices in the St Martin's Lane – Charing Cross Road area, so my day would begin by catching the Underground to the West End and dropping in on those with whom I had made contact in the hope that they would remember me and offer me a job. On this particular day I was at a low ebb. The established agents had been grandly uninterested and even the tattier agents were rude or dismissive and I was getting nowhere. As I was crossing over to the Leicester Square Underground, the only two coins I had in the world slipped through a hole in my pocket and fell through a grating in the centre of the road. Down below me I could see the two half-crowns glinting in the light of the street lamps. I hurried into the station and managed to speak to a supervisor who told me that the only person who had access to the area where my coins lay had gone home. I explained that it was all the money I possessed in the world, but he shook his head – there was no way he could help me. I would have to come back first thing in the morning to claim them. I took a deep breath and walked back to Swiss Cottage. It isn't particularly far but it had been a trying day and I was tired. When I got to Winchester Road, I was relieved to find that there was still something like sixpence worth of gas left. I lit the fire to warm my feet and smoked a cigarette. I had no money for food, but remembered the food parcel my mother had sent me, which I had stored in the wardrobe. There was a packet of raisins dried in the South African sun, a tin of tongue which I didn't like, and a tin of guavas which I did. I treated myself to a handful of the raisins only to discover that mice had been there before me. The rest of the evening I spent carefully sifting the raisins from the mouse-droppings, then running them under the tap before eating them, washed down with guava juice. I set my alarm for five the next morning and walked back in the dark to the Charing Cross Road. When I presented myself to the day-shift at the Underground the money had gone.

In my heart of hearts, I wanted more than anything to do what my father had suggested, even though it had made me angry at the time. 'Don't forget, you can always come home,' he'd written in a postscript to one of my mother's letters. It had made me more determined than ever to stick it out. I remembered too what Ivor Jones, the *Cape Times* critic I had sought out in order to say goodbye, had so waspishly implied. 'See you back in six months.' It only strengthened my resolve. Cramming another handful of raisins into my mouth, I put on my hat, coat and woolly muffler and trotted along to the Embassy Theatre. There was a club upstairs where patrons could get a meal after the show. I needed company and the manageress had always been friendly. I'd have a chat with her and cheer myself up.

She turned out to be a godsend. 'You look as though you could do with a good steak and kidney pie,' she told me, eyeing me with concern. I told her that I couldn't possibly afford it but she brushed this aside. The steaming plate of food she brought to the table warmed me up and brought me back to life. 'I can do that every night for you, love, if you'd like. Just keep quiet about it or I'll get into trouble. Come round about this time when most of them have gone and I'll see what I can do.' She was as good as her word. Oscar Lewenstein, the theatre manager, saw me eating there one evening. Luckily he didn't ask how I could afford it, but wanted to know how I was getting on. I did my best to sound optimistic but he saw right through it. 'We need a call-boy,' he told me. 'Five shillings a performance.' I took the job. There was no alternative.

It was a time when actors were called to the stage personally, a tradition which changed with the arrival of the tannoy system. Tap, tap on the door: 'Half an hour please, Miss Kann.' Yes, she was back. 'Act I, beginners please, Miss Kann.' 'Curtain up on Act I, Miss Kann.' 'Your call please, Miss Kann.' 'Stand by for the final curtain, Miss Kann.' At the end of the week, as was customary, I hovered near the stage door for any gratuities which actors might feel disposed to hand me. Miss Kann swept past me that Saturday night. 'I was going to give you half a crown,' she announced, 'but I didn't want to insult you' – and she was gone.

In another two weeks, with the production over, I was out of work. I had no idea where my next job was coming from. I began to get frightened. Late one night, the phone rang. It was a welcome call, my old friend Jobie Stewart ringing from the Library Theatre in Manchester where he was working. 'They're looking for someone to understudy Owen Riley in a tour of *Ring Round The Moon* – twelve weeks' work, Nige! How about it?' I was thrilled and relieved, of course, though it meant that I would have to get my skates on and leave the following day. Nervously, I approached my landlady to explain the situation, telling her that I had no money to spare apart from the train fare to Manchester so would be unable to pay the rent immediately, but as I was about to be earning the princely sum of £8 per week, if she'd agree, I'd save up and pay her back as soon as I could. To my astonishment the wonderful lady said yes. I was off on a twelve-week tour in one of the best plays I'd seen since my arrival. Well, not exactly 'in'. Understudying, as I was to learn, didn't mean 'in'.

7

Hiding Place

I hadn't had the time, when Jobie telephoned me, to ask whether or not he too was going to be on the tour but when I got to Manchester, he told me that he wasn't involved in the production and would be staying on at the Library Theatre. Although this was most disappointing, I had no time to brood on it as, almost immediately, I was being despatched to Southport, our first date, there to join the other members of the *Ring Round The Moon* company. But first, he and I squeezed in a quick tea and Welsh rarebit at the Kardomah and regaled one another with stories of our adventures. I couldn't have wished for a better tonic than hearing the sound of his laughter once again. It was a precious link with my past which I was loath to sever, yet both of us knew that the career we had chosen would take us further and further apart. There was so much to discuss, so many anecdotes to embroider, that we tumbled over one another in the telling. Had we only stopped the flow to listen, how much more precious those moments might have been – how much more lasting. The really comforting thing was that when we did meet again we would always be able to pick up where we'd left off.

In Southport I met the company. In the Margaret Rutherford part was a cut-glass aristocrat of actresses, Helen Haye, who had begun in the companies of Ben Greet and Frank Benson and was now in her late seventies. She appeared rather aloof to begin with but I quickly saw how splendid she was going to be as Madame Desmortes. Miss Haye's elderly companion, with whom she shared her home in Milner Street, Chelsea, was a chatty, bridge-playing, chain-smoking and highly individual woman called Eva Fenton, who solemnly told me on the day we met how dependent Churchill had been on her during the war. Owen Riley, whom I was to understudy, clearly relished the opportunity of playing a dual role as the twins Hugo and Frederick – one an extrovert the other an introvert. While being rather too short for true elegance and wearing a hairpiece on stage to disguise a receding forehead, he nevertheless had a lively intelligence and his immaculate diction was a real bonus. The remainder of the company included Thelma Ruby doing the famous tango scene and the dynamic Rachel Roberts as the bitch. By and large a talented and eccentric collection of actors, though the production itself was a pale shadow of the one in London. Lacking the Oliver Messel touch, this was a makeshift, cheap touring version, which was perfectly acceptable had you not caught the West End production, and left you feeling short-changed if you had. It was a strange experience for me to hang around watching them all beavering away and know that I had nothing to do except sit there and wait for Owen to get ill.

By the time we reached our next port-of-call, Southsea, Owen had introduced me to golf which, until then, hadn't entered my horizons. Neither of us was much good, but Helen and Eva – or Madam, as she was nicknamed – announced that they were keen golfers and wished to make up a four. I felt very honoured to be asked to socialise with the leading actors, but soon found that they were pretty easy to get on with and not in the least thrown by the fact that I was just an understudy. Helen's golf was under-powered but nonetheless the rest were no match for her. She seldom hit the ball more than a few yards, but it was as straight as a die. Owen and I, on the other hand, were pretty wild, tending to swipe into the trees, lakes and particularly the bunkers, while I got the feeling that Madam wasn't particularly interested in the game, going along with it as it was Helen's passion, but really preferring to chat. What an odd quartet we must have made! We played most weekdays throughout the tour except when we had a matinée, and through it all, cigarette dangling from her lips, Madam regaled us with her preposterous stories of espionage, how she had tangled with Burgess and Maclean, and taken an active part in the invasion on D-day. She certainly had us all open-mouthed with her experiences while testing the atom bomb over the Yorkshire moors. Helen, smiling benignly and fiercely loyal, was emphatic that every word was Gospel truth.

Owen and I began to spend a lot of time in each other's company. This started as fun. He was naturally flirtatious, and I suppose there was something flattering about being courted by the leading man. I didn't find him attractive except as a companion, which was just as well as I knew him to be married, with children.

One day, during an understudy rehearsal, I had just exited into the wings as Hugo – or Frederick – when I almost crashed into Helen. 'I've been watching you work,' she told me in her crisp way. 'I think you have a real talent, and I'm going to do what I can to help you.' There was no time to encourage her to enlarge on the offer or even to thank her as my next entrance was upon me, but as I went through the lines of the play my mind was on other things. Nobody had ever said anything like that to me before. How was she going to help me? I wondered. How could she help me? Well, the truth of the matter was that she couldn't and didn't.

It's very difficult for one actor to help another. Producers and directors have their own ideas about whom they want – oh, they'll agree to see you on someone's recommendation, but that doesn't mean to say they'll give you a job. Helen's great friend and fellow bridge player was the agent Miriam Warner. Everyone in the business knew her name and to many she was something of a joke. As an agent, Miriam was very low down on the pecking order. Her office was high above the traffic of Cambridge Circus and her second-in-command, a bespectacled, kindly man called 'Smithie', sat guard in the outer chamber and let through only those who had the stamp of approval. Miriam was a short woman in long dresses. Most actors knew her as a persuasive business woman with an obsessively mean streak. Normally, they would deal with her – or she with them – on the phone or at the other side of her desk, but should you be lucky enough to see her on the move, which was rare, you couldn't help but notice that, standing up, she was considerably shorter than when she wasn't – a sort of female Toulouse Lautrec.

Miriam handled twice-nightly reps, second-rate tours and 'special weeks', where an actor would join a company for a single production or perhaps two. There is a famous story about her. She had telephoned one of her 'artistes', offering him a job with a repertory company. He asked what money he could expect. 'Well,' she is alleged to have replied sadly, 'it's small rep, dear. What's your lowest?' 'Well,' he sighed, 'I've got a family to support, I couldn't do it for under fifteen.' Back came the reply, 'Small rep, dear.' Reluctantly, the actor began to come down in price until he got to £10 a week and there he stopped. 'I may need the sodding job, Miriam, but no, I'm sorry, I'm not that bloody desperate!' And as Miriam launched into her litany, 'Small rep, dear . . .', he hung up on her. Later that day, he happened to be walking down Charing Cross Road when who should he see on the opposite pavement but the lady herself, Miriam Warner of Denton and Warner. He waited until he had caught her eye then gave her a savage V sign. Miriam smiled sweetly back at him across the road, shook her head sadly and lifted a solitary finger in return.

On Helen's recommendation, I was invited to the office in Cambridge Circus for an interview. Miriam didn't seem overly friendly but said that she would do what she could. Without allowing my mind to dwell on what or where that might be, I disappeared into the outer office to off-load all my CV details and some copies of the Landseer photographs to 'Smithie' (who studied them critically, comparing me with the photograph, then the photograph with me without commenting), then caught the train back to Cambridge where we were playing that week. I had rather hoped that the coincidence of Cambridge and Cambridge Circus might prove an omen, but no such luck. However, it was a chance for me to visit my father's old college, Clare, and to look up his name in the archives. It transpired that he'd won his half-blue in water polo, a detail I knew, but it said that he was the goalkeeper – which I hadn't known – and had let in quite a few goals, too. No wonder he'd kept quiet about that period of his life.

The twelve-week tour was over almost before it had begun. Owen didn't miss a single performance so I had no chance of contacting anyone influential to see me working and perhaps advance my career. However, the £8 per week, even though I had to pay for my own accommodation, was enough to enable me to send the rent I owed to my ex-landlady in Swiss Cottage. I was used to living frugally. After all, I had saved up the boat fare to come to England on a weekly salary of £4, though to this day, I'm not sure how I managed to do that.

Back in London, Owen invited me to his home in Bayswater to meet George, which was the curious name of his wife, and his young family. As I had nowhere to live, Owen arranged for me to have a room in the house of a grossly overweight colleague of his, who was appearing in the West End. My landlord, like me, was homosexual, and I rejected an advance he made almost the day I moved in – he didn't hang about. One evening, I got in quite late, and on clicking the lock on the front door, heard his voice calling out my name. I'd had a terrible lift back to London which had ended in a row with Owen, who had drunk too much and had been driving appallingly, and so, being in no mood, I hurried by his room grimly muttering 'Go back to sleep, you old queen!' and firmly closed my door. 'Nigel! . . . Nigel . . . !' I could hear him calling as I brushed my teeth and climbed under the blankets. 'Nigel . . . !' When morning arrived there were police in the house. The man had been discovered dead in his bed and, though I couldn't possibly have known, he must have been calling to me for help. I was asked a few questions before they moved away to continue their investigations somewhere further down the passage. Foul play had not been an issue; the poor man had died of a heart attack.

I sat on the edge of my bed, deeply shocked yet strangely removed from reality. It wasn't that I was callous or unfeeling, but it was as if none of it had really happened, that it was all part of a dream or a scene from Agatha Christie, in which I was a peripheral character – the Young Man from the Colonies.

I was less disturbed by my landlord's death than by the presence of the police. I'd come from a very law-abiding family. As children we didn't steal and we didn't lie. Not that in this case I was guilty of anything, I told myself, feeling nevertheless a gathering guilt. This was, after all, my legacy from the Christian Brothers. That man might still be alive had I gone in when he'd called. There might have been something I could have done – raised the alarm, phoned for an ambulance. The police were leaving now and someone was letting them out of the front door. I heard them drive off down the hill. What happened after that I don't remember – the facts have conveniently erased themselves through the years. I can't even think who else was in the house, nor who remained with the body except that someone did – and that it wasn't me. I had taken the easy way out. Excused myself from the scene. Went for a long walk to clear my head.

A day or two later, Buxton was offered again, although it was already a quarter of the way through the season. As was the case throughout my life, an escape route would open up at the very moment when I expected to confront reality. The big attraction for me this time was that I wouldn't be required to stage manage, I was being employed solely as an actor. My short stay in London had been miserably unhappy. Apart from everything else, Owen's continued interest in me was mounting to persistence, aggravated, I suspect, by my obvious availability and resistance to his advances. He quite simply couldn't understand it. So it was with a feeling of intense relief that, once again, I gulped in the Derbyshire air and stepped through the Playhouse stage door to embrace some of my old friends and meet some new ones. Shaun and Ba Sutton were back, so there was plenty to talk about. Rehearsals for *The Cat And The Canary* were due to start in the morning. It was a comedy-thriller and I was looking forward to it, and to the sound of laughter. The theatre had organised accommodation so, with eleven weeks' work at £8 per week ahead of me, I splashed out and summoned a taxi to take me to my new digs.

Owen Riley was waiting for me in my room, and there was an unopened suitcase on the bed. He explained that he'd telephoned the theatre for my address, turned up at the house and the landlady had told him it was all right to come in and wait. I was so shocked I didn't know what to say. 'You don't seem very pleased to see me,' he said. He was quite right, I wasn't. The atmosphere between us had become tense, and I knew from experience that weekly rep was a demanding job. I didn't want his being there to distract me from my work, and told him so. 'You won't even know I'm here,' he assured me.

This was very far from the truth. Although I managed to persuade him to move digs further up the road, his presence was constant and I longed to be left alone, yet he'd insist on hearing my lines, meeting me at the pub and driving me around the countryside in the afternoons when, strictly speaking, I should have been learning. It would be unfair of me not to admit that I sometimes enjoyed his company, but it was proving a strain having him around. All things considered, the second season turned out to be far less fun than the first. The portly Raymond Lovell, who had been Horace Vandergelder in *The Merchant Of Yonkers* at the Embassy Theatre, joined us to play the cream of the leading roles. Raymond was a great friend of Tony Hawtrey so we were all on our best behaviour. As luck would have it, by the time he arrived Owen had been cast in a West End thriller, which obliged him to return to London to begin rehearsals, so, at last, I was able to get on with my life. We ended the season with *The Barretts Of Wimpole Street* which provided a terrific role for Ray and even quite a good one for me. I was Captain Surtees Cook, who arrives at 50, Wimpole Street resplendently handsome in his scarlet, brass-buttoned tunic and tight-fitting breeches. Unfortunately, what arrived from the costumiers was a far cry from my expectation. The uniform had faded to a dirty pink through constant use, didn't fit anywhere, and was pockmarked with moth holes. Never at ease with needle and thread, I spent the whole of Sunday taking in the breeches, patching up the jacket and shifting the epaulettes which were somewhere half way down my back. On the opening night I had no option but to wear my sports jacket under my tunic to fill it out a bit. The week ended, we all said our farewells and, once again out of work, I went back to London and signed on at the Labour Exchange in Lisson Grove.

So far, I couldn't boast a major change of fortune since my arrival but I had managed to keep going, which in itself, I suppose, was something of an achievement. Nobody had rushed up to me puffing at a fat cigar and waving a lucrative contract under my nose. Perhaps Leonard Schach had been right all those years ago, things were going to be slow. The odd thing about the theatre is that you never know what may be round the corner. Keeping going was important. My bank balance hadn't swelled, in fact I was no better off, but I was beginning to find my feet in the profession, beginning to feel part of it. I hadn't distinguished myself in any of the roles

I'd played and in some I am quite sure I was dire, but I was learning by degrees.

I went to Oxford to see Owen, who was touring in his thriller before coming to London. In my superior way, I thought the play a load of old twaddle, and infuriated the people round me in the audience by guessing the murderer on his first entrance and blowing his identity to everyone within earshot. Afterwards, in the pub, Owen alarmed me considerably by telling me that his wife had claimed to have discovered some letters I'd written him, was suing for divorce and would be using the letters as evidence. I was appalled, though I couldn't for the life of me think I'd written anything of an incriminating nature. Also at that time, homosexuality still being an imprisonable offence, for the next few months I fully expected a knock at the door from someone in a pin-striped suit clutching a dossier. Fortunately, it never came and the whole matter, like Owen's and my so-called relationship, began to fade into the mists of time.

Barely had a month of signing-on gone by when Miriam Warner despatched me to the Grand Theatre in Southampton which was a weekly rep. When I arrived, I found out that performances were advertised as playing twice nightly, which she had omitted to tell me. It meant that the texts of *Poison Pen* and *Laburnum Grove* – the two plays for which I was contracted – had to be abbreviated considerably to fit in. In those days, we often worked from what were called 'part scripts', in which each actor's copy contained only the lines his particular character had to speak, with the last three or four words of the previous speech as a cue. This meant that it was perfectly possible to take part in a play without ever knowing the plot or what most of the other characters were talking about – if, indeed, you knew who they were. Rehearsal time was correspondingly limited and I confess that, after the first day, I felt rather crestfallen. To complicate matters further, Jobie had written to say that he had been accepted

Dr Charles Hawthorne
in masonic regalia.

Mrs Rice, grandmother, artist and
mentor. A shy person who found
solace in a world of plants.

Rosemary Hawthorne in
her seventies, Cape Town.

The house built by Dr Hawthorne to house his family and surgery in Victoria Road, Camps Bay.

Rosemary Hawthorne with the twins Janette and John in the pram, and Nigel and Sheila at Newlands, Cape Town.

Right: A view of Clifton, Camps Bay and the Twelve Apostles in the 1960s.

Below: John, Janette, Nigel and Sheila at Camps Bay. It was a magical place to grow up.

Aged 28 at Clifton, Cape Town.

Cockpit, a University of Cape Town production in 1949, with Job Stewart (seated).

The Landseer portrait that failed to create a star.

Northampton Repertory Players 1954:
First stranger in *The Little Hut*

Orlando in *As You Like It*

Dick Whittington

Varville in *Last of the Camellias*

Beyond the Fringe, South Africa style, with Ronald Wallace, Siegfried Mynhardt and Kerry Jordan

Below: With Elspeth Bryce in *Summer of the Seventeenth Doll*. The National Theatre, Johannesburg 1957.

Below: A reluctant Pantomime Dame at Hornchurch

Left: *Try for White*, Cockpit Players, Cape Town 1959. A controversial play on the subject of apartheid. Directed by Leonard Schach with Marjorie Gordon and Jane Fenn.

Bruce Palmer in the paint shop at
Northampton Repertory Theatre
1954.

Anthea Cross. Still glamorous in
1997.

In the homemade beard which was used to win
a small part in the film of *Young Winston*.

As You Like It with Gorden Kaye as Audrey. National Theatre Tour of America in 1974.

Below: As Prince Albert in the revival of *Early Morning* at the Royal Court Theatre in 1969, with Moira Redmond and Shirley Anne Field.

Oh! What a Lovely War, both national and East and West Germany tours. Joan Littlewood's Theatre Workshop 1964.

Joan Littlewood who opened so many doors.

As Major Flack with Joe Melia in Peter Nichols' *Privates on Parade* in 1977. An RSC production – his performance was to bring him the first of many awards in the years to follow.

by the Old Vic and was changing his first name to the more sober, classical version – Job. While being overjoyed at his good fortune, I couldn't help feeling just a little bit envious at the way his career was shaping – and mine wasn't.

My next play was to be in Walthamstow. Under the banner title of 'The Savoy Players', patron of the arts the Countess Mala de la Marr had, in her infinite wisdom, taken over the Palace, an old variety theatre there, in an attempt to win over the locals to straight plays such as *While Parents Sleep*, which I watched on a complimentary ticket when less than twenty paying customers were rattling around the huge auditorium. Some of these people were undoubtedly parents and a good many of them appeared to be asleep. I was there to appear in Patrick Hamilton's thriller, *Rope*, which Hitchcock later turned into a film. During the last act, the aesthetic Rupert Cadell points challengingly at a wooden chest which the audience has to believe, through the entire play, contains the torso of a murdered boy, and demands that the perpetrators of the crime reveal its contents. When they refuse, with a deft twist of his cane he forces the lock and opens the lid. Although the audience couldn't see into the chest, they could certainly guess the contents from the actors' horrified reactions.

For our final performance, the Countess had decided to throw open the gallery. It should be borne in mind that normally the public would pay the princely sum of 1/6 for a seat up there in the 'gods' but that particular night it was free, so while the rest of the theatre was virtually empty because of the smog that smothered London, the gallery was crammed to bursting point. The evening was, at best, a bumpy ride, but when Rupert flamboyantly prised open the lock of the chest to confront the murderers with their crime, the whole chest capsized like a pack of cards, revealing that there'd been nothing in it in the first place. Most of us thought we were lucky to get out with our lives. With difficulty I made my way to the Underground by following the white line in the middle of the road. The smog stung my eyes, dirtied my clean collar and got into my throat. We read in the local paper that an estimated four thousand people had died from respiratory problems that winter of 1952.

During the week I had auditioned for a new play called *For Better For Worse* which was to feature Geraldine McEwan and, in his first starring role in the West End, Leslie Phillips, whom I was to understudy. I had to cover two other members of the company as well: Ken Riddington (who was also the stage manager) and a gentleman among actors, Anthony Sharp. At £7 per week, I was on familiar ground, but at least I would be in London and not having to pay for two lots of digs. We opened in Blackpool in December. It was snowing. The audience was enthusiastic. Both Geraldine and Leslie were skilful at comedy and, despite the flimsiness of the play, invested it with great warmth and fun. At the end of the second act, Geraldine (as Ann) has left a clothes horse across the door. Leslie (as Tony) races in with some good news, sees the obstacle too late and does a spectacular dive over it. On the first night, he flew through the air, fell, lay still and they brought down the curtain. With one accord the management amongst whom I sat swung round and wished me luck. I hadn't even read the play. Luckily, Leslie protested that he had only been acting and, after a short break, picked up where he'd left off – but he'd given me a very nasty turn.

The West End opening at the Comedy Theatre just before Christmas 1953 was triumphant – 'an oasis of sweetness and light in this cynical old world', declared the *News of the World* in a rare burst of lyricism. Little did I know then that it would run for eighteen months and that I would never go on for any of the three people I understudied. As an endurance test it was a salutary experience from which I learnt patience and stoicism in equal measures.

Once, fairly late on in the run, I did have a close shave. By that time, for an extra £1 a week, I had been persuaded to join the stage management. As prompt I 'sat on the book' for half the play. One night, Leslie stumbled over his words, a most unusual occurrence which made me perk up and pay particular attention, for sitting there night after night listening to the same old thing gave the mind licence to wander into more interesting areas. I pulled myself together with a jolt. Then he forgot his lines. I prompted him, clearly and discreetly as I'd been taught. He didn't respond. I repeated the line. He remained silent, then suddenly pitched forward on to his face and lay still. I gave the cue for the curtain to be brought down. However, the stage crew were all in the pub, so I raced through the door to the dressing rooms, yelled out for Ken, the stage manager, who came running. 'Leslie's fainted. Bring in the curtain!' As Ken dashed round to do so, I made my first West End appearance, entering through the centre door, going down on one knee before an astonished audience, hoisting the leading man into my arms and carrying him off. Geraldine had backed away against the scenery not knowing quite how to react, and unsteadily the curtain came in. Dumping Leslie in his room, I dashed upstairs to get ready. The clothes were all standing by, just in case. A little hastily-applied make-up which was *de rigueur* then, and down the stairs in time to meet Leslie coming from his dressing room with a 'Bad luck, Nige', on his way to the stage. That was the closest I got.

Understudying is a soul-destroying business. In a long run nobody in the cast really welcomes a different interpretation of a familiar characterisation, you want what you're used to. The audience doesn't want it either. If they've paid to see Leslie Phillips then Leslie Phillips is the one they want to see. Many's the time I've heard a concerted groan go up when the announcement is made that the star is indisposed, and there's usually a stream of disappointed patrons scurrying up the aisles on their way to get their money back. I remained the plain boy in the dressing room at the top of the building who was at a loss to know what to do to establish himself. I had no clear idea of how to turn the background into which I was fading into a foreground.

1953 was the year Sir John Gielgud was arrested and fined for importuning. He had been knighted in the Coronation Honours list, a citation many thought long overdue, and his name was outside the stately Haymarket Theatre as acting in and producing *A Day By The Sea* by N.C. Hunter. The play, written in an English Chekhovian style, was in rehearsal. I remember seeing the small mention in the *Evening News* that Mr John Gielgud, employed as a clerk, had been fined a tenner for soliciting. Clerk? The poor man with his reputation at stake must have been at his wits' end to have invented such a transparent porker. For the next week or so the posters outside the theatre were smeared with 'Dirty queer' graffiti and there was talk backstage that the knight-errant had been set up, with the policeman who arrested him positioned as a decoy. When he reported for rehearsal the following day, he was advised to enter via the front rather than through the stage door where there were reporters. The cast working on stage in his absence paused mid-sentence as he made his awkward way down the aisle. It was Sybil Thorndike who broke the tension, stepping forward and wagging her finger with a 'Who's been a naughty boy, then?'

It was the time of the Lord Montagu scandal, and the whole closet was a-tremble as to who would be next on the list. In those days there were certain clubs for homosexuals. They had names like the Rockingham, the Music Box and the A and B which stood for Arts and Battledress. They were West End havens, though seldom heavens, where you could meet people of your own kind without arousing comment from the outside world – with the constant danger, of course, that they might be raided by the police. The Rockingham we all thought piss-elegant because of its Regency wallpaper, its pianist, who tinkled away at the baby grand, and its clientele which boasted the famous playwright Terence Rattigan and his friends. I didn't drink there often as it wasn't my style; besides, you usually got the impression that a battery of lorgnettes were being raised as you went in. A number of Rattigan's plays (to those of us in the know) had homosexual characters thinly disguised as heterosexuals like the Major in *Separate Tables*. The stage was the perfect hiding place for the homosexual. He or she could spend their careers convincingly passing off as heterosexuals. Some of the most romantic leading men were 'queers', like Ivor Novello, who had an army of female admirers and who, like Coward, wrote parts for himself where he was surrounded by desirable and adoring women. Actors had licence to pretend.

In the Fifties intolerance reached its zenith, and with the law so hostile to our proclivity, it was small wonder that we were forced into an underworld. I entered it with reluctance, a stranger in a foreign land who barely knew the language. There were those who relished the danger and the excitement, an area which had no appeal for me. I used to frequent the 'A and B', mostly because it was approached along a narrow alley just off Leicester Square where there was little chance of being seen. When the coast was clear, I would dart into the doorway like a spy on a mission and make my way up the steep stairs which reeked of fried scampi filtering through from the restaurant down below. The club was on the top floor. This had a beamed, Tudor look to it and there was someone at the top of the stairs to vet your membership card and turn you up in the files – the same files which were frequently turned up by the police in one of their raids. Lining the walls of the two rooms which comprised the club would be men young and old but seldom any women. They did nothing more than look. Even if the new arrival was a friend, no embrace was acceptable, the most permitted by the management being a nod or a manly handshake. It was perfectly usual for me to nurse a drink all evening and not address a word to a living soul. Usually I left alone at closing time. When the bell sounded for Last Orders, the bouncer stationed at the entrance would don an enormous picture hat, and with a deep-throated 'Time, boys and girls please', parade his way through the customers collecting empty glasses. It was extraordinary how some of them delighted in this moment, a token gesture of femininity which somehow unified them.

I've never been comfortable with men pretending to be women. The only 'drag' acts I could tolerate were Dame Edna, Old Mother Riley or Mrs Shufflewick because they remained male and weren't impersonations. I've sat stony-faced through drag shows – embarrassed and feeling like some distant disapproving relative. I myself certainly never wanted to dress as a woman. I once played Dame in pantomime at Hornchurch and have seldom been more embarrassed nor, I suspect, more embarrassing. I wasn't an obvious 'pansy', I was somewhere down the middle. Until I was 'outed' by the press in the mid-Nineties, I didn't ever discuss my sexuality with those who weren't 'gay', as we were now called. It was quite simply nobody's business what I did in the privacy of my home and, if they guessed, how they reacted was up to them. Whatever ingredients I have in me which make me what I am I can honestly say were there from my birth. I didn't order it like that. From an early age I knew myself to be different, yet my behavioural patterns weren't forced upon me. They were always there. Hard though that has been to accept, I do so. I could have married, for there were opportunities, but it wouldn't have been fair on the woman. I would have loved nothing more than to have had children but it was not to be. Through the years I have turned into a contented person. The painful years, the unhappy years, were earlier, in the beginning when I was struggling in a hostile world to come to terms with my life. It must be hard for those who write us off as deviants and perverts to accept us and there is to this day an alarming amount of bigotry and hypocrisy. The dark days of the Fifties were rife with it, so we ventured further and further into the shadows to avoid cruel exposure and a brush with the law.

The run of *For Better For Worse* was coming to an end. We were told that there was to be a short provincial tour. I explained to Harold Boyes, our production manager, that I would find it very difficult to exist on £8 a week as I would have my bedsit in London to pay for as well as living expenses on the tour. 'That's all right,' he answered brightly. 'We'll get someone else.' What price loyalty? Astonished that, having worked for the production for eighteen months, I could be so effortlessly discarded, but mindful of my catastrophic mistake in dismissing myself at the Embassy Theatre, I capitulated. Shortly before we left for Leicester, coming out of the public library in the Charing Cross Road, I met someone called Robert.

We both stopped in our tracks. I had a matinée that day so we agreed to meet when it was over. He told me that he was off to Venice the following morning. A week later I received a note with his photograph in black and white taken by someone alongside the Rialto. When he got back, he didn't answer my letters or return my messages. Our tour finished and my long association with the play and the actors over, I found myself wandering around the University of London campus where he was studying in the hope that I might bump into him. But I never did. Nor did I see him again – except once, many years later, travelling on a Number 15 bus. I must have frightened him off.

I was interviewed for a part at the Royal Theatre in Northampton. The play was a wobbling old farce called *The Sport Of Kings* by Ian Hay. I was offered the job for £10 a week – things were looking up. I needed to get away from London, fight off the gloom and practise my craft. It had been so long, I was getting rusty. I found digs with a Mrs Lyman, who announced proudly that she chucked out

Errol Flynn when he was with the rep way back in 1933 for dragging back a girl in the dead of night. She seemed to be implying that a repetition of that sort of behaviour wouldn't be advisable. I reassured her and went down the road to the enchanting little theatre in which I was to work, sitting that night in the auditorium where audiences had applauded Irving, Frank Benson and even Charlie Chaplin.

It was the opening night of the current production, T.S. Eliot's *The Cocktail Party*. The Royal Theatre which had opened in 1884 was the perfect size and shape. It seated about 850 and had been lovingly tended through the years, particularly by its resident scenic designer, Tom Osborne Robinson. The play I saw may have been weekly rep but the standard was extremely high and I went for a drink at the interval exhilarated. Across the bar, a pair of dark, beady eyes caught mine and held the look.

The next morning, he was backstage where we all congregated for coffee break. He came over and introduced himself as Bruce Palmer. I saw from his overalls that he worked in the scenic department. I had no time to improve on our acquaintance as we were summoned back to rehearsal but we met in the pub for a drink one evening and talked until I had to excuse myself to go back and study my lines. Bruce was everybody's friend. He had a naughty smile, loved his job at the theatre and seemed to look upon life as something not to be taken too seriously. His home, I learnt, was in Jubilee Crescent in nearby Wellingborough, he'd fought at Arnhem and been invalided out with phosphorus burns, was an agnostic and sometime jitterbug champion of the Midlands. He didn't get on with his family and ignored all their approaches at reconciliation. He had come to hate his father, who had reputedly ill-treated his late mother of whom he had been very fond. It all seemed to pour out of him. I warmed to him that evening while, at the same time, being wary. I didn't want to get involved. Not one bit. Little did I know that I would be spending the next twenty-seven years of my life in his company.

When next we met, he told me a hard luck story, that he was being obliged to share a bed at his digs with his landlady's only son, an attractive young man but as straight as a die. He and Bruce had been friends for years but the landlady's cooking, in which almost everything was fried, hadn't improved the state of Bruce's ulcer and what with the fatty food and the narrow, uncomfortable bed the upshot was why didn't we find something together? It seemed like a good idea at the time. I had just been invited to stay with the company for the rest of the season, it was a good way of celebrating, so we went down to the local estate agents to talk about renting a flat.

My performance in *The Sport Of Kings* continued to improve, though the local critic wrote that I was too inexperienced for the role. (I found out later that *she* was still at school.) I felt that I would be happier here in Northampton than at Buxton. I was a bit more confident for one thing and more at ease with people than before. We found a first-floor flat in a run-down Edwardian terrace near the racecourse. It was in an appalling state so Bruce and I threw a wallpapering party, providing the drink and some food, as well as scrapers for removing the yellowing, elaborately patterned paper which clung like grim death to the walls. We went to the auction rooms and bid for some furniture. Home-making seemed like fun when you were sharing it with someone else.

Then one evening, Bruce told me that he was in love with me. Why did he have to spoil everything? For a short while we pretended to have an affair. I say 'pretend', as I was a dismal failure as a lover. Bruce simply didn't turn me on, nor would he admit to my failure. It concerned me that he was becoming extremely possessive. I had told him that I couldn't reciprocate his feelings, thinking that my frankness would do the trick and that we could just be friends. I was to learn that he didn't give up easily. It didn't seem to count that he had liaisons with others in the town, but let me so much as look at anybody else and all hell would break loose.

Still, sharing my life with someone, however complex the circumstances, had its pleasures. The loneliness that I had felt since I had been in England was beginning to fade with this new security in my life. We'd go to the market to buy pieces of Staffordshire pottery at the antique stalls and fresh vegetables and fruit to last us the week. Once a month, we'd get a bus on a Sunday morning and go to his home town of Wellingborough where his friends Billy and Jose Marsh lived. We'd have roast and two veg. with them before Billy went out beagling, after which Jose, Bruce and I would sit round the log fire talking theatre. Jose ran the local dance school and choreographed the amateur pantomime each year. They were kind people who welcomed us in as though we were family. Visits to their home every so often took away from the routine of weekly rep and the long bus ride was always fun – neither of us drove. The months slipped by. Some plays worked, some didn't. Some were happy experiences, others less happy.

For our two-week break in the summer, we went to Spain. I'd never been to the Continent, I'd not been able to afford it. We went on a Frames Tour to San Sebastian, which in those days under Franco was a puritanical seaside resort where attendants patrolled the beach and whacked your leg with a cane if you were sunbathing facing the promenade – the implication being that you could see up the girls' skirts. As we weren't permitted anything as brief as swimming trunks, we used to swim out to the raft in our regulation shorts, peel them off on arrival and sunbathe in our trunks to get the maximum possible tan. We went to Pamplona where I watched my first and last bull fight. It was disconcerting to see, as we sat in our bus waiting for the driver, the butchers' vans arriving empty and leaving fully stocked. There had been something exhilarating about seeing the matadors and picadors going about their balletic routines, yet our concern for the poor wretched bull and our shame at being part of such a barbaric display overrode any appreciation of the spectacle. We came away chastened, though it was amazing how quickly that feeling dispersed while riding through the Pyrenees in the late afternoon sunshine on top of the bus.

After some months the demanding nature of my relationship with Bruce was starting to worry me. Beginning to feel trapped, I had made up my mind not to stay too long at Northampton and told Jobie so when we spoke on the phone. A week or so later, I was called into the producer's office. There was a rumour going round town that I was leaving. Was it true? By that time, I had decided to stay another three months so I was able to deny it, but couldn't help wondering where the story had come from. I was soon to find out. I was on the phone to another friend when I became aware that there was a third party involved at the other end of the line. I could hear breathing. I put two and two together. One of my fans, a young girl called Jill, had begun to work at the Post Office. I made a guess. 'Jill? Is that you?' I asked. There was a long pause. Then a breathy voice replied, 'Yes.' 'Have you been listening to my conversation?' I asked. 'Yes,' came the reluctant reply. 'I always do.'

It was difficult to go back to London and face being out of work after eighteen months of solid employment. I found accommodation first in Clapham, then in Pimlico, and went about the debilitating business of doing the agents. I returned to 'Smithie' at Miriam Warner but there was nothing doing, dear – besides, I didn't want another spell of touring, nor could I face twice-nightly weekly rep after the luxury of once nightly. I wrote masses of letters, though seldom had a reply. Eventually, the director at Bromley Rep, which was weekly, agreed to see me. 'Yes,' he decided. 'You do look like Frankie Howerd.' Seeing that I was uncertain whether or not to take it as an insult, he hastily explained that Mr Howerd had agreed to take part in a farce called *Tons Of*

Money and a look-alike was required. Frank, as he preferred
to be called, was a slumped, lugubrious man who turned up
for rehearsal in a chauffeur-driven car. He had a slender grasp
of his lines by opening night, though that didn't seem to impede
him. The play began with a breakfast scene. As he made his
first entrance down the stairs, Frank would pause for the
applause to die away, bend down and peck Sheila Hancock,
who was playing his wife, on the cheek – 'Morning, wife.
Good morning, mother-in-law. Good morning, toast. Good
morning, marmalade . . .' – then go straight down to the
footlights to address the audience. 'Now, I expect you're
wondering what all this is about.' He would then proceed
to tell them the entire plot of the play. When he had reached
the end, he would hold up his hand – 'Quiet for the actors,
please' – and go back to more or less what the author had in
mind when he wrote it. I'd never met this sort of anarchy in
the theatre before. I rather liked it.

Another star who came to Bromley was Binnie Hale, who
was famous for revue. Playing opposite her in an extremely
silly play by Ivor Novello called *Full House* was an actress
called Pamela Lane. Without realising that she had been
married to John Osborne, I urged her to go to the Royal
Court to see *Look Back In Anger* which had recently opened.
The play had made a huge impression on me, seeming to blow
all the cobwebs out of the theatre, spurning the French window
world we all knew only too well and dragging us all kicking
and protesting into the mid-Fifties. She came into rehearsals
one morning so distracted that I asked her if she was all
right. She told me about Osborne, about their rows and his
vituperation. 'Every word,' she said, 'is as I remember it. I even
have the squirrel at home.'

Pantomime time came round again and Bromley were doing
Cinderella. I was asked to play 'Old 'Enery', a yokel in a smock
with a tattered straw hat and boots who had a duet with one of
the Ugly Sisters, 'Say Something Sweet To Your Sweetheart'. It

wasn't exactly the proudest moment of my career but it took me over Christmas and half way through January. After that, I managed to get a few walk-on jobs on television, some lines if I was lucky, a week in rep here, a week in rep there. I was getting nowhere fast. Apart from Miriam Warner, I hadn't been able to get myself an agent. At least if I had I might have been put up for jobs instead of having to traipse around cap in hand from office to office, wearing out the soles of my shoes. The more I thought about it, the more demoralising I found it to be and the more I wondered why on earth I was doing it.

To add to my depression, Helen Haye had died. I had lost a dear, strange friend. In the last few years of her life, she had enjoyed a personal triumph playing the Dowager Empress in *Anastasia* at the St James's. I remember going round to her dressing room after the performance and kneeling before her as though she were royalty. Madam, as to be expected, was puffing away in a corner. Helen took the adulation in her stride and made no protest that I should return to my feet. On the opening night, her exit towards the end of the second act had provoked the audience into such prolonged applause some claimed it had lasted a full five minutes. There was a memorial service in St Martin in the Fields to which I went. Laurence Olivier made the eulogy. He said that it was tragic that, having made the greatest success of her career in the stage play, when they came to make the film, the casting people made a mistake, misheard the request and contracted the American star Helen Hayes for the role. It was perhaps an understandable error. Miss Hayes too was a fine actress with a formidable reputation but she was short and dumpy, lacking the majesty and incisive delivery of Helen Haye. Poor Helen missed out and now she was gone – to the great golf links in the sky.

Bruce would come down from Northampton some weekends. He loved nothing more than strolling amongst the Saturday night crowds in the West End, feeling at one with their spirit of revelry. He found it exciting – I hated it. They gave me agoraphobia. I would far rather have spent a quiet evening in my digs, but he was on a high, there to see the sights and the twinkling lights. Now and then, I would catch the train and go back to the flat in Northampton for the weekend.

On one of these trips Bruce had invited a couple of friends to drop in for coffee after their game of tennis. One of these was someone I shall call Martin Anders. Bruce remarked afterwards that I barely spoke to anyone else in the room the whole time they were there, and that I'd seemed preoccupied by him, which I hotly denied. It was true that we had talked about some of the things like music and literature which didn't interest Bruce, though he was sharp enough to notice that I found him fascinating. What he didn't know was that we had agreed to meet the following morning. We went for a gentle stroll down by the River Nene, a romantic enough setting but, early on in our conversation, Martin dropped a bombshell – he told me that he was emigrating (it would appear that my spell of bad luck wasn't completely exhausted) and leaving for Canada the following morning. That seemed to be that, though we exchanged addresses.

For the next five years, there being no chance of meeting, we wrote to one another. The letters were, I suppose, a form of courtship – or became so. I was infatuated with the thought of this young man and, as time went by, managed to convince myself that I loved him. It was an absurd situation, though I didn't think so at the time. A romantic fantasy was a passable substitute for the real thing. Our acquaintanceship was so brief it could have had no foundations. It was wishful thinking. Uppermost in my mind was the need to hide from Bruce the fact that I was exchanging letters with someone else. Martin was my secret.

Back in the real world, things weren't improving. I'd started to dread going back to London, not because I wanted to stay in

Northampton and be with Bruce, but because it was beginning to look as though, as an actor, I'd reached a dead end. I began to think more often of ditching the whole thing and even had a mind to return to South Africa, something which only a few months previously I would have been too proud to consider. I'd applied for all the auditions – Stratford, H.M. Tennent – got up and did my pieces and didn't get a look-in. Not once was I recalled. Was I that bad? Were they trying to tell me something?

Sometimes, when we reach moments of frustration tinged with despair, something does happen to change the course of events. So it was in my case. Leonard Schach got in touch with me, asking whether I'd go back to Cape Town to play Cliff in the play which had knocked me sideways when I'd seen it at the Royal Court, John Osborne's *Look Back In Anger*. Although I knew that in many ways accepting the job was an admission of failure, it didn't take me long to make up my mind. I had been away for six and a half years, and couldn't wait to get back. I needed the comfort of blue skies and old friends. I missed my family. The prospect of leaving behind the grey of London with its disappointments and lack of opportunity rejuvenated me. It was almost as though I was on the very brink of my career. There was, however, Bruce.

I needed to hear his reaction, so I rang and told him of the offer. Leonard Schach was sitting beside me as I spoke. There was a vacancy for the job of scenic designer. Would he like to come with me? Bruce had been in a bit of a rut so it sounded an exciting opportunity and he didn't need much persuading. He gave in his notice at Northampton and travelled down to South Africa House in London to apply for a visa. Neither of us had any money. None at all. Strictly speaking, Leonard Schach, as producer, should have brought us over – he promised to loan us the fare – we could pay him back later.

Was I off my trolley? It had all been arranged so hurriedly, I hadn't given myself time to think of the implications. By inviting Bruce, I was walking smack into trouble. Looking back on those days, I know it would have been far wiser if I'd followed Martin to Canada or at least gone on my own and not encouraged Bruce to give up everything and join me. If I'd wanted our relationship to end, and there was little point in its continuing, it would have been far more sensible. Even today, I have no answer as to why I did what I did. I was fond of Bruce and we'd had good times together but it wasn't more than a friendship, nor realistically had it ever been. Yet, I knew that if I were to leave him, not only would there be a major confrontation, but he would go into a decline. While giving an external display of huge confidence – the life and soul of the party – not very far from the surface was someone deeply vulnerable. He was so easily hurt, I suppose I just didn't have the heart to do it to him. That makes me sound like a martyr. If I were to be more honest and dig deeper into my motives, I would find that my old demon, 'guilt', was dwarfed by my craving for companionship. No question about it, Bruce and I both needed the same thing, to share our lives, but there was a difference – he was emotionally involved and I wasn't. Not having a physical relationship but someone to come home to suited me – it was a compromise, but it would do. I didn't have to commit myself. I could take life as it came. And if it didn't, well – perhaps it didn't matter. Not all that much . . .

8

Whites Only

Less than a week before we sailed in 1957, the loan from
Leonard still hadn't arrived. We were frantic. Although we'd
put down a deposit, the Union Castle Line people took to
phoning on a daily basis asking for the balance. Eventually
we called on Leonard's best friend, the concert pianist Lionel
Luyt, who was living in London at the time. He was extremely
angry on our behalf and sent a telegram to Cape Town which
amounted to an ultimatum, telling Leonard in no uncertain
terms that, unless he wired the money by return, he would
sever their long friendship. It came.

During those few anxious days before we left, Bruce and
I had pooled the little we had to buy suitcases and some
lightweight clothes, short-sleeved shirts and swimming trunks
while I telephoned my parents in Camps Bay to let them know
that I was coming back – but wouldn't be returning alone.
They were aware of Bruce of course, and knew that he and
I had been sharing the flat in Northampton. I had absolutely
no idea what they might have suspected of our relationship,
nor, if they had suspected, whether or not they would have
minded. They would have been wrong, anyway. However, this
latest development was, being on their doorstep so to speak,
a bit different. My mother sounded surprised but genuinely
elated and put me on to my Dad. 'I can't hear a word you're
saying,' he complained. 'Refuse to accept the call. Speak to
the exchange, ask for the supervisor, tell him they've given
you a bad line.' I tried to explain that the call was costing
me £3 a minute but that only made it worse. 'It's a bloody
disgrace. Tell them you won't accept it.' I tried to reason that

all I needed to say was that I was coming back home and was looking forward to seeing . . . but, in his outrage at the injustice of it all, he'd slammed down the receiver.

The voyage turned out to be pleasurable enough, though I knew from my previous experience of travelling on a mail ship that it was better to avoid getting too chummy. In a confined space over a two-week period, everyone gets to know everyone else's business, so we agreed to isolate ourselves from the other passengers, particularly when it came to deck games, which, in any case, Bruce, not being sporty, refused to play. I did, however, put my name down for the deck quoits competition. I rather fancied my chances at deck quoits. I was just getting into my stride in my second match (having won the first) when a skinny man with spectacles and long shorts strolled over to watch. Every time I called out the score, he corrected me. Even if there was the slightest dispute whether or not the quoit was inside the line he declared my opponent, clearly a friend of his, to have won the point. I put up with this for a while until a quoit landing well outside the base line was given 'In'. I suggested rather tersely that the man might go elsewhere for his entertainment. 'I'm the chairman of the sports committee,' he announced. 'I don't care whether you're the captain of the bloody ship!' I told him. 'Bugger off!' This outburst didn't go down at all well so I took my name out of the competition and settled for a book which I'd already read from the lending library. While I was there, I seized the opportunity to write to Martin. There wasn't a great deal to say, just the ramifications leading up to our journey. Bruce caught me at it. When he asked to whom I was writing, I didn't lie, nor did I elaborate. He may well have guessed the reason for the letter but mercifully this time there were no histrionics.

On our last night before landing we were bullied into joining the fancy dress competition, several passengers ganging up on us saying that we were the only ones who hadn't entered, and as we were 'supposed to be professionals', how about it? We had to think quickly as the contest was less than two hours away. I let Bruce, the designer, take control and he decided on *commedia del'arte* clowns. We slipped into white trousers, draping sheets around ourselves in an Italian sort of way, smeared our faces with shoe whitener, then outlined our lips and painted on tragic eyebrows with a make-up pencil. I thought we looked rather good. On our way there, we bumped into Catherine the Great – not, I think, in a costume she had improvised on the spot. 'What are you supposed to be,' she squeaked in an accent I knew only too well. 'Ghosts or something?' At that moment I realised that there was no getting out of it but we hadn't a hope in hell. Other passengers, even the purser, kept trying to penetrate our disguise without success, and when we told them they just looked blank. We weren't even contenders for the booby prize, though, rather irritatingly, Catherine walked away with the Silver.

The next morning most of us got up early to watch the famous skyline come into view. The sun had only just begun to rise and the city at the foot of the mountain was veiled in a mystical blue haze. It looked like some fantastical kingdom, the haunt of giants and goblins from an Arthur Rackham illustration. How good it was to see the mountain again. I felt safe once more. I was back with my old friend, the companion of my childhood, undemanding, unchanging, unchallenging – dominating but protective. Bruce and I leaned over the ship's rail, rubbing shoulders with other excited passengers as the mail boat steamed into dock. It seemed to take for ever. By now the mists had lifted, revealing the city bathed in morning sunshine, windscreens of cars on de Waal Drive glinting in the light as they processed in single file bound for the office – but still we meandered. We seemed to be drifting further away rather than closing the gap. What were they playing at down there in the engine room? Why should I be so impatient when I had the rest of my life to spend there? I watched Bruce perusing the landscape about which I had so often enthused.

How would my family take to him? I wondered. He could be brusque almost to the point of rudeness if he wanted, and he quite often wanted. I worried less about my mother and Bruce than my father and Bruce. She and he would get along fine. Sadly, she wouldn't be there to meet us. We'd had a message on board a few days earlier saying that she was in a nursing home having an operation to an arthritic kneecap, that she was in a bit of pain but that there was nothing to worry about. Dad would be there in her stead.

'I think I can see him,' I told Bruce as we filed into the customs area. 'Right at the back – bald head, red face.' Tentatively I waved in greeting in Dad's direction. He didn't acknowledge this but thrust his way through to where we were standing. In those days you could wander all over the place without breaching security. He'd aged considerably since I'd been away, his head sinking into his shirt collar like a tortoise. We shook hands – nothing as emotional as an embrace – and I introduced him to Bruce. He barely acknowledged him. 'How much longer are you going to be?' he demanded. 'Well,' I explained, 'we still have to go through customs. We shouldn't be more than a few minutes.' I smiled reassuringly, aware of his impatience. 'Well, I can't hang around here all day,' he said. 'I've got things to do. You'd better make your own way home.' And off he went to where he'd parked his car.

Bruce and I were stunned. He had been the only member of the family to meet us. I suppose that the others had been at work or were otherwise committed, and anyway we'd meet up some time later, but, I remember thinking, after my having been abroad for six and a half long years, surely he could have stayed just another fifteen minutes or so? I did my best to hide my dismay, explaining to Bruce that Dad still had a practice to run, that there was obviously an appointment he had to keep, a patient to visit, so – um – well, we'd better start looking around for a taxi. As they'd all been nabbed, we had no option but to lug our suitcases all the way up to the main road and wait there for a bus which would take us to the nursing home where my mother was recuperating and see how we went from there. So far, as a homecoming, it hadn't been too promising.

There was to be no improvement later. At supper that evening there was nearly a stand-up fight when Bruce left some pie-crust on his plate. 'You haven't finished your food,' noted my Dad, nodding in the direction of his plate. 'Yes, I have,' said Bruce politely enough. 'I couldn't eat any more.' 'Nobody,' said my father, reddening in the face, 'nobody in this house leaves a dirty plate.' 'Well,' said Bruce lightly, 'there's got to be a first time.' My father snapped. 'Damn and blast your eyes, when you're in my house you'll do as I say.' Bruce kept calm, 'I don't want it, thank you,' and pushed the plate to one side. The atmosphere in our dining room was frosty. It wasn't that my father had finally met his match or anything so conclusive, but my instinct was correct that he and Bruce were not destined to be the closest of friends.

Mrs Rice, my dear old Gran, was still very much alive and I was overjoyed to see her for, when I'd left, a reunion had seemed unlikely. As always, she was intrigued to hear about the theatre work which I was preparing, though the play, *Look Back In Anger*, meant nothing to her. She got to know Bruce and they chatted about where he had studied and how he would interpret the scenery. My mother returned from the nursing home. Tragically, the operation to her knee had been bungled and she was in considerable discomfort. She was to spend the rest of her life in some pain, unable to play bowls or even, eventually, to drive a car. Old age happens so precipitously. It isn't something we recognise when we're young until we return, as I did after an absence, to find that the middle-aged have become elderly, the elderly old and very often unsteady or, like my mother, ailing.

There were a few days before rehearsals began – time to get acclimatised, time to take stock. Bruce and I needed to get a place on our own – with so many egos flying around it seemed safer – and began looking for a flat in the Clifton area. It wasn't then quite the glamorous millionaires' paradise it is today with its luxury apartment blocks and smart hotels, but it was still pretty good after a damp basement in Pimlico where every time it rained the mark of the outside steps would show through the wallpaper. Clifton consisted of four wonderful, sheltered coves with snow-white sand, and, towering above, the phallic shapes of rounded granite mountain boulders. We found a modern block called Marivan perched on concrete stilts on the precipitous sea side of the main road. The flat was only one room with a kitchen and bathroom but it had a verandah which hung over the sea, where we could sprawl in the evening to watch the sun go down and the stars light up. At night as I lay in bed, the sound of the waves lapping against the rocks below would lull me into a peaceful sleep. The record player, even turned up to full, made no impression. All you heard was the sound of the sea. How happy I was to be back! Or was I? There was something wrong. I had a great need to escape from London, to put behind me those dark winter afternoons when I felt impelled to go down on my knees and implore God to turn up the light, to suck in fresh air unadulterated by smog, to justify my choice of career by being in a really good stage play with an adequate rehearsal period where I could show people what I knew I was capable of doing, to be once again with my family – perhaps it would have been impossible to have fulfilled all these needs. Perhaps my expectations were too high and beyond reach. I'd come back wanting everything to be perfect and it wasn't. To begin with, there was apartheid.

'For Europeans Only' – the signs were everywhere, on the buses, the trains, the beaches, the park benches! Even the modest sub-post office in Camps Bay had an absurdly unequal division down the centre of the small room. Let there be a queue of a dozen or so coloured people waiting at the counter to buy stamps, then let a white come through the door, the clerk would instantly drop whatever he or she was doing and go over to serve the privileged newcomer. It was a rude shock to arrive from England and walk smack into attitudes so devoid of humanity, so dismissive of people's sensibilities. It was going to take time to adjust. I did my best to fill Bruce in with this strange new world, though it was so complex and one-sided a system he remained baffled throughout the length of his stay. South of the Limpopo River the country was divided into four ethnic groups, black, Asiatic or Indian, coloured and white or European. There were over a million Cape coloured people, yet they were denied access to any but the most out-of-the-way beaches, and forbidden to use the theatres, cinemas, cafés and hotels frequented by the whites. Their destiny was to tend to the white man – to work in his offices and factories, wash his dishes and his toilets, polish his shoes and clean his streets – yet they had no rights. The franchise was reserved for the master. The days of slavery were not, after all, all that distant. This was the world to which I had returned.

The iniquitous apartheid policy was in full swing. The word literally meant separateness or segregation, not 'separate development', the convenient euphemism circulated by government sources. By being there, by having agreed to work there, we were in theory condoning the system. Yet neither of us had any more sympathy with racism than the man in the moon.

The Wentzels, patients of my father, were Cape coloured people and rather beautiful at that. They were kind and gentle. Their home, under the shade of scented eucalyptus trees up the road from where we lived, was without warning reclassified as a white area, and under the Group Areas Act they were obliged to pack their bags. It was happening all over the place, families shunted about with no thought for how it would affect them, and the barren Cape Flats – sparse of trees and cold of comfort – which was their usual destination was filling up. Many of them accepted the upheaval with their accustomed good humour – 'I've got a better garden, now', 'I'm nearer the shops', 'We've got a dining room. We don't have to eat in the kitchen any more' – but there were others who were angry. You couldn't help being aware that the equable situation couldn't last. The volcano would one day explode.

The bile which so many of them must have felt at the injustice of life was as nothing beside that which flowed from Mr Osborne. *Look Back In Anger* showed a world of ironing boards, forlorn Sundays and a cramped environment which fuelled aggressiveness, a world totally unfamiliar to the average South African. It was surprisingly well received at the Hofmeyr Theatre where I had given my first performance as a professional actor. As a director, Leonard had gained in experience as well as in reputation. He was known for choosing interesting new works and presenting them with integrity. Over the next decade, that reputation was to gain strength, each of his productions given with his own particular stamp of class. Bruce's sombre stage setting with its green walls and sloping attic roof was atmospheric and considered by public and critics alike to be wholly appropriate. I was now beginning to enjoy myself more than I had for some time. The role of Cliff suited me and I had a good working relationship with Leon Gluckman, who was playing Jimmy Porter. Although the political situation was uncomfortable for Bruce and those of us, like Leon and myself, who had returned, within our cushioned make-believe world of rehearsals, half-hour calls and cramped backstage conditions it was easy to be blinkered about what was happening outside in the real world.

Leon, in his other hat as a director, invited me to be in his production of *School For Scandal* for the National Theatre. Old Crabtree isn't much of a part; he's one of the gossips, an avuncular fop who has chosen as his soul-mate one Sir Benjamin Backbite, an arch-bitch as indicated by his name. During rehearsals, the actor playing the wayward brother Charles Surface dropped out, and the management was in a state of panic trying to find a replacement. All likely candidates who could approximate to standard English without a thick Afrikaans accent scything the air were already employed. Word got round that we had a problem. One night as I lay in bed, the sea below cutting up rough and hurling itself at the rocks, I had a brainwave. 'Eureka! I've cracked it!' I could scarcely believe my own ingenuity. So many decisions made in the small hours come a cropper in the cold light of day, but this one I was certain could survive. I would double the roles of Crabtree and Charles. One old, the other young; grey wig – brown wig; ordinary nose – false nose . . . In my excitement at this stroke of genius, although it was something like three in the morning, I pulled on a dressing gown, went into the bathroom so as not to wake Bruce, and waded aloud through the text, carefully allowing time for the quick changes of both costume and make-up, and finding, with my heart beating at a rate which made further sleep that night impossible, that it could be done. Just about. Leon's face was a study when I put it to him. He inhaled deeply on one of the long, dark brown cheroots he imported specially from Switzerland, rolled his mournful eyes to the ceiling, then dissolved into a gurgle of delighted laughter. So that was how it turned out. We toured every town and village, every town hall, every building that even remotely resembled a theatre, with most of the country's leading actors playing the main parts. Joyce Grant, who was to become one of my best friends, was a superlative Mrs Candour, and every night I, for no extra money and through my own impetuosity, hurled myself into an absurd number of exhausting quick changes, none of which I for a moment regretted.

Leon was a Johannesburg man who wanted to work with Africans, use their natural gifts for singing and dancing and create with them an original musical. That musical turned out to be *King Kong*, the sleazy, township story of prize-fighters and shebeens which, because of its toe-tapping music, its simple charm and the virtuosity of the performers, all Johannesburg turned out to applaud. The police developed a mean trick of lying in wait for the actors as they arrived for work, and if they happened not to be carrying their passes, took them straight down to the police station and locked them up. Minimum effort, maximum number of arrests.

The musical was brought to London, where it had success to match that in Johannesburg. I admired Leon's initiative and envied him his rapport with the African performers he had transformed into musical stars. After so short a time back in his homeland, he was absorbed in a project which was both worthwhile and fulfilling, sharing his expertise with those who could ill afford to help themselves.

That was Leon Gluckman's contribution, but what was mine? I wish I could say that my own anger at what I was seeing all around me was channelled into so personal a crusade to change things for the better. I can remember a row I had with an actress at a party given in my honour when, feeling uncomfortable because the conversation kept veering towards the political and from there to the racial, I decided to make an early departure. I'd seen a Cape coloured man on the promenade at Sea Point leaning over the railings watching the whites frolicking about on the beach which he wasn't allowed to use, and the injustice of this really got under my skin. I couldn't get the man out of my mind. He seemed to me to epitomise the whole travesty which was apartheid, to represent everything that made the system so offensive. As I got to the door on my way home the actress called out, 'You know your trouble, Nigel, you're a humanitarian!' She meant it as an insult. I remember at the time being stopped in my tracks by what she said, yet I have come to see now what she meant. I was all talk and no action, suffering from a bad case of political inertia. I thought, I hoped, I was doing everything right – behaving with respect and fairness towards the coloured people with whom I came into contact, and confident that my attitude towards them was in no way different to how I behaved with my fellow whites – yet, I was at heart a wishy-washy liberal who made no stand on their behalf. It was easy for me to come from another world – and a borrowed world at that – and criticise, but I hadn't had to live with the situation, and now that I was here, and didn't approve, what was I prepared to do about it?

Once again I found myself in an emotional tangle – though, as was my wont, I was able to elbow it on to the back burner using, as a convenient excuse, the fact that my work took so much of my time. It was true that I was working hard, though there always was time to play – if not to think – and we lived in a corner of the world which was, for the whites at least, a perpetual playground. At last I began to relax, feeling more at ease with the people around me – after all, I'd grown up amongst them. Added to this, because I was appearing in fashionable plays, I was being accepted socially. The carefree way of life in Cape Town seemed to attract homosexuals, both the male variety and the female, and they came from all over South Africa to settle there. Yet, although there was no shortage of jollity and mirth, I still was far from being totally contented.

Letters to and from Martin continued to fill the emotional hole in my life. He had moved to the United States and news from him in his distinctive copperplate handwriting was always a pleasure to receive. I had begun to lose hope of seeing him again, feeling that, although wanting, my new life back in Cape Town was far more satisfying than anything London could offer. My relationship with Bruce was not an easy one. He was making the uncomfortable discovery that his lack of intellect was hampering his progress as a stage designer. Bruce, in many ways, was a simple person and, heaven knows, the world of theatre can be very snobbish. The only people who can get away with being simple are the actors as their contribution is, broadly speaking, interpretive, but designers are expected to come up with things such as concepts and this was where Bruce fell down. As a scenic artist, he had a certain talent. He was gifted without being brilliant. Well schooled, there was an honesty about his work which was immensely appealing. He was practical, conscientious and always delivered on time, though, like an actor, better as an interpreter than a designer. The management, however, expected him to be more exceptional, to enter into lively discussions with them about the issues debated in the plays, and when he couldn't scramble up to those giddy heights, they wrote him off as 'reppy' – second-rate. It hurt him deeply and sometimes, unwisely, he would retaliate derisively in self-defence. These outbursts were quite often rude and usually received with mild astonishment, but they strengthened the barriers around him and made it even more difficult to break through to him than previously. Also they did little to enhance his reputation as a young man of promise.

It wasn't easy to give Bruce encouragement without his feeling patronised. He found it hard to accept that people were just being complimentary, always feeling there must be a hidden motive. That said, he thrived on praise. It was a measure of his perversity. He was as stubborn as a mule – God, was he stubborn! Once he'd decided on something, or formed an opinion about someone, he couldn't be shaken. As people we were very different. He was gregarious, liked parties and gatherings, while I preferred my peace and quiet. A man of strong opinions, he was, because of his deep insecurity – much of it stemming from his background – enormously vulnerable. In our private world away from things theatrical, he could be suffocatingly possessive. Then there was Martin. Our letters to each other were the sort you could show your mother – not steamy and full of bottled-up passion, but newsy, sober and touched with romanticism. Intellectually speaking, we fed off one another. Our relationship was growing stronger by the day even though we were only pen friends.

Meanwhile, the closeness to my family, which had been so much a part of my childhood, had suffered a setback. Even my mother, with whom I'd had such a wonderful and understanding relationship as a youngster, seemed to delight in putting me down, while I, in turn, was aware of how irritating she could be. In other words, I was in a bit of a mess. I didn't know who I was, where I was. I thought I was coming back to paradise and it had all gone wrong. Once the euphoria of my return had worn off, the hard reality was beginning to show through. Perhaps a happy relationship would have waved the magic wand and made it better, but the only fairies I met were the ones on the beach or at weekend parties, and they appeared to have no magical properties whatsoever.

Try For White was a play about apartheid. It was the first time that a Cape Town audience had witnessed a dramatised indictment of the system under which they were living. At last the arts in South Africa were beginning to grow up, to make a statement about the injustices and prejudices which were so abhorrent to the rest of the world. Basil Warner's play featured a bus conductor called 'Hockey' Jagger who had been living in a poor white area with his mistress, Muriel Jordan. In the kitchen, passing the dishes through the hatch, is the Cape coloured maid, an elderly woman who is in reality Muriel's mother. When during the action of the play 'Hockey' is given the news that the woman with whom he's been sleeping for nearly twenty years is not, as he is, 'European' but Cape coloured, he hurls her to the floor, spits on her, reviles her and walks out, never to return. The play had a particular significance in Cape Town where so many passed for white. My role was the dullest in the play, that of Muriel's son who has been living in the Transvaal and returns to his mother for Christmas as witness to her humiliation. But I was proud to be part of it all as it was dealing with contemporary issues which, for so long, had been swept under the carpet. Needless to say, the biggest irony was that by law no Cape coloured person was allowed to see the play. Also, because the apartheid laws forbade whites to appear on the same stage as Africans or coloureds, several of the actors had to black up in order to be even remotely convincing. We were expected to go with it to London and eventually travel to the 1961 International Theatre Festival in Paris but, just as most of the financial backing had been raised, South Africa pulled out of the Commonwealth, the backers, fearing a backlash, withdrew their support – and that was that.

Apartheid was a stockpile of absurdities, except, because of the seriousness of the context, it was often hard to find any of it amusing. In Bruce's scenic department was a Cape Malay carpenter named Gamat Orrie. He was an amiable man with gaps where teeth had been, who had a prodigious capacity for alcohol. At a coffee break during one of our rehearsals for *Try For White*, as was customary, he joined members of the company, helping himself to one of the mugs from the tray on the forestage. An English actress who was playing the Cape coloured mother and should have known better admonished him, 'Shouldn't you be drinking from your own mug?' The poor man, feeling every eye upon him, instantly replaced the one from which he'd been drinking, sobered in a second and slipped away. It seemed extraordinary that we should be breaking new ground with the play and yet have our feet planted so very firmly on the old.

Meanwhile, I was gaining valuable experience playing leading roles – which, through lack of opportunity, I hadn't managed to achieve in England. Already I had appeared in *Summer Of The Seventeenth Doll* for the National Theatre, *Waltz Of The Toreadors*, *The Matchmaker*, James Thurber's *The Male Animal* and the epic *Long Day's Journey Into Night* by Eugene O'Neill, all for the Cockpit Theatre. We took some of the plays to Johannesburg for a season, and Bruce and I decided to stay for a while as there was more work, and the chance of making a bit more money than Leonard Schach would have considered paying.

It was while we were away that my dear Gran died. She was eighty-nine. She'd been having problems with her sight for some years.

She had continued to explore new themes with her water colours, but latterly her touch had been clumsy and lacking in detail, reflecting the increasing problem she had in seeing with any definition. She could just about cope with her deafness, though it entombed her in a world of silence, but if she could see, then at least she could paint. Painting was her life.

They told her the trouble was cataracts but that she was too old to have them removed, particularly as, in convalescence, she would be expected to spend long periods in the dark without moving. The specialist's words were like a red rag to a bull. I used to come across her lying down with the curtains drawn, practising being still, determined to prove to everyone that she could do it.

The day the bandages were removed, I went to visit her in hospital. As I came through the door, her face lit up. 'Nigel!' she exclaimed. She hadn't been able to see with any clarity since I'd left for England and her exuberance at this new gift of sight was matched by ours at seeing her cured. But sadly the end was in sight. Not long after the operation, she developed arthritis in her painting hand, gave up and died.

In her spiritual home, Kirstenbosch Gardens on the slopes of the mountain, a tree was planted in her memory. It's an *Ilex mitis* – a modest tree for a modest lady – tucked away at the back; you wouldn't find it unless you happened to know it was there, which I'm sure is the way she would have wanted it. There's a small plaque at its foot with her name and dates and a quotation from William Blake:

> 'To see a world in a grain of sand,
> And a heaven in a wild flower'

In Johannesburg, Bruce and I rented a modest flat in a 1930s block alongside Joubert Park at the corner of Quartz and Koch Streets. It was a rough area even then and the streets were dangerous at night. We trod the pavements warily. There were frequent electric storms and earth tremors in the city, the latter shaking the whole building, rattling the windows in their Thirties metal frames and unsettling the pictures on the walls. Blissful in our ignorance, we watched the storms with fascination from our vantage point high in the apartment block, never imagining that we might be in danger. Bruce got himself a job at the Alexander Theatre where I did a couple of plays and we made friends in both the hetero- and homosexual communities, being shown the most wonderful hospitality. With neither of us able to drive, we bought a car and encouraged people to take us out in it if we paid for the petrol, so Sunday excursions to country homes with swimming pools and tennis courts at Hartebeestpoort Dam were a regular occurrence.

I agreed to go on a National Theatre tour of a piece by William Saroyan which some of my mother's friends might have written off as 'artsy-craftsy'. It was called *The Cave Dwellers* and was about a bunch of tramps who live in a disused theatre. The characters had names like The King, The Queen and The Girl. In the unlikely part of a punch-drunk boxer I managed to get some good reviews and, with our success firmly established, we set off on the road. Our vehicle was a Volkswagen minivan in which we travelled thousands of miles visiting parts of the country I'd never seen before. I navigated, while at the wheel was Brian Proudfoot, who played

The Bear. Yes, The Bear. On stage, he was obliged to wear a full and furry skin including the head. It was stiflingly hot. He lived on a diet of salt tablets, and would frequently wander off stage at inappropriate moments to have a swig of water. He often had dizzy spells, he told us, and during one memorable matinée, The Bear keeled over in a dead faint and we all had to gather round and revive him. Being a subsidised company, it was our happy lot to play the soul-destroying run of town and school halls, so we seldom got much feedback from our audiences other than a lot of raucous laughter, a good deal of which, I suspect, was richly deserved.

There being a small gap in our schedule, we decided to pause in our travels and visit Basutoland, as it was then called. Not having ridden since childhood at Camps Bay, I became obsessed by the desire to ride one of the Basuto ponies. They were quite small but as adept as mountain goats at climbing the hilly terrain. Our hotel in Maseru was very picturesque. It comprised the main block which housed administration and the restaurant, while each guest was allotted a chalet in the exotic garden which surrounded it. I persuaded three other members of the company, including Brian the Bear, to come riding with me, but unfortunately the only stable we could locate had just three horses. Seeing our disappointment, the owner ran out into the main street, pulled an unsuspecting passer-by from his mount, and then we had four. We agreed on a price for a two-hour ride and off we went.

On our return, I went to settle with the owner. To my consternation, he insisted that we had agreed double the amount we had, in fact, settled on. The four of us argued the point until I noticed out of the corner of my eye a bunch of hefty Basutos moving in our direction. 'Into the car, quick!' I called and, as we drove off like greased lightning, we saw the group gathered alongside the owner staring after our vehicle in a threatening manner. Our hotel was a little out of town so we felt quite secure and, dismissing the incident from our minds, went off to shower and get ready for dinner.

As I stepped from my chalet en route for the restaurant, a black policeman stepped from behind one of the bushes. 'Why won't you pay this man what you owe him?' he wanted to know. At his side was our old friend, the owner of the horses. 'Because it wasn't the amount we agreed on,' I said. 'You'd better come with me,' he announced, and I was led to a police car and driven down to the station. It was no more than a hut and the whole town seemed to have gathered to watch. Night had fallen and some guttering candles provided the only illumination. Through the windows peered the people of Maseru; inside the benches were jammed. I was the only white person present. In a tense atmosphere the case began. As none of it was conducted in English, I felt a little disadvantaged, but the policeman obligingly translated for me from time to time. The argument seemed to be becoming very heated but I stood my ground until I remembered my vulnerability, and that of the other members of the company, isolated in chalets, in the middle of a garden – anyone could walk in . . . I raised my hand to speak. The hubbub in the courtroom died away. I got to my feet. Charles Laughton couldn't have done it better. 'I'll give him the money on one condition,' I said. You could have cut the atmosphere with a knife. 'On one condition – that you explain to him that he's not entitled to it. It was not the sum on which we agreed and I have witnesses. But I'm giving him the money because I don't want trouble.' As I sat down to open my wallet, my words were translated by the policeman to the crowd around me. There was the briefest silence before an ear-splitting roar went up, threatening to lift the roof and sending a shiver of terror up my spine. From all sides people ran towards me. For a moment I thought they were going to lynch me, but apparently I must have said the right thing, for I was hoisted into the air and carried over their heads to a waiting horse. On to the saddle they lifted me, guided my shoes into the stirrups. All the way back to the hotel, the people chanted and danced, leading the animal along the dusty, unlit streets. At the hotel, they helped me dismount and, shouting salutes of, 'You are a king!' – as it was later translated to me – they danced off down the street taking the horse with them. I watched and waved till they were out of sight. Silence descended as I walked up the path to the restaurant with my empty wallet and pride in tatters. 'We were getting worried. Where have you been?' said the others. When I told them, they didn't believe me.

Bruce was anxious that I should meet some of his new friends, but despite the hectic social whirl, I couldn't warm to Johannesburg with its mine dumps and rectangular concrete buildings – especially after the simplicity of the Cape – so when, in the summer of 1960, Leonard told me that he'd managed to get hold of the rights to Harold Pinter's *The Caretaker* and encouraged me to return to Cape Town to play the troubled Aston, I jumped at the chance. The production became a huge success and we toured with it all round the country, into what was then Rhodesia and on into the Copper Belt in the north.

It was here, in the little mining town of N'dola, that I made the mistake of remarking to my hostess that I enjoyed a game of golf. The play was due to open that evening but she made a quick phone call and then, overwhelmed by her success, gushingly announced that she'd arranged a game for that very afternoon, which hadn't been quite what I'd had in mind. My opponent, and I think that's probably the correct word, was the local theatre critic. At the first tee he hit a spectacular drive right down the fairway and as he wheeled round in my direction to catch my approval, I noticed the look of triumph in his eyes. True to form, I whacked mine into the belt of trees which, rather curiously, was behind me. After twenty minutes' searching for the ball, I could sense his impatience. 'Throw one over your shoulder!' he kept saying, so rather than make an enemy for life I did. Having begun so unpromisingly it was hard to clamber back. By the half way mark, I was playing so atrociously and he so sublimely that it was no contest, and I was becoming more and more despairing. However, from then on the pendulum began to swing in my favour. It wasn't that my playing improved but more that my bad playing was unnerving him to such an extent that he began to play badly himself. Once he'd caught my disease he couldn't shake it off. I remember our being within sight of the clubhouse at the last hole. 'Please,' I heard him mutter to himself, 'all my friends are watching me!' Needless to say he walloped it into a tree and I rounded off the afternoon feeling that Helen would have been proud of me, while my poor wretched opponent slunk off in total disarray, surely the butt of clubhouse ribbing for many months to come. Peculiarly, he gave *The Caretaker* a rave review and singled out my performance as being outstanding. Perhaps I should always play golf on opening nights.

Thoughts about returning to England to have another stab at success were beginning to keep me awake at night. A flicker of hope that it might provide me with an opportunity of seeing Martin again, if we could coordinate our trips, fanned the flame. I had always known that, to be rated as an actor, I would have to pit whatever talent I had against the best. It was what had taken me to London in the first place and, even though I had failed then, this time I would be better equipped, hopefully have saved a bit more money, and gained confidence. But, before I could telephone my family with the news and book a flight, I was offered another job, the revue *Beyond The Fringe*.

The re-creation of this phenomenal West End success was far from straightforward. On one of his many visits to London in search of new material, our producer, Leonard Schach, had been offered the rights and, on an impulse, decided the show might work well in South Africa and bought them. As there was no written text, at that early stage – we were the first company in the world to perform it outside London – Leonard persuaded the management to let him pop a tape-recorder in the wings of the Fortune Theatre in Covent Garden. When he returned to South Africa he proudly presented me with the result and gave me the sweeping directive that I should transcribe it into the script we lacked. The assistant stage manager, Paddy Canavan, and I didn't quite realise the challenge which was before us. As the tape had been recorded during a performance, a huge percentage of the words were obscured by the laughter and applause of the audience. Even though she and I nearly wore the wretched tape out trying to make sense of it, sometimes we would have to settle for what we *thought* we heard rather than what the actors actually said.

For days we toiled. I was never very expert at typing, accomplishing things with two fingers rather than two hands, but eventually we presented Leonard with a working script and off we went. We had absolutely no idea of the impact the show would have. At the Hofmeyr Theatre in Cape Town where we opened, *Beyond The Fringe* was ecstatically received: 'A whip-lash brand of satire, at times savage and biting', 'Recommended without reserve'. The audiences poured in and the little theatre shook with their laughter. It was decided to send the show to Johannesburg for a season and then to put it out on tour. Wherever we played, the result was the same. Whatever the takings at the tiny Fortune Theatre in London, we must have made the Fab Four collaborators (Peter Cook, Dudley Moore, Jonathan Miller and Alan Bennett) a fortune. Sometimes the theatres we played seated two thousand people, and every night we were packed to the rafters. Leonard had taken a gamble – not for the first time – and it had paid off.

Martin wrote that he feared his mother was beginning to go blind, and was thinking of returning to Northampton to see her. When I replied, I told him of my own thoughts about having another go in London, and suggested that it might be good were we to contrive to be in the UK at the same time. It had been over five years since we had seen each other. Our romance already had reached romantic novel proportions and, like all good stories, it had to be played out to its conclusion.

As the end of the tour of *Beyond The Fringe* approached, I let my friends know that I'd be leaving for England for a second time to try my luck. The night before I flew off, they gave me a wonderful farewell party, and early the next morning, feeling rather the worse for wear, I set off for the airport. I left Bruce ensconced with Alpha Films, a Johannesburg-based company which made commercials. As he had another six months of his contract to run, in a way I was being made a gift of my freedom. I need hardly say that, as usual, I didn't embrace the opportunity.

It wasn't easy saying goodbye, nor did I know whether I'd have any better luck this time than I'd had before. This time I had stashed away just about £1000 which I thought would see me through a certain amount of unemployment, though times had changed and things were more expensive, and, as before, I had no job to welcome me nor an agent to represent me. But Martin was due to meet me at Heathrow on arrival, and Kerry Jordan, one of the actors in *Beyond The Fringe*, had very kindly offered me his flat in Swiss Cottage, where we could stay together in blissful harmony when Martin wasn't at his mother's.

On my arrival at the Johannesburg customs, I was asked for my exit permit. I didn't know what the man was talking about and explained that, having been on tour for several months, I had acted on the advice I'd been given by a friend of a friend who told me I needed only the tax clearance which I had already presented. The official returned this to me. No, it wasn't enough. I wouldn't be allowed out of the country until I had the correct documents. His verdict was final, his attitude unfriendly. I argued until I was blue in the face that I was being met at Heathrow. It was imperative I was on the flight. Eventually he walked away, while I had to get a taxi, trail all the way back to the flat in Johannesburg to wait four endless, nail-biting days before I had legitimate documentation. I had no opportunity of contacting Martin in London to let him know of the delay.

I arrived in London in the late, fierce winter of 1962, when the snow fell to settle and everything froze. There was a dramatic moment, not long after I'd unpacked, when the pipes burst and I had to retreat to the public baths in the Finchley Road in order to wash or shower. It was a rude awakening after the clear skies of Africa where we left doors and windows ajar to admit the breeze. It felt strange being back. I'd forgotten how crowded and grey it all was in London – how even the red splash of the buses made little impact and how people seemed happier moving at a slower speed. They gave the impression of being tired, as though they'd taken on too much and were hoarding their natural energies and enthusiasms for some imaginary holiday when all their strength would miraculously return and their troubles evaporate.

My priority was to get to Northampton and to trace Martin, who would have no idea what had happened to me. When we pulled in at the station, I pored through the local telephone directory under 'A' for *Anders*. There were quite a few of them dotted about. I copied down the addresses, armed myself with a map and set off on foot. At my sixth attempt, the front door of a modest terraced house was opened by an elderly lady wearing dark glasses. I asked whether she had a son called Martin. He wasn't in, she told me, but playing the organ in the church. I was on the right track. When I asked which church, she shook her head sadly. She wasn't sure.

Off I went again, discovering, at long last, a church near to the racecourse, which had Handel's glorious Toccata and Fugue overflowing on to the pavement outside. Seated at the organ was Martin. He was astonished to see me. We were shy with one another – perhaps not surprisingly after such a long time – guarded as though not quite knowing what to say nor how it would be taken. I felt nothing. Just a bit flat. It was most disappointing. This was certainly not the meeting of young lovers. He seemed like a total stranger. There was a lot of chat about how cold it had got, the delay of my flight, whether or not I'd had to pay any duty, how he'd not known what to do when I didn't arrive, and so on, but the important thing was that I'd found him and, after five years, we'd met up again. I secretly suspected that the love bit would emerge when the dust had settled.

The next day happened to be my birthday, and I suggested that we go for a celebratory dinner to L'Escargot in Soho. It might have been better had I remained that night in Northampton where Martin had to stay with his mother who was on her own, but I chose instead to go back to London. The following evening Martin joined me and we passed among the dimly-lit tables of L'Escargot to take up the reservation. Our napkins were shaken out, the candle was lit, we had some champagne – after all, this was a special occasion – placed our order and settled back to do some catching up. I wish I could say that the chemistry we had generated five years ago hadn't diminished. He was curious about my decision to give up a position of security in South Africa and have another go at sticking my head over the parapet. He asked about Bruce too, and how he was getting along. The first course arrived. The food at L'Escargot was always superb, and they'd done us proud. As I took my first mouthful, I happened to glance up at Martin. He was literally shovelling food into his mouth as if there were no tomorrow. I can't think of another way to describe it. He ate like a pig. At that moment I lost my appetite. Whatever I had ordered sat unmolested on the plate. 'Aren't you hungry? I'm starving' – the two phrases run together as if one – he slurped the juice, spoke with his mouth full, crammed his plate with everything within range and finished the lot. I looked up at him and Charles Laughton as Henry VIII looked back. Five years of love's young dream went sailing out of the window of the restaurant like a flabby balloon. I sat in a daze. I tried to dismiss his gluttony as trivial. I can cure him of that – it's only table manners for goodness' sake – and thought that some more wine might anaesthetise me. The bottle of Chablis wrapped in a napkin rested in one of those silvered coolers to one side of the table. I looked round for our waiter but he was nowhere to be seen. I wasn't sure of the protocol. Though I was paying for the meal, was I allowed to help myself, or did I have to wait for him to pour it for me? Martin solved my dilemma by suddenly leaning forward, recharging his own glass, then, in an assertive way, plonked the bottle down alongside my glass. 'Have you tried Californian wine?' he asked. 'Now that's *really* good.'

Back at the flat in Swiss Cottage over a cup of coffee, he confessed that, because of the delay in my arriving, he'd gone to one of the clubs and met someone else. Our long-awaited, emotion-packed affair was not to be. I felt an overpowering sense of relief. I'd had an extremely lucky escape! Our father had brought us up so strictly that bad table manners have always brought out the prude in me, though I was taken aback at how rapidly my vision of paradise had evaporated.

West End theatre beckoned. I invited Hilda Kriseman, who had left Cape Town with me in the theatrical exodus over ten years earlier, now a highly esteemed radio actress, to see – my first choice – *Beyond The Fringe*, managing to get seats right in the front row. Only inches in front of us on the little stage were the originators, Peter Cook, Dudley Moore, Jonathan Miller and Alan Bennett. I sat back determined to enjoy myself. To my deep embarrassment, I soon found that the dialogue to the unravelling of which Paddy and I had so assiduously applied ourselves bore very little resemblance to the real thing. Time and again, words and phrases which I was quite certain we had reported accurately were different. Often wildly different. The miracle was that, even with the wrong words, we'd managed to get genuine belly laughs. A number of the scenes I had totally misinterpreted. Tag lines to jokes, people's names, even long-winded descriptions were embarrassingly different. Afterwards, Hilda and I went backstage to meet the four. We'd had a wonderful, exhilarating and quite surprising evening. I had ended up weak with laughter and admiration, only too aware of how inadequate by comparison we in South Africa must have been. Where they brushed aside the comedy as though it were some mildly tiresome insect, we'd biffed it on the head with a mallet.

Some weeks later, word got round that there was to be a new cast, so I applied for an interview. I was told to prepare two pieces; it seemed appropriate that they should be from the show. I chose a couple of monologues (with appropriate amendments) which Jonathan Miller had written for himself and which, for the past nine months, I had been performing. I was at home with them and confident that I could present them with practised familiarity. This confidence evaporated immediately I walked on stage and saw that, instead of being interviewed by either the director or the producer which was normal, sprawled out on the seats below were Peter Cook, Dudley Moore, Jonathan Miller and Alan Bennett. As I stood gawping at them in horror, one of them, and I haven't the faintest idea who, asked, 'What are you going to do for us?' 'Nothing,' I said, 'nothing . . .' Stammering in my nervousness, I explained that while it was true that I'd prepared two extracts from the show, 'I couldn't do them in front of *you* – it's just not possible – you're the *originals*!' There was a comforting chuckle from below. 'Don't worry about us,' they sang out, trying to reassure me. It was as though my feet were wedged in wet concrete and my mind a tangle of wool. Finally, to put an end to my misery and probably theirs by getting it over as soon as possible, I launched into the first piece, hearing my voice rattling round the empty auditorium and being achingly unfunny. My performance was received in silence. It deserved no better. I essayed the second. There was little improvement. They gave the job to Joe Melia.

I managed to get an audition with Arthur Storch, a Method director from New York, who was casting a double bill of William Saroyan plays heavy on symbolism. The blanket title of the evening was *Talking To You*, the name of the first play in which, unexpectedly, I was given the rather splendid part of an American crook known as Fancy Dan. I found that I was at ease with Arthur's style of working, even though it was my first attempt at improvisation, and much enjoyed the feeling of freedom he generated, encouraging the cast to explore its imagination. In the leading role was a wonderful black actor, Johnny Secca, who came from Dakar in West Africa. He and I got along well and, while on tour, shared digs. Embarrassed by the number of letters from South Africa greeting me at the theatres we visited, I decided to come clean with Johnny rather than have him find out for himself my sinister origins. 'I should have told you – I come from South Africa,' I announced bravely, 'but as far as I know I have no colour prejudice whatsoever.' There was no hesitation from him. 'Well, if you had,' he answered, 'I would be the first to know it, wouldn't I?' The plays opened in London at the Duke of York's and were thoroughly abused by the critics. They jumped up and down on them. Saroyan himself had come over for the celebrations but didn't stay for the wake. The producer, on the other hand, did. Anna Deere Wiman, in turn the daughter of a famous American producer, was a sickly woman who walked with the aid of crutches. When the closure of the play was announced she was at the stage door, propped against the wall – her crutches within reach in case of an emergency – bravely apologising to each actor as he arrived for work that the show was to end a lot earlier than expected.

It was in this production that I met Thelma Holt, then a carrot-haired actress with enviably defined cheekbones, but these days a daring and respected producer though the bones haven't altered (or even the hair come to that), whom I found lived diagonally opposite my borrowed accommodation in Fairfax Road. The coincidence seemed like fate and we became friends for life. When *Talking To You* had completed its disastrous run and most of us were back on the dole, she persuaded me – as a special favour – to join her on an extremely tatty tour of the West Country with two plays, Ibsen's *A Doll's House* and a Russian comedy, *Squaring The Circle*. In the Ibsen, alas, neither she nor I played the leading roles, though we were eminently suited, while Bruce, who had now returned from South Africa and was staying in my flat, was given the unenviable task of revitalising for the umpteenth time the geriatric stage flats which wobbled alarmingly whenever anyone approached within six feet of them – the whole room threatening to collapse like a pack of cards when Nora leaves home at the end of the play, famously slamming the front door. It was what was known as a fit-up tour and I don't think I've ever quite forgiven Thelma for having involved me.

There was news of a Beryl Reid revue to be called *All Square* and, as I'd met Beryl in South Africa where she'd gone to work, I managed to wangle an audition. In order to keep body and soul together, I was doing the occasional play at a weekly rep theatre back in Bromley, Kent, but as the audition was awkwardly slotted for five in the afternoon and I had a performance that same evening, I asked to be seen first, and it was agreed. I had decided to sing 'You Always Hurt The One You Love', one of the Inkspots' classics, as a sadist. It was a pretty feeble idea but I thought it might help disguise the fact that I was no Pavarotti. I got to the audition in good time to be met by a middle-aged man who claimed to be the accompanist for the session, and would I like to run through my piece before they all arrived? I thanked him but declined. With only one joke, it wouldn't do were the big brass to get there early and catch me at it.

Finally they settled in their seats and, after a flurry of introductions, I began to sing. To my consternation it seemed as though the piano behind me had a life of its own. After only half a dozen bars or so I stopped and swung round to the accompanist. 'What are you doing? Whose audition is this, yours or mine?' There was some impatient muttering from the stalls. 'Just get on with it, please, if you're wanting to get away . . .' I tried to explain why I'd been forced to stop, that I was doing one tune and the piano seemed to be doing another while the accompanist glared at me over the top of the music, but finally I capitulated. 'Thank you. I will get on with it – but only if he sticks to the tune!' The joke, had there ever been one, had been long since sunk without trace but I soldiered on to the end. 'Thank you, Mr Hawthorne,' came the voice of Charles Hickman, the director, amid a certain amount of chortling. 'Back to Bromley!' And that was that. Once again, unsurprisingly, the job went to someone else.

Things could have been better. I had no job, no private life and I was smoking nearly fifty Senior Service a day. I managed to get Bruce an interview at Bromley where he was accepted. He joined the company as scenic artist, so at least one of us was in regular employment. The working conditions for him were pretty terrible. The antiquated theatre, which was in a parlous state, had been built above some old public swimming baths, the basic structure of which, including the tiles, still remained. The paint shop being directly beneath the floorboards of the stage and, with no trace of ventilation, the smell of the size (glue made from melting down goats' hooves) used on the scenery greeted us at the stage door and remained with us until we left, penetrating our hair, our clothes and our lungs.

There were moves afoot to demolish the borrowed accommodation in Fairfax Road, so I began to look round for a substitute, eventually finding something suitable in Elgin

Crescent, Notting Hill Gate. With hindsight this would have been a golden opportunity to part company with Bruce, once and for all. Call it cowardice in the face of unarguable persistence, I allowed myself once again to include him in the muddled equation of my life. The justifications, as ever, were that it was better to be un-lonely with Bruce, whom I knew so well, and despite everything genuinely liked, than sulking on my own. The flat consisted of two rooms on the first floor and a hallway which could be used as an eating area. At the rear were the communal gardens, while at the front was the busy main road along which passed the frequent No. 52 bus and the not so frequent and considerably less reliable No. 15. While Bruce was working away down at Bromley, I began decorating our new home. One evening, at the end of a long day, I happened to catch sight of my face in the mirror. All round my lips were traces of the paint I'd been using. I believe it was called 'Magnolia'. Each time I'd taken a drag from a cigarette, some of the paint had stuck to my skin. I looked at the ashtray crammed with butts of different lengths. I couldn't remember having smoked any of them. When I returned the following morning to continue work, I positioned the full ashtray alongside the can of paint, so that every time I wanted a cigarette, the ashtray in front of me with its disgusting contents stopped me in my tracks. It may not have been the conventional way of giving up smoking, but it certainly worked in my case; I haven't had one since.

The flat in which we were now living in Notting Hill was within a stone's throw of the famous Portobello Road market. In the early Sixties you could buy quite handsome antiques for very little so Bruce and I furnished our flat and settled down to enjoy the invasion of the hippies who, every Saturday, crowded the streets. It was the early days of the Beatles, flared trousers and beads and the air reeked of pot. For Bruce and me it was a reasonably contented period, despite the fact that neither of us was attached, apart from to one another, nor

bringing in much money. I worked but only spasmodically –
Bromley, Hornchurch, bits on television – but for very little
remuneration, and the work was seldom fulfilling. It paid my
share of the rent and that was about it.

In between jobs I found work as a domestic cleaner at
ten shillings for a half-day. The company was called 'Your
Servant' and operated from a smart address in Half Moon
Street, Mayfair. The room where my interview took place was
certainly impressive and spacious, yet there was almost no
furniture. A plain desk, behind which sat the interviewer, was
positioned across a corner at the far end, with a simple chair for
the interviewee. The only other furniture was an unmade bed.
'What are your hobbies?' asked the interviewer, who, apart
from the occasional vowel lapse, could have persuaded me
he'd had a public school education. He smiled in an agreeably
interested way. Suspicious of his motives, I told the man that I
was in the theatre and very much liked art and music – mostly
classical. 'Then, I believe I'll suggest you to Mrs Heidler,' he
said with a sage nod. 'She's very musical.' Bewildered about the
relevance of this to a cleaning job, off I went to Mrs Heidler,
somewhere off the Finchley Road, and knocked at the door.

There was much rattling of chains and turning of locks and
bolts so that I half expected Marley's ghost to open the door
with appropriate eerie creakings, but it was Mrs Heidler who
was revealed. Her reaction to me was unexpected. 'What are
you doing?' she yelled, her eyes almost popping out of her
head. 'What?' I replied in panic. 'What is it?' 'The shoes!' she
screamed. 'The shoes! There'll be mud all over my carpets.
Wait there!' And she slammed the door in my face, leaving me
on the threshold. I had been given no time to volunteer that,
as one of my jobs was to vacuum the carpets, she needn't be
too concerned, but stood shivering in the drizzle and waited
for her return. The door opened again and she threw down
a pair of bedroom slippers. 'Leave yours outside!' she said,
and was gone. Wisely turning my own shoes upside down to

prevent their filling with rainwater, I pulled on the slippers which were a couple of sizes too small and went indoors. She was a stickler for cleanliness, being most particular about her bathroom. 'Listen carefully,' she instructed. 'I'm not going to tell you again. Take the broom and sweep the floor. There's a dustpan and brush in the cupboard by the sink. Now. There's Jiff on the shelf but use it sparingly. Flash on the floor and the bath and Vim in the basin, never the other way round, Gumption on the taps. There's a soft cloth in the cupboard, wet it first so you don't make scratches, Harpic in the bowl and Windolene on the windows but don't leave streaks and Pledge on the furniture – NOT the dining table which is walnut (a smile – brief but proud). Use beeswax – it's in the cupboard. I'll check your work at the end of each morning to see you've done it properly. Don't just stand there, that's not what I'm paying for!' and off she went down the passage, leaving me dazed. Before me the array of tins and aerosols. Now, let's see . . . Gumption on the floor . . .

Wallis, the dress shop syndicate, took me on for a spell which I'm sure they regretted almost as much as I did. My job was to sweep out their shops in the King's Road, Knightsbridge and Oxford Street, the last coinciding with the lunch hour when the street was packed, pushing the muck, with a muttered 'excuse me, please', between the ankles of shoppers, out across the pavement and into the gutter. For some reason, I found this embarrassing. I suppose that I imagined some famous impresario like Binkie Beaumont confronting me and shaking his head sadly. I did suggest sweeping the dirt into a neat pile in the doorway and then scooping it all up with a dustpan and brush, but they wanted it in the gutter. Their shop in the King's Road had a linoleum floor which was quite difficult to clean because of all the hanging clothes. It was on several levels with a number of metal uprights supporting the display structures. One day the handle of the polisher I was using snapped off, and, before I could stop it, the machine had spun out of control amongst all the trendy frocks and shoppers. I chased after it in an attempt to cut it off before it did any damage but the wretched thing was elusive. Round and round it spun like a dervish. It was like a thing possessed. With muffled screams, the shoppers and assistants scattered. At long last the cable wound itself like a boa constrictor round one of the uprights and the polisher shuddered to a halt – forced to capitulate – though not before it had terrorised the entire shop, including me. I offered to pick up some of the garments which were strewn about the floor and somewhat creased but the offer was declined.

One of the grander ladies I cleaned for was Cicely Berry, voice coach at the Shakespeare Memorial Theatre. She and her husband Harry Moore, who worked for the BBC, lived in Earls Court. My first chore was cleaning their hallway which was laid with black and white tiles (Flash again) that showed up every speck, therefore needing to be tended several times a week. As they had a young family there was always plenty to do, plenty of things to pick up off the floor and stash away just out of reach of prying fingers. Mrs Moore cautioned me not to attempt her husband's office as there were 'scripts all over the floor', but one day I was given the go-ahead to enter the holy of holies. The 'floor' in question was covered with coconut matting which is always the devil to clean and, having made a reasonable job of that, I set about the dusting, positioning myself so that I could glance idly at the title page of the top script which was now set neatly encased in a transparent folder to one side of the table. It was the libretto of a musical written by Dan Farson and, by a strange coincidence, not only was I to be in it, but *The Marie Lloyd Story* was to be instrumental in altering the whole course of my life. Though that was all some way off.

9

Stratford Beckons

Having tried on innumerable occasions to extend my limited classical experience by joining the august company of Shakespeare wallahs at Stratford-upon-Avon and getting a thank you but no thank you for my pains, it was ironical that my quest for excellence should have steered me not towards the quaint market town in Warwickshire with its spiteful swans and inglenook tea rooms but to its distant cousin, Stratford-atte-Bow in the East End of London. This may lack some of the clout of its namesake on the Avon but amongst the architectural gems tucked in amongst its post-Blitz muddle is the charming Theatre Royal, made famous by the legendary director, Joan Littlewood.

At long last I had an agent – Barry Krost, a friend of a friend who took me on without even expecting me to sign a contract – which let both of us off the hook. It was a convenient arrangement, whereby either one of us could break free if we wanted to. I'd been offered a play called *The Albatross* at the Theatre Royal. As it turned out, it was significantly named. It was to be presented by Howard Koch, and in no way was connected to Joan Littlewood's Theatre Workshop. It was about Charles and Mary Lamb and their literary friends, amongst whom was Samuel Taylor Coleridge, who had written 'The Rime Of The Ancient Mariner'. The actor entrusted with impersonating the poet having dropped out, I was shunted in to take his place. The opening night with its jokey good-luck cards and eccentric floral arrangements was upon me before I could catch my breath. I knew my lines, the auditorium was buzzing with important people, my head that auspicious evening bulging with dreams of being discovered. Dreams of being found out might have been more appropriate. My first scene passed without mishap. Like all seasoned actors, I cleared my throat and checked my flies before making my entrance, Mary Lamb guiding me to a chair on which I perched, elegantly flicking my coat-tails and stretching my legs, my feet splayed in the accepted classical manner. I rather fancied myself at this 'period' stuff and the audience seemed attentive enough until, that is, the second half of the play when I was required to enter white-haired and dazed through opium abuse. Mary Lamb, shocked beyond measure this time round at the change in her dear friend, was heard to gasp, 'Samuel! Where have you been?' My response was the epitome of calm under fire; a heavenward flick of my bloodshot eyes and an accompanying gesture of despair capable of moving a granite heart as I muttered the single, immortal word, 'Everywhere . . . !' It stopped the show. I couldn't fathom what they were all laughing at. Now I come to think of it, we'd probably been getting the warning signs for quite some time without being fully aware, titters kicking up from various parts of the auditorium, but this single word was the catalyst. A great roar of laughter went up like a firework and the evening was never the same again. Matters worsened when Mary, in an effort to change the subject from opium to something in a lighter vein, turned to me with touching innocence to enquire, 'And how are the Wordsworths?'

It was several minutes before the audience could recover. Hysteria had set in. Friends there on the opening night told us later that a number of people were helpless – clutching each other, literally crying with laughter. The next day, quotes were given prominence in all the reviews and, later that week, coachloads came down from London to revel in our misery.

Yet the little Victorian horse-shoe auditorium, the venue for our humiliation, was a delight to play in, intimate and friendly. In fact, the whole building radiated good nature which I had to assume was due to the influence of Miss Littlewood, though I'd heard she could be a bit on the awkward side. It would be another year or so before I would have the opportunity of working there again and on that occasion, not only would the circumstances be rather different, but they would change my life for ever.

Oh! What A Lovely War was a musical set during the First World War, featuring a troupe of pierrots and pierrettes arrayed in white satin with black pom-poms who sang the songs of that wasteful, terrible war against the background of slides made from contemporary photographs and a ticker-tape which raced across the stage at intervals listing news of the casualties and the amount of land gained or lost. It was one of Miss Littlewood's greatest achievements and, as a slice of anti-war propaganda, it had no equal. It enjoyed a huge success when it opened at Stratford, then transferred to Wyndham's in the West End before going on to conquer Broadway. Joan, I think, would have been perfectly satisfied had the show never left the East End but there were more commercially-orientated forces at work to persuade her that *Oh! What A Lovely War* could be a major money-spinner. A tour was being set up first around England, and then over the Channel to Holland, Belgium and Germany. It was to have a spanking new cast and my agent Barry, never one to let a good idea slip through his fingers, telephoned one afternoon to suggest that I went down to Stratford at 10.50 the following morning to meet Joan Littlewood.

Joan Littlewood! What was I thinking of? And agreeing to? I must have been off my chump. I'd never worked the way she worked, whatever way that might be, nor did I want to. Rumour had got round that it was some sort of free-for-all. Every man for himself. I liked to know where I was supposed to be at any given moment, where I was going to go and, if it was my turn to speak next, what I was going to say. I couldn't operate in anarchy. In any case, I wasn't a musical actor. Far too self-conscious. I wasn't a dancer, never had been. Or singing come to that. And all that improvisation! The whole thing was absurd. Whose bright idea was this? I rang Barry. 'You got me into this. Now get me out.' 'I think you should go,' he said. So I did.

The pubs opened at 10.30 but, in a total blue funk, I somehow managed to down six bottles of Guinness, not something I would do as a matter of course, before presenting myself at the stage door. Miss Littlewood, I was relieved to hear, wasn't in the building, she was still in America. However, Gerry Raffles, with whom she lived, was, as well as Kevin Palmer, who, in her absence, was directing. I don't remember much about the audition except Gerry Raffles's booming laugh which rattled the foundations when I impersonated my agent Barry, whom he knew – and that I landed the job. I'd heard that Guinness was good for me, but I had no idea that it could perform miracles.

Rehearsals began. They were serious affairs. We were slowly to be indoctrinated into the Theatre Workshop approach. First we were given research, during which no page of any tome on the subject of the First World War was left unturned, no anecdote passed by. Some of the lines improvised by the original cast, now in New York, were scripted and deemed to be sacrosanct, but there were other stretches to which we could offer up our own thoughts. Joan wanted the dialogue to sound as though it was our own words, not especially written for the occasion – the unexpected taking precedence over the predictable. Contrary to popular belief, the music hall approach long identified as being favoured by Joan was fine as long as it stuck to the rules. To give the appearance of reality we spoke to one another face-to-face, for instance, and not flat on to the audience. Like all good intentions, it didn't always work out quite that way in performance but, none the less, as a theory, its virtues were undeniable. There were many contradictions. She appeared to despise the trained singer, actor or dance performer, yet valued his or her stability and technique. Like Fellini, she would have preferred a cast of amateurs off the streets. Stuck with us, she welcomed our dedication, our ability to sustain and our punctuality. As part of an ensemble, no single actor was notified in advance what line of parts he would be playing. He had to prove himself. And information was seldom forthcoming. We were expected to use our own resources, dig deep and come up with something original. Although Joan had yet to set foot on the scene, these we were warned were some of the qualities she would be expecting on her return from the States. It was a system guaranteed to bring out the introvert in many – me in particular. I froze up just as I always had when I knew that something was expected of me. Exhausted after a strenuous rehearsal, I would seldom find it easy to sleep. The music from the show would be going round and round in my head, the dialogue repeated a million different ways. I even tried to visualise my first encounter with the great lady and, such was my paranoia, how I would react to her stinging criticisms. The more I thought about it all, the worse it got until, finally, the inevitable conclusion stared me in the face. I was in the wrong job – way out of my depth. As if to confirm this unhappy suspicion, I was becoming increasingly aware that Kevin, the director, seemed markedly unenthusiastic about me.

Perhaps he'd not wanted me in the first place – been talked into giving me the job by Gerry Raffles – but day after day I would arrive for rehearsal to find that my appearances in the show had been whittled down until I was doing virtually nothing. The morning we began the first run-through Kevin took me on one side. He'd decided, he told me, that I wasn't right for the title number and was taking me out of it. 'But it's a company number,' I protested. 'Everybody's in it.' He was adamant. A little later, I sat disconsolately doing the crossword in my dressing room, baffled as to why I had been chosen as the whipping boy, and on the brink of despair while over the tannoy I could hear them all belting their lungs out. I felt like doing something unmanly like running away and never coming back.

Then Miss Littlewood returned from America. I remember her coming down the backstage stairs in her sailor's cap and frilly shirt, a disarming smile on her face. 'You're not going to put on a show for the old girl, are you?' she asked in her croaky but unexpectedly genteel voice. No! Certainly not! Nothing like that! Forfend! We all knew of her passion for spontaneity and kept well away from anything which might be construed as expected. Shyly, she went round to the dress circle in her flat white shoes, cigarette dangling from her mouth, to take her place alongside the giant, photographic blow-up of Lord Kitchener pointing fiercely in the direction of the stage, 'Your country needs YOU!' The tinny little band under Alfie Ralston struck up and we began her show – in front of her. Despite the sense of occasion, I could honestly say that I felt no part of it all. If Kevin thought I was so terrible why should the great Joan Littlewood's opinion be any different? Yet, when it was all over, I could detect no glaring signs of disapproval. She treated me like the rest, took us all for a drink at the pub down the road. We needed it. 'We've got work to do, kinders,' she whispered conspiratorially, 'but that can wait until Monday, can't it?' Of course it could, of course. No problem at all. We were devastated by her sweetness. If a tigress was lurking, she was well camouflaged.

Monday morning dawned and we all assembled to await Joan's arrival. Kevin, the director, seemed not to have altered his attitude towards me, so I was feeling bolshie and demoralised and, despite the imminent presence of the magnetic Miss Littlewood herself, vehemently resistant to the show and just about everybody connected with it. In those days, I was rather prone to black depressions – and this was a humdinger. To add to my peeve, the first thing she wanted when she came in was an exercise – and my least favourite exercise at that –

improvisation. I might just as well have gone home. We were all to be, yes, surprise, surprise, here we go, jolly pierrots and pierrettes arriving at a jolly seaside venue. 'Out into the street, my lovelies, and I'll let you know when to come in.' Oh! What fun this is all going to be! All of us mugging away like crazy, bending over backwards to please her. My worst fears about the woman were about to be confirmed. The company surged out on to the pavement, quivering with anticipation. I lagged on behind, a solid wall of resistance. The stage manager came out to give the signal. There was a stampede. Load of bloody sheep, I thought in splendid isolation. In a matter of seconds it was as if nobody had been there. The entire company had gone back inside and, apart from me, the pavement was deserted. A wave of loneliness washed over me. Even if I *did* go in, what was I going to say? As if actor's block wasn't bad enough, I'd now got thinker's block as well. I was totally at a loss to know what to do, my mind a blank. I might just as well go home. I knew that the others were cart-wheeling about, telling jokes, doing magic tricks and impersonations of utter brilliance because I could hear all the whooping and roistering in the distance. I couldn't think of anything, and seldom felt so ineffectual. In my misery, I just wanted out. I knew it would be a pity to squander an opportunity of working with the great Miss Littlewood, but at that stage, I didn't care. Enough was enough.

Taking one last look at the mournful streets of Stratford before wending my way back to the station, an idea began to take shape. It was so simple as to be almost pathetic. I found instead that my feet were being invisibly guided back through the theatre door which, only seconds before, I was convinced I'd never enter again, and from there into the auditorium. Inside, it was apparent that the others had rather worn themselves out and their exuberance was considerably diminished. One of the younger actors came up to banter with me in a Theatre Workshoppish sort of way. 'Who are you then, you silly old git? What do you want?' It was like a red rag to a bull. 'Get me the manager!' I demanded. 'Do as I say. Not yesterday. Now!' The auditorium went quiet. It seemed as though I had all the time in the world. An actor improvising the theatre manager came up to me. I cut him short. 'The name's Hawthorne. Shakespearean monologues. Top of the bill, man, you should know that. Number One dressing room, if you'd be so kind.' The rest of the company did its best to appear outraged and gave me a lot of stick on my way through, though I held my ground.

That evening, back at Notting Hill Gate, the telephone rang. It was Joan Littlewood. She told me that she was considering reapportioning some of the roles and how many did I feel I would be able to tackle? 'What about the other actors?' I asked, knowing from experience how painful it was to be rejected. 'Leave the other actors to me,' Joan said, fully in command, and I could hear her flicking through the script, muttering as she did, 'You'd better do this, you'd better do that.' By the time she'd finished, I was just about playing all the leading parts. This wasn't going to make me very popular.

First thing next morning, she began unravelling all the details so painstakingly arrived at by Kevin, and then slowly stitched it all together again, scene by scene. Contrary to my expectation, she was surprisingly insistent upon symmetry, and it was fascinating to watch her working at full throttle. It was planned like a military exercise. Scenes dovetailed with one another so that there was minimum break in continuity. It was best to watch the show from the dress circle or higher up as it would give you some idea of the director's dexterity when she created a location with no scenery, making the audience fall back on its own resources and use its imagination. A scene involving two or three people would give way to an ensemble scene where the actors would take up carefully marked positions, moving into shafts of light which only seemed to increase the numbers and suggest far more space than in reality. She had devised mathematical stage patterns crucial to her concept and we were expected to work freely, yet never to ignore this overall structure.

Now and then she would employ the dreaded improvisation as a way of clarifying a complex area. My fear of launching forth into unfamiliar territory without knowing what was going to come out of my mouth slowly began to disperse. I even began to find improvisation helpful. I watched her rescue some of the girls who were struggling with attitudes which today no longer exist. There was a tiny scene in which she felt that the actresses playing French country girls were being too modern in their approach to the Tommies. They were gathering round a group of soldiers, bringing them gifts of bread and wine and flirting with them. We knew it as the 'fraternisation' scene. The band begins to play 'Mademoiselle From Armentiers' and they pair up and, wheeling round and round, totally at ease in one another's company, dance off into the distance. So Joan invented an imaginary convent, just a few chairs and a table for the altar, and with the rest of us pretending to be devout nuns chanting in the background, each girl was asked to bring a posy of flowers down the aisle of the 'chapel', shyly present her gift to the Mother Superior and receive her blessing. Then Joan made them return to the scene itself. The difference was remarkable – it made sense for the first time. It sounds simple enough, I know, and there'll be cries of 'Anyone can do that!' The painful truth is that anyone can't.

Littlewood was the most important influence of my life. I owe her everything, even though sometimes what was achieved struggled through the swirling mists of confusion – and was frequently acrimonious. Her encouragement stimulated me and transformed my work as an actor. She taught me to be truthful. She made me take risks – the high diving board was always in evidence – though, to begin with, she was at hand to provide the gentle though persuasive shove which made me jump. I was to learn to confront challenges, that anything was possible. For the first time, I came to understand the contribution I could be making to my chosen profession, and learning that, after all, there might be a place for me. Slowly but surely I began to feel more secure about things – even to enjoy what I was doing.

It was time to go on tour. We sallied forth with our sheepskin coats and woolly mufflers into an English winter with an undisguised feeling of pride at being associated with this famous and wonderful company. We all worked well together and became friends. My apprehensions about being victimised because Joan had reshuffled all the roles and given some of the best to me were mercifully without foundation. The second leg of the tour involved visiting Rotterdam, Antwerp and then Brussels. Then, into Germany which, after all, had been the enemy in both wars and was the bad guy in our show. The reaction was ecstatic wherever we played. In Zurich in the late afternoon prior to our opening performance we were greeted by worried faces. The scenery and costumes hadn't arrived – bad weather had resulted in their being held up at the border. The theatre manager was in a fine old state. The cream of Zurich society was arriving in all its finery, the theatre was sold out. We could do nothing but wait. The audience, dressed to kill as expected, began to arrive – and still no news.

The actors came up with a suggestion. We volunteered to entertain the audience until such time as the trucks arrived. Had we gone raving mad? The manager stepped before the curtain, made the announcement to cheers and handed us the empty stage. We told jokes, we sang songs, we had competitions, we told the same jokes in another way, sang the same songs with different words, held a quiz, a word-game, 'I Spy', anything. It was just as well the deadline arrived when it did for we had all run out of steam. The audience had been magnificent, joining in the spirit of the moment with huge gusto, but there was a limit to their endurance. We checked our watches for the umpteenth time. The scenery and costumes hadn't arrived, it was 9.30, so the manager stepped in front of the curtain and broke the news that he was obliged to cancel the performance. Half way through his speech, like one of those melodramas when the reprieve arrives just in time, there was an urgent hammering on the metal doors at the back of the stage. The trucks had arrived! Someone went forward to prod the manager, the curtain was taken up and, with a huge blast of icy air, the dock doors were lifted and the skips, the costume rails, the Sam Brownes, the scaffolding for the ticker-tape, the lighting equipment, the sound equipment, the musicians' instruments, the slide camera, the crates of rifles and tin hats were all brought in and dumped on the stage to a mighty cheer from the audience. Working as though we had been drilled, we all helped to erect the set and hurriedly got ready to do the show. What a night to remember! I think we finished at about 1.30 in the morning. No one in the audience went home until it was over. We all knew that we'd been part of a very special experience.

Wherever we took *Oh! What A Lovely War*, the houses were sold out and the curtain calls cheered. So successful had the show been that Joan and Gerry decided to send it out again, this time to East Germany. With a hastily convened company, most of whom had played it before, off we went to the savagely bombed Dresden, KarlMarxstadt, Leipzig and also the east and west sectors of Berlin. We were reputed to have been the first show to have played both sectors consecutively. In the mid-Sixties, the contrast between the city's halves was extraordinary: the west, propped up by American money, ablaze with light and as vibrant as New York, the east, dimly lit, not many people and not much traffic. The eastern sector was by far the more interesting. Each night, those of us who had elected to stay there had to pass through the checkpoint at Friedrichstrasse. My hotel bedroom looked right over the railway station and I could sit in my window and watch the trains from the western sector racing between the platforms of waiting passengers – for they weren't perm... back to the west. The waterways around us were stuffed... coils of barbed wire to prevent escape – there were not many trying to get in – while the chilling no-man's-land either side of the Wall was patrolled by armed police with dogs.

Having watched Brecht's starkly impressive version of *Coriolanus* in the unexpectedly pretty theatre with its gilded cupids and the fire curtain of the Dove of Peace designed by Picasso, we had dinner as guests of the Berliner Ensemble. Wolf Kaiser made a speech in halting English saying that for years the Ensemble had believed itself to be omnipotent, yet here were these young English actors who, he said, 'make us look like amateurs'. As we listened, modestly swivelling our eyes towards our plates rather than risk any direct contact, it was left to me to put my foot in it when Wolf Kaiser turned round with the question, 'How long did it take you to rehearse this masterpiece?' I should have known better than to tell the truth. 'Oh, ten days,' I replied airily. I might just as well have slapped them all in the face. Rehearsals in Germany were seldom completed in under nine months.

The Marie Lloyd Story featured Avis Bunnage as the middle-aged music hall performer who rebelled against the establishment, Joan predictably being drawn to someone on the way down rather than someone on the way up. Marie's songs were considered too risqué to be allowed at the first Royal Variety Show so instead she gave a Command Performance of her own in the theatre down the road and Dan Farson, the writer, structured his musical around this episode and the events which led up to her tragic death. Joan wanted me to be in the show but warned me that there was no big role for me, 'just a lot of bits and pieces, an old lag, a hanger on, someone in a queue and a recruiting sergeant'. Rehearsals were enjoyable though not, I think, for Dan, who felt that his text had been butchered by Joan. Hardly a line of his remained by the time

...ugh with it. The opening number was excised ~ very first day, dissolving the poor man into floods of tears. Joan was merciless. 'How do they all know the tune? How do they all know the words?' Her re-creation of a band call at a provincial variety theatre was almost documentary in its detail.

Playing one of Marie Lloyd's beaux was an actor called Jimmy Perry. We shared a dressing room where he would regale me with stories about the television scripts he'd written. One day, he came in and announced with great pride that the BBC was on the point of commissioning his latest effort. I asked what the subject was. 'The Home Guard,' he told me. I remember thinking at the time that it was about the worst idea I'd ever heard and had about as much chance of making it as flying to the moon. *Dad's Army* proved me wrong. At the height of its phenomenal success, I bumped into Jimmy on the platform at Notting Hill Underground station. He looked supremely affluent in a white, fake fur coat, white trousers and shoes and a huge white fedora hat. I was just wearing my usual and looked very out of work. He seemed delighted to see me again and, before we parted company, had offered me a part in the series. I told Bruce the good news. Perhaps from now on we wouldn't need to worry. Agent Barry rang to discuss the offer. 'Just accept it,' I told him airily. I knew everything would be all right – Jimmy was a friend. The script arrived. To begin with, I couldn't find the part. It was only after I'd begun reading it for the third time that I was successful. It was one line. Angry Man: ''Ere! That's my bike!' That was it. It was a dismal experience going into a well-established series with so little to do and, with the exception of Clive Dunn, nobody was very friendly, including Jimmy and David Croft, the director. The embarrassing thing is that nowadays they keep repeating the episode on television, and people come up to tell me, 'Saw you in *Dad's Army* last night!' It isn't a period of my life that I remember with much affection.

Cicely Berry and her husband came to the opening night of *The Marie Lloyd Story* and I was introduced to them afterwards at the drinks party. They didn't seem to associate me with the out-of-work young actor who had swabbed their black and white hallway in Earls Court. Perhaps all the changes of disguise had confused them. Harry, her husband, was one of the producers but, although there were whispered rumours of a transfer, we remained rooted at Stratford E15.

Despite the helpings of humble pie which were my constant diet, my luck was about to change. In the audience one evening was Bill Gaskill, the Royal Court Theatre director. He was looking for actors to play Victoria and Albert in a new Edward Bond play called *Early Morning*, which because of its subject matter had been hopelessly censored by the Lord Chamberlain's office. Bill had decided instead to give just three Sunday performances under club regulations, where thanks to a legal loophole, all such censorship could be ignored. Moira Redmond was cast as Queen Victoria and myself as Albert. The principal offending section was an hilarious scene in which Victoria and Florence Nightingale appeared as lesbian lovers, the latter played by Marianne Faithfull, being ordered by the Queen to dress up as John Brown in a carrot-red beard and kilt.

The first two Sunday performances passed without a hitch. The critics were to be admitted on the third. However, at the last minute, the Director of Public Prosecutions stepped in and placed an outright ban on any further immediate performances. Ever defiant in the face of injustice and despite a row of police stationed outside the front of the theatre, Bill saw to it that the audience were smuggled into the auditorium through a side entrance. As I was in the opening scene, I was warned by the theatre manager that during my first dialogue with Disraeli a member of the constabulary might step from the wings and clap me in irons, yet it all passed without incident, leaving me feeling a bit cheated. Within a year, the censorship was repealed and the Royal Court mounted a new production without restriction, but for all the world I wouldn't have missed the excitement of that one performance.

I've always had a soft spot for the play. It was witty, wildly abstract and full of wonderfully imaginative ideas: the tug-of-war between the warring armies of Victoria and Disraeli on Beachy Head, and the bizarre spectacle of the Siamese twin sons of the Royal couple obliged to go everywhere together, locked in conversation, joined at the waist. When the younger is killed, his brother carries round the steadily disintegrating skeleton until only the skull remains. The play had a mild success despite its sensational qualities but it helped launch the careers of Kenneth Cranham, Dennis Waterman, Jack Shepherd and Bruce Robinson, who would one day write *Withnail and I* and *The Killing Fields*. A young man called Trevor Bentham was stage manager – tall, tousled, with an irreverent sense of humour. We liked each other on sight, but it was to be ten years before we worked together again.

Mrs Wilson's Diary was described as a 'lampoon'. It was written by John Wells and Richard Ingrams of the magazine *Private Eye* and was pretty much a broad political satire with some rather feeble, undergraduate humour and a few rumpety-tum songs. The characters were cartoons. It had been announced that there was to be a new Chancellor of the Exchequer in the Wilson government and Joan asked me if I'd like to join the show, currently enjoying a successful romp at the Criterion Theatre, to play Roy Jenkins, whom she thought I resembled. I needed the work, and readily agreed. If I remember correctly, I was invited to report to the stage door on a Thursday afternoon at five, immediately after I'd been to the costumiers to sort out what I'd be wearing. On arrival, I was handed two scenes, the first some four pages long, the other shorter. I was asked to sit in the stalls while Joan invited each member of the cast to step on to the stage and read my part. Finally, I was allowed to read it myself. 'That's fine,' she announced. 'You can go on tonight.' She'd taken my breath away. 'But I don't know the lines!' I protested. Joan looked at her watch. 'Well,' she said, 'you've got an hour before curtain up, you'd better go and learn them.' That's what I mean about going in off the high diving board!

Joan was right; with my hair parted low down and pomaded across my forehead, I did look like Roy Jenkins, and replacing my Rs with Ws made me sound like him too. The audience applauded my entrance and it seemed that I could do no wrong. I'd never been particularly interested in politics and wasn't even sure what Mr Jenkins looked like, let alone having time to study his mannerisms in any detail, but I was accepted and the show continued to be quite successful so at last I was able to relax, having the security of a long run to bolster me. The play had its hazards, however, and one evening I made the mistake of going on stage without having read the evening paper. As I made my entrance, Bill Wallis, who was playing Harold Wilson, said, 'What have you been up to then, Roy?' It was an unscripted line. I was used to that, but I hadn't the foggiest idea what he was talking about and said so. Bill didn't let go. Again and again he cross-examined me about what I was supposed to have said in the House that afternoon, eventually coming to the embarrassing conclusion that I wasn't just pretending I didn't know what he was talking about, I genuinely didn't know. I learned my lesson that evening. Never go unprepared to a performance.

Joan would see the show once a week, and every Monday afternoon we would be called in to rehearse, as she was a great believer in keeping the show fresh. The notes she had taken were Sellotaped down the walls leading from the stage door so that any visitor curious enough could read them. I got in one Monday for rehearsal to find my name splashed across some half a dozen of the pages. In her meticulous printing, she made mincemeat of me. A few minutes later, at the rehearsal, she totally ignored me, and it didn't end there. She kept it up. Six long weeks went by, and the writing on the wall wasn't improving. If only I could have sat down with her and talked it through, but Joan never let you get close enough to her to discuss things. If she wanted to speak to you, she sought you out. She didn't want to speak to me. At the end of an interminable rehearsal where, once again, I had been treated like a leper, I began to feel that Vesuvius was due to erupt within me and there was nothing I could do to prevent it. She was castigating me as usual, not that I was able to hear what she said; I only knew I had to stop it before it went any further. I got to my feet. 'I don't know what I've done,' I began, 'for you to treat me like this. You don't have to get up on this stage and do the bloody play every night. What do you think that's like? Six weeks you've been ignoring me. I know you think you can break me, I know you like to break people. But you're wrong. You won't. I'm stronger than you are.' I sat down. I hadn't worked out what I was going to say, it just came out. I was so nervous there was hardly any power to my voice, but it did the trick. Joan came forward, a beatific smile on her face. 'Dear, darling Nigel,' she said. 'What are you doing after the show tonight?' 'Nothing,' I said defensively. 'Let's go and have dinner,' she said.

That night in Soho over the meal, peace was restored. Without hurting my feelings – I suppose she thought she'd done enough of that – she tried to explain that actors in a long run get stale, that I was being predictable, unadventurous. I looked as though I knew what was going to happen next and I shouldn't. Everything should be a surprise. When someone knocked at a door, I shouldn't automatically know which door. It might be any one of three. I promised to try to be better.

At their elegant home in Blackheath, Joan and her partner Gerry would give memorable Sunday luncheon parties. Bruce and I were often invited. The tables groaned with food. Gerry was a superb cook and, each time we went, the menu would be drawn from a different country, Greek, Moroccan, Indian, Turkish, while down in the garden there'd be a bouncy castle and donkey rides for the children. One Sunday, Joan took Bruce and me on one side and asked whether we'd like to go for a walk. She led us down to the Maritime Museum where she revealed to us her intimate knowledge of history. She wasn't showing off, she so enjoyed the subject it made her want to enthuse us in the same way. She seemed perfectly happy to be away from all the noise and jollity and made no attempt to hurry back to her other guests.

The last time I was to visit the house was when Gerry, a diabetic, tragically died on a boating holiday in France. He'd come away without his insulin, collapsed, and the people who found him didn't know what was the matter with him. He had never been one to bother with tags indicating his condition. Joan threw a massive party in celebration of his life. In the garden they erected a marquee and an entertainment was given by members of the Theatre Workshop team – poems and songs which Gerry had loved. Joan was nowhere to be seen. I happened to go up to the house to visit the loo and nearly bumped into her rounding a corner. It was the first time I'd seen her since Gerry's death. I put my arms round her, kissed her and asked how she was. She didn't reply but pushed past me down the corridor. It was also the last time I was to see her. She washed her hands both of the theatre and of England with its bureaucratic problems about grants, her interminable wrangles with the Arts Council and the government, packed her bags and went to live in France.

What was it about this dumpy little matron with her jaunty sailor caps and working-class aspirations which drew me to her? Not her intellect certainly – I wouldn't have dared cross swords with that even over a friendly pint; not her warmth as she could be an ice cube, nor her friendliness and sense of fun. She kept her distance and was gregarious only when it suited her. Not her talent, formidable though it was, barring those occasions when she let her innate good taste topple over into prat falls and banalities. Possibly it was a sum total of all these ingredients with a little bit added. Basically, I suppose, I'd never really had a teacher before, not one who believed in me.

She was aware of how necessary it was to stint on praise. Encouragement was one thing. Not that she was grudging, but sparing. 'An improvement this morning but you can do better' sort of thing. Not a single Christian Brother had breathed such encouragement. She found my voice. Perhaps that was what she wanted. She made me stand up to bullies, but I should have booted her in the backside the first day she began having a go at me – in the accepted Theatre Workshop tradition. Quite simply, there's nothing I wouldn't have done for her.

The years went by and I knew that I missed her. Although I had only been in three of her shows, and ones at the very end of her creative life, she meant a tremendous amount, and I was envious of fellow actors whom she sought out, sending messages in the hope that they'd get in touch. She had been the rock on which I'd built my whole career. Without her there I felt considerably less secure. I used to dream of her frequently and still do. The dreams are affectionate, which is odd considering how turbulent our relationship had become. Some years ago, on *Desert Island Discs*, which she happened to hear, I talked about her with affection to Michael Parkinson, but admitted that, at times, she could be 'a bit of a monster'. She wrote me an angry letter saying she heard words coming from me which one would expect to have been said only after one's death, to which I responded with fury, the pen scoring into the notepaper so that when I held it up, I could see the daylight through it. How dared she assume I didn't respect her . . . and so on. Unfortunately, very shortly afterwards, I'd made the mistake of giving a second interview in which I said more or less the same thing. I received another letter and another rebuke. There was to be no escape from the listening ear, which I found oddly comforting.

After many false starts, when everything I said served only to make matters worse, finally it was my illness that touched her. Her letters lost their hostility and a generosity and affection broke through. I shan't want to take it any further – perhaps for fear of spoiling things – happy that peace has been restored. These days she lives in Paris, calling herself Joan Petitbois, a sure sign that her sense of humour, seldom of a conventional nature, hasn't deserted her.

10

Freedom

The landing of the *Oh! What A Lovely War* contract was a turning point in several respects – it meant that, because of the welcome burst of financial security and the fact that I was working with someone as renowned as Joan, my family could breathe a sigh of relief on my behalf. Not having had much to write home about for so long, there now came a torrent of excited news about my experiences in the show, and a noticeable reduction of the padding in my letters. The new mood of cautious optimism must have been catching as my mother's responses, invariably communicated by air letter, became correspondingly more up-beat. Not that I was out of the wood yet, both sides knew that, but there was a discernible tilt in the right direction. Each week my mother managed to deal quite systematically with all my news and queries on the first page of her pale blue air letter then, on the half page used for folding, she crammed all the minutiae of home life, sometimes vertically in the margin in order to accommodate everything she needed to report. Her loyalty in the face of my one-time despondency had been so total, her concern for my welfare and her thinly-disguised disappointments at my various rejections so touching that, each week, when the post was delivered, her letter was like the arrival of a food parcel in a prison camp, so welcome was it; though I was beginning to lose track of who in the family was married to whom, how many children there were and what they were all called.

Her old schoolfriend, Doreen Widgery, lived at Bramhall in Cheshire, so a trip to the United Kingdom was set in motion with the excuse that my mother could visit her, and 'drop in' on me at the same time. The bungled operation to her arthritic kneecap after many years of wrangling had led to a settlement and, with the money she was awarded, my mother treated herself to her first visit 'home' for over thirty years. London, as I had discovered for myself, was, to put it mildly, dissimilar to Camps Bay so it took her time at first to adjust to the differences – particularly the crowded streets and the traffic. Bruce and I showed her the sights and made a fuss of her. We introduced her to the delights of the Portobello Market, where we bought our vegetables and ambled round the antiques of a Sunday morning, picking up and putting down, never buying because of the inflated prices. My mother had spent most of her life tightening her belt. She had never been in a position to have money – so to be extravagant was totally foreign to her. By nature, she was inclined to judge by appearances, so the down-at-heel appearance of the area – the road itself bulging with litter, paint peeling off walls, the ramshackle stalls – meant that the antiques on display were written off as 'junk'. I was proud of Notting Hill Gate, a trendy, lively area with its mixture of races and cultures in which we lived, though my mother's opinion differed: 'A bit of a slum'. Well, I had to concede that it was a bit, though I can't say that up till then I'd really noticed.

We took a trip down to Greenwich on a tourist boat, and I once had a photograph of her standing astride the meridian line at the Observatory, not squarely but with her right heel dug into the paving and her toe aloft, striking a pose, a perky smile on her face. I'd always enjoyed her sense of fun; she could be quite a show-off at times, and indeed loved being the centre of attention, having an infectious cheek about her, a twinkle in her eye, making sure nobody took things too seriously. In the photograph, without her noticing, Bruce is mimicking her stance in the background. He too had a mischievous sense of humour, although when he was relaxed he tended towards rudeness – something of which my mother would never have been guilty. I don't really think that my family understood quite who he was or why he was always around. 'Nigel's flatmate', that's all he was. And for once, they were right.

It was now some fifteen years since I'd ventured into acting and nearly eighteen since I'd begun to live away from home. Because I was in my mid-thirties and still unmarried there was often the predictable enquiry as to whether or not I'd 'met someone', for which I had a ready answer. I had become quite adept at keeping a 'straight' face. Nobody cared in the world in which I worked, of course, but when it came to relatives or long-standing family friends living in this country I avoided too close a contact, my experience being that they'd magic up Bruce's name in the conversation, either out of genuine interest or just curiosity, and I wasn't sure that I wanted them putting two and two together and making five. I suppose matters might have been different had Bruce and I been an 'item', which is what most people had concluded. As a subject of conversation we were a minefield and I'd learnt that it was safer to tread with care.

In later years, when I began my life with Trevor, I realised how wonderfully proud I was of our relationship. It gave me huge pleasure to show him off to my family and friends. I lost the embarrassment I'd felt before with Bruce. We were sharing our lives in a way I'd always wanted but had never achieved, so I could afford to be open and not skulk around thinking up ways to put people off the scent. I still didn't really want them to get too nosey about us, but that was, I presume, partly because of the way I'd been brought up, partly because of the times in which I lived, where relationships between people of the same sex were considered taboo. Trevor was another matter – ours was a happy time, whereas the twenty-seven-year liaison with Bruce was strewn with unhappy memories and stretches of loneliness. Perhaps it was understandable that, when people who couldn't really be expected to sympathise insisted on prying, the portcullis slammed into place.

Bruce and I had many things in common, yet as people we were poles apart. He craved to be the centre of attention, liked entertaining, was excited by parties and opening nights, wanted to be seen in the company of famous people – all areas which I, despite my strong theatrical connections, resisted. I should have packed my bags way back in the mid-Fifties when he first told me that he'd fallen in love with me and I'd had to explain as gently as I could that it couldn't be reciprocated. But because the need to share my life was so very powerful within me I let the situation drift and wound up feeling trapped, though, paradoxically, I think it worked for Bruce. The more successful I became – and it was still on a pretty modest scale – the more he could bask in reflected glory. He thrived on my growing popularity, my friends becoming his friends. Yet, each time the escape hatches opened and there was an opportunity for me to strike out on my own, conveniently it was overlooked – we were both guilty – and we kept going as we were, maintaining the pretence of domestic harmony.

Anthea Cross was a stunningly beautiful model I knew from my days in South Africa. We'd taken part in a charity revue, I remember, where she had sung a bewitching song about the Lorelei. I heard she was in London working in the fashion industry and got in touch with her. I took her to see *School For Scandal* at the Haymarket Theatre and I picked her up at the flat she was sharing in Mount Street with two other attractive models. Anthea always took time getting ready, in other words we were invariably late for everything (the compensation being that she looked like a million dollars), so we arrived at the theatre to take our seats just as the lights were beginning to dim. It was a packed house. I noticed that in our row an elegantly-dressed woman and her escort had occupied the wrong seats, leaving an empty one on either side, so as we picked our way along the row in the vanishing light I asked them if they would kindly move up one as clearly there was a mistake, which, obligingly, they did. When we returned after the interval they were back in their original seats, so again I asked whether they'd mind doing the honours. 'We prefer these seats, thank you,' snapped the woman, and refused to budge, so Anthea and I were obliged to watch the whole of the second half of the play separated by this poxy woman and her escort. 'Only in England,' grinned Anthea afterwards with a certain amount of justification.

We went out together, the beginning of an odd romance for we both knew the obstacles. There was the trip to Paris, staying in a tiny hotel in the rue Lepic. We enjoyed one another's company, laughed a good deal, yet remained at a respectful distance. Then, just as it began to look as though it might be developing into something more serious, it fizzled out. She returned to South Africa, married and raised a family. My homosexuality was always to be a barrier between us. We were certainly extremely fond of one another and have remained so, and I've often wondered whether we could have made it work – by that I mean marriage. I wanted children. Having none would always be a disappointment to me, but I suspect that, had Anthea and I been braver and taken the plunge, despite the strong sense of humour we both had, it all would have ended in tears. No, if there was to be domestic bliss, which at the time seemed unlikely, my partner would have to be male.

Bruce, meanwhile, had settled into a promiscuous sexual life. I wasn't looking for a casual encounter in a dark alley, I needed a partner. The more I searched the more elusive that person seemed to be. Sometimes, as a game, I would walk down a crowded street in broad daylight confronting passers-by, young, old, male or female, catching them full in the eye, literally defying them to return my gaze. Was no one prepared to give me a second glance? Was I so unattractive that no one found me appealing? No one at all? I don't think I was being self-pitying, then or even now, but I was intrigued. Perhaps they were terrified out of their wits as clearly I was barking mad. I was never one for doing things by halves.

Let it be said that, as a subject for discussion, loneliness is socially unacceptable. Nobody wants to listen – they've got their own problems. Also, it's very difficult to shake off. The more you try to be less lonely the more lonely you get. You scare people off because they can see you coming on too strong and run for cover. Even though I avoided the bars and off-the-beaten-track cruising areas favoured by a high percentage of homosexuals because I felt out of place, I was absolutely convinced that somewhere – coming round a corner, waiting for a bus, feeding a pigeon in Trafalgar Square – was the right person for me.

My mother had come to see *Oh! What A Lovely War!* when it was at the Hippodrome in Golders Green. I wasn't really sure whether or not she enjoyed it but she did say later, 'It wasn't like that, you know – the war'. I supposed she meant that the soldiers wouldn't have been able to crawl round the muddy trenches wearing white satin pierrot costumes, so I tried to explain the premise to her. I wasn't totally convinced she got it. It was only a brief stay, but visits to members of the family widely spread from Land's End to John O' Groats somehow had to be squeezed into the itinerary, while the reunion with her old friend Doreen was one which she would treasure. A lot of memories had been stirred, and the latent affection she had for England had been rekindled. Much as she loved the place where she now lived and to which she was now returning, its scenery and climate, her friends at the bowling club, I knew this wouldn't be her last visit.

Not long after she got home I had an air letter thanking us for our hospitality. On the flap was a rare and surprising postscript from my father. He would like to come back himself in their winter – our summer – could we put them both up at our flat in Notting Hill? I could hardly believe I'd read it. I'd always assumed that Dad never had any intention of returning. But, even taking into account the fact that his handwriting, like most doctors', was virtually illegible, there it was in black and white. My father had made up his mind and when that happened there was precious little anyone could do to change it. There were only two rooms and not much storage space for luggage, so it was going to be a bit of a squeeze.

Bruce, meanwhile, had not been very happy in his post as scenic designer at the New Theatre, Bromley, although by designing and painting stage sets and costumes, he was doing what he wanted. The scheduling was alarmingly tight, a different production each week, and somehow the management always managed to slip in a musical like *Robert And Elizabeth* or *Half A Sixpence* with all the trimmings which, on top of the annual pantomime with its dozens of cartoon backdrops and transformation scenes on a budget of coloured beads, nearly killed him off. The work was tiring, only occasionally rewarding – and smelly.

I had been working off and on in television. The roles weren't anything particular, a few lines here or there, the scripts pot-boiling stuff, but I began to enjoy being in front of the camera with its different sets of disciplines, and the opportunities it gave to re-do something you found unsatisfactory. One day, Keith Lyons, a colleague of Bruce's during his Northampton days, bumped into me at Elstree television studios where he held the television equivalent of Bruce's job. On hearing of Bruce's discontent, he offered to help by taking him on at Elstree as a senior assistant. Such are friends. It wasn't too much of a departure for Bruce as, while in Johannesburg, he'd run the scenic department of Alpha Film Studios which turned out commercials for the big screen. The change was a happy one all round and, when Keith moved to Thames Television in Teddington to be nearer his family,

Bruce was elevated to his position. All in all, despite the lengthy train journey and grizzles about staff problems, he welcomed the move. It was a huge relief for me to see the boost it gave to his self-esteem. He was a different person.

As my mother was reluctant to fly, my parents came to England by sea and I went down to Waterloo Station to meet the boat train. I had no idea where they might be sitting; indeed it took me some minutes racing up and down the platform to locate them. By the time I'd caught up with them, my father, purple faced and rather the worse for drink, was threatening one of the porters. 'You take your bloody hands off my suitcase!' he yelled, snatching his arm. In the nick of time, averting a crisis, I stepped in hastily with a conciliatory fistful of coins. With me that day were the Hedley-Proles. My Uncle Laurence, as I knew him, had been my father's best friend during the First World War, though they hadn't seen each other since the early Thirties. Yet, despite the long separation, the greeting was perfunctory. Dad looked as though he had more important things on his mind. I didn't have any more success than Uncle Laurence. 'Oh, there you are, Nigel!' Dad said reprovingly, as if I'd been posted missing and had unexpectedly returned. 'Where's the nearest pub?' Ah! That's what it was all about. I ushered them all down the platform to the main hall of the station, they chattering away nineteen to the dozen, I carrying as many of their bags as was humanly possible. Family reunions always seemed to be like this – nobody particularly warm and welcoming or even emotional. A bit surreal, in fact. 'Good thing you were with me, Nigel,' confided my father, choosing a moment when my mother was regaling Mrs Hedley-Prole with stories about the trip. 'Hedley's changed so much I'd never have recognised him!' Hedley was to say more or less the same about my father a few minutes later. Huddled around the little table in the station pub, the precious luggage arranged in a sprawl about our feet, my father unveiled his Grand Scheme.

'I'm here to collect the Freedom of the City of London,' he announced. If, for a fleeting second, I'd had the fancy idea that the purpose of his visit was to see how his eldest son was getting on, I would have got what Dad used to describe as 'another think coming'. He explained that the honour was connected with the Royal Society of Apothecaries. He'd read somewhere that there was a clause in some ancient statute which decreed that when you held the qualifications my father did it was yours. So, in a word, he'd come to collect what was due to him. Nudging jokes about free rides on the trains passed my Dad by as, once again, he was struggling to his feet agitating to make a move. All the way to Notting Hill in the taxi, after we'd said our abrupt goodbyes to the Hedley-Proles, Dad, barely interested in the London he'd not seen for so long flashing past the windows, interrogated me about the area he'd be expected to go to to collect his honour. I remembered that I had a London *A to Z* in the flat and promised that when we got back there I'd look the place up.

It turned out to be just off Ludgate Circus in the City, a stone's throw from St Paul's. 'We'll take a cab,' I offered gamely but Dad wouldn't hear of it. It was to be a bus or nothing. Throughout the years, I'd never known my father travel on a bus even though, in Cape Town, the A 1 stopped right outside our front door. There was only one snag. Dad had no intention of waiting. When he said he wanted to go he meant ASAP.

Bruce wasn't best pleased watching us gulp down his carefully-prepared lunch, especially as he'd taken time off from work to get it all ready, but then he rather surprisingly volunteered to come with us, for which I was grateful. With their suitcases still piled in the little hallway, we downed the pudding and, seconds later, were off to the other side of the road to await the arrival of the No.15 bus – a service which was known to be erratic. We perched ourselves in a row along the little whitewashed wall belonging to the house opposite and every time a red double-decker bus stopped at the traffic lights on the corner of Ladbroke Grove, we would all crane forward expectantly like some weird chorus line until the lights changed and we were able to identify the number. Without exception it was the wrong one for the next hour and forty minutes. Although Bruce and I were becoming increasingly agitated, not to say embarrassed, my parents were surprisingly calm. I thought I understood why. This was a big moment for my father. Throughout his long life titles and honours had been important to him. For some reason, he believed they changed people into something special. There was a noticeable difference in his attitude to people of importance compared with the man in the street. Like many officers who had fought in one or both wars, he liked to be addressed as 'Captain', though his days of fighting had long since passed and he was no longer in the services. Sadly, he died some twenty years before I was knighted though, now I think about it, perhaps it wasn't such a bad thing after all. The excitement would certainly have been too much for him.

At long last round the corner came the No. 15, and our journey could begin. We sat on the long seats at the back of the bus, Bruce with my mother, I with my Dad. In Paddington, the bus stopped to let a stunningly beautiful black lady embark. She found the last seat on the lower level directly opposite my father. Dad just couldn't take his eyes off her. Sensing her embarrassment, I tried all I could to distract his attention. He kept staring. We had only just rounded the corner from Praed Street into the Edgware Road when, using my knee for support, he leant forward and, in the loudest voice he could muster to combat the noise of the engine, blasted off a stream of Swahili, or an approximate equivalent, complete with 'clicks'. It created quite a stir, other passengers swivelling round in their seats to see what was going on. At last he ran out of steam and paused a moment for her response. The unfortunate lady shot me a rather helpless, apologetic smile. Dad settled back in his seat and our journey continued. 'She doesn't understand me, Nigel,' he said, shaking his head sadly.

Though the traffic was horrendous finally we arrived and, map in hand like some Victorian explorer, I led the search for the Royal Society of Apothecaries. The towering dome of St Paul's was ahead of us, to our right the glistening Thames. London basking in the late afternoon sunshine was at its most handsome. The bus journey had been tiring and disorientating with all the stopping and starting, especially as we'd been sitting side-on to the view. Poor old Dad looked worn out, and watching my mother limping over the uneven paving stones made me realise what pain the disastrous operation to her kneecap must have given her all this time. Suddenly, there it was, a small but handsome building quite in keeping with the historic city soon to provide privileged and unlimited access to my father. This was an occasion of which we as a family could feel justifiably proud, a moment to reach for the champagne. I rang the bell and we waited to be received. There was no response. It was only then that I noticed the fateful placard: 'CLOSED FOR THE MONTH OF AUGUST'.

In many ways this visit was to be unsatisfactory. Obviously, Dad's disappointment at not being given the Freedom coloured the whole stay, and I only wished that I could have waved a magic wand and made it all happen for him. It mattered so much. A sensible phone call or a letter sent before they'd both set out on their six-thousand-mile journey might have made all the difference. To organise the trip so impulsively was a little reckless. On the other hand, who would have thought that such a large organisation would have shut down for a whole month? From that day on, all the scampering about trying to see the sights and visits to relatives and friends succeeded only in wearing him out. My mother was similarly frustrated. She who so loved to talk was shunted about from one side of the country to the other, never having enough time to do what she really wanted, which was to sit down over a cup of tea and have a really good natter. During their short visit – only three weeks – it must have crossed my mind many times that this might be the last time I'd see either of them. When they'd gone back I realised that, like them, I hadn't found the time – the time to say thank you.

We so seldom talked to one another. If we did, it was usually idle chatter, arguing or discussing what had happened at school or work that day. It was never in depth, never a serious discussion about art, music, politics. I wish we'd been encouraged to speak at meals, for example, one of the few times in the day when we were lumped together as a family, yet more often than not we were told to shut up or mind our own business. The sad result was that we never really knew one another.

The next time I saw my father he was to be incontinent, the victim of a series of strokes, and shortly to die. My mother, maid of all work as I had always known her, was nursing him, at her wits' end, frightened and lonely, but insistent that she could cope. It's fashionable to blame our parents for our shortcomings. I can't find it in me to apportion blame. I was the lucky one to have these two as my parents. An odd couple, if you like, but good people, honest as the day is long. I loved them both very much in their different ways, and probably even more now that they're no longer alive. I have regrets, of course, and not having found the time to get to know my parents better is one which most afflicts me. They taught me what they themselves had been taught – to speak when you were spoken to, to keep yourself to yourself. To get on with things instead of complaining. To mind your own business. To keep your elbows off the table. To do as you were told, and not to ask for help however much you might need it. It taught me independence right enough, but for many years kept me introverted and awkward in the company of strangers, not in any way equipped to venture out into the great, wide world. My Dad was self-absorbed, my mother the opposite. He was the breadwinner and slotted into the category of Typical Victorian Father; the housework was allotted to my mother while he held the purse strings. She handled the staff, prepared the children for school, organised the meals and tended to the garden. Dad didn't know an hibiscus from a camellia. As such, it was a conventional marriage of the period, though it was hard to tell whether or not they were happy.

On their last evening in England, I took them to see the film *Cleopatra* with Elizabeth Taylor and Richard Burton. The reason for this particular choice was that, when I was a schoolboy, I had taken my parents to see *Caesar And Cleopatra* with Vivien Leigh. My father hardly ever went to the cinema. A lot of American films were shown in Cape Town and he couldn't come to grips with the accent. *Caesar And Cleopatra* however had been the best choice I could have made. Dad loved it and talked about nothing else for weeks. It totally converted him and he became a regular cinemagoer. Not a Saturday went by without he and my mother going to the Adelphi or the Marine in Sea Point. Knowing that the film had been produced by J. Arthur Rank was a huge plus. With J. Arthur's man banging the gong, nothing would keep him away.

Cleopatra, however, was an American film with a sprinkling of British actors – and not only extremely long but boring. Dad watched transfixed throughout the screening – by which I mean he wasn't actually snoring – coming to life about five minutes from the end. Pointing to the actor on the right of the screen, he asked in a loud stage whisper, 'Who's that supposed to be?' I told him that it was Richard Burton who for the last few hours had been playing Mark Antony. He made no comment. Several more minutes passed by then, once again, he tapped me on the arm. 'Terrible acne,' he said and returned his attention to the picture.

They went back to Cape Town on another of the Union Castle liners with, if I'm honest, a certain amount of relief all round. Bruce and I reshuffled the flat in Notting Hill Gate roughly to what it was before, and got back to relative sanity and thoughts of work.

Having only recently been associated with Theatre Workshop in a minor way (not during what might be called Joan's 'golden' period, but just after that), it now became my fortune to be connected in a minor way with the Royal Court Theatre in Sloane Square. Again, not quite its hey-day when the place was buzzing with the likes of George Devine, and Olivier, Plowright, Wesker and Osborne were flavours of the month, but shortly after they'd all left, though Osborne staged a comeback. There was no curtain on the proscenium arch, or, if there was, I never saw it. It wasn't the fashion in the late Sixties to have one. Instead, the lights would fade down to blackout and come up again as required. Scene changes were accomplished in the dark or, at the most, a dim glow from the safety lights. The stage staff would stumble on, their eyes struggling to get accustomed to the dark, and do their utmost to set the articles they were bearing, properties or furniture, in the required position. It was a foolish convention, as the audience could see the shapes quite clearly, and the changes took minutes rather than seconds. Besides, every so often you could hear them drop something or crash into one another or the scenery. The audience's imaginations worked overtime and introduced them to a world of amateurism we could have done without. It would have been far more sensible to have on some decent light, done the change and got on with the show, instead of pretending the scene change wasn't happening.

Another quirk of this particular theatre was provided by an interior decorator who advocated that the auditorium should be painted either black or dark chocolate brown – I can't really remember which – unrelieved, apart from a splash of red here and there, the building's reluctant admission that it embraced things theatrical. It set a sombre note for the season ahead.

Its situation in the very heart of Chelsea meant that it was not only a focal point to the whole area but fashionable, in addition to which, the actors – and often members of the audience – found it handy for the underground, the shops and restaurants. Indeed, so handy was it that during performances, the rumblings of the District and Circle lines were a major irritant to audience and actors alike.

Glancing back at the time I spent at the Royal Court doing plays by such diverse luminaries as Bond, Christopher Hampton, John Osborne and Congreve, I couldn't help being aware that the parts they allotted me were either bordering on caricatures or just plain dullards. Hidden in there somewhere is a compliment. 'Here's a rather boring character, let's offer it to Nigel. He might be able to do something with it.' They were lightweight roles; I wasn't entrusted with anything meaty.

The theatre was run by a team of director/teachers who were occasionally skilful at picking out a well-written play from the duds. Amongst them, there was a common attitude to theatre, a consensus about what was important and progressive; even though, understandably, their tastes were inclined to differ. They were much less successful in their handling of people. The Royal Court had an 'us' and 'them' feel to it. Should an actor happen to stray into the front-of-house where the offices were situated, voices would be lowered and, even were his visit to be perfectly legitimate, he would be made to feel an intruder. It was like having stumbled upon a secret society which didn't want anyone outside the chosen circle to get too close, or even to know what was going on. Cards were held very close to the chest. Actors were selected by a process which was relatively new. A casting director was employed who would draw up a list of possibilities and then present this list to the director in question. After a lot of shuffling and sorting, another list of actors would be compiled. These would be invited to an interview which would be either successful or unsuccessful. Not many years previously, a casting director was considered necessary only for films and perhaps television, but in the theatre it was expected that the director would know the people with whom he'd like to work and make his own choices. This new system cut corners but the personal touch had gone for good.

Directors at the Royal Court, at the period I was there, were inclined to dither. Bill Gaskill, a man of high intelligence and renowned for his teaching ability, had his own list of what he considered the cream of young British talent. After inviting them to take part in his Edward Bond season, he let it be known that he had it in mind to form a permanent company at the Royal Court – which would have suited a lot of us very nicely. We were told not to consider any future employment without first consulting him. We never heard another word.

The schoolmasterly approach was considered essential as, by keeping an iron control over these wayward children entrusted with performing the precious new works, the directors could use their power to persuade those who might be given to experimentation to adhere to the straight and narrow. It was very much like being back at school with the Christian Brothers, the welcome difference being that we weren't beaten with a strap for missing our cues.

I had only recently come from Joan Littlewood, whose attitude to theatre was the antithesis of this. She encouraged us to use our imagination; in fact, we were considered useless if we didn't. It was hard for me to understand why this new breed of directors in Sloane Square held her in such enormous esteem. It was as though they admired the freedom of her working methods, but were too timid to follow suit. It marooned the plays in arid and infertile soil, thirsting for nourishment. Having selected a bunch of young people bursting with vitality it seemed perverse to stifle it. The directors – Lindsay Anderson, William Gaskill, Peter Gill, Anthony Page, Jane Howell and Robert Kydd amongst others – turned out productions which tended to be austere and reverential, drained of both fun and emotion. Sometimes this suited the plays, sometimes not, yet the house-style remained. I had the feeling that, lurking beneath the humourless mask assumed by Edward Bond, was a hugely imaginative jester exploding with comic potential. But this aspect of his talent was suppressed because comedy sadly carries the label of second-class citizen, and there was a danger that it might vulgarise the intellectual issues on display.

Whatever our age, we were treated like drama students. Couldn't do this, couldn't do that. Constantly scolded. Held up as examples of how things shouldn't be done. Our imaginations, bursting at the seams through lack of use, were seldom brought into play and every single morning we were thrust into an improvisation class (that word again) where discipline rather than freedom of expression was sought. We were instructed to make statements when we acted, to cut out anything which was extraneous. It was like working in a straitjacket. Being a 'writers' theatre', the lines were to be delivered word perfect (I was once held up to ridicule for playing a comma instead of a semi-colon) and we were all discouraged from doing anything as indulgent as 'inhabiting' a role. It's small wonder that so few acting 'names' emerged from those seasons at the Royal Court. We weren't there to enhance our reputations but to get across what the writer wanted to say. There is, of course, a certain value in this approach to things, but to drain theatre of the excitement upon which it thrives just doesn't make sense. From Stratford East where everything was opened up to the Royal Court where it was all bottled up made for variety but I certainly was in no doubt as to which style I preferred.

I I

Time to Make a Change

In the late Sixties, I was asked to be in several plays at
the Royal Court, the first of which was *Total Eclipse* by
Christopher Hampton. The writer had been 'discovered' by a
young assistant called Robert Kydd who had been told to trawl
through a large pile of dusty scripts. He uncovered a play called
When Did You Last See My Mother? which he read, liked
and got permission to direct for a Sunday night performance.
The play transferred to the Comedy Theatre in London for
a respectable run, so when Christopher's new play dropped
into the office with a recommendation from Peggy Ramsay,
the doyenne of theatrical agents, it was a natural progression
that Bob Kydd should be asked if he'd like to direct it . . .
The play was the story of the relationship between Rimbaud
and Verlaine. Rimbaud, the exquisitely beautiful young poet,
was to be played by Victor Henry, a precociously talented
young actor from the north of England with dyed yellow hair
and an appalling squint which was partly concealed by thick
pebble glasses. (Members of the audience, a little imagination
required here please.) Opposite him there was John Grillo,
who had recently made a success playing the mad monk in
The Rasputin Show for the Footlights Club in Cambridge,
which meant that he needed only to trim his beard and give
it a shampoo in order to play Verlaine. The two actors were
chalk and cheese, Grillo being mild and kindly while Victor
was flamboyant, abrasive and highly volatile. It was he who
was indirectly responsible for the existence of the Theatre
Upstairs at the Royal Court, which had operated as a club
bar until, one terrible night, he got roaring drunk and smashed

the place up. There was a lot of tut-tutting and finger-wagging and finally the club was disbanded and turned into a popular studio theatre, if you didn't mind the stairs.

Victor would goad John mercilessly, every evening making a point of bursting through the stage door and yelling in the direction of the dressing rooms, 'Twelve professional actors supporting one Cambridge undergraduate!' While the rest of us would glance anxiously at one another, his target remained passively resistant, not rising to the bait. If, during the performance, Grillo had a long speech to deliver, Victor would somehow position himself in front of him, and with his back safely to the audience, pull faces or ape his lines as he spoke them in an unsuccessful attempt to provoke. It was childish behaviour, but those in charge did nothing about it. Blind eyes were shut for the chosen few. One evening Bill Gaskill, on his routine tour of the dressing rooms, put his head round the door to say, 'Oh, by the way, Victor's drunk.' It was thrown in so casually we asked if he was joking. 'Wait till you see him!' came the reply.

The curtain had risen only seconds before, and Kathleen Byron, who was playing my wife, nodded expectantly in my direction as the maid announced the arrival of M. Rimbaud. There was a very sticky pause and no sign whatever of Victor Henry. Finally, in desperation, we began to ad-lib – seldom a comfortable substitute for the real thing. Just as the audience were getting a bit fidgety, we were startled to hear a wail like a wild animal in distress coming from behind the couch on which we were sitting. Victor, puce of face and clearly not just drunk but legless, using all the strength he could muster, hauled himself to his feet and, clinging to the furniture for support, began to intone the dialogue, slurring it so badly it was impossible to understand. It is probably fair to say that, as the evening dragged by, clarity improved – though not by a great deal. That performance we managed to add an extra forty minutes to the running time, and customers missed their trains home. I was embarrassed, and indeed furious, particularly as I had friends watching the show. When they presented themselves backstage, I hardly knew where to begin, how to apologise, how to control my rage. Finally, in the most nonchalant voice I could muster, I managed to ask, 'What did you think of Victor Henry as Rimbaud?' There was no hesitation. 'Brilliant!' they enthused. 'Best thing in it!' There's no justice.

The poor man had a tragic end, though, and it wasn't from drink but an accident. A London bus lost control and swerved on to the pavement where he was walking with some friends. Victor was hit and left brain-damaged. He survived for several years with loyal support from his family, and friends like actor Jack Shepherd (later to be with me in the Bond season), who travelled up to the hospital in Yorkshire on a regular basis to see him. He died in a coma, stripped of any quality of life for far too long. He is remembered both for his talent and his craziness. With his passing went one of the 'greats' of the Royal Court – but my God he could be difficult!

Early Morning was presented in the late Sixties together with *The Narrow Road To The Deep North*, Bond's sparse, stylish play about the Japanese poet Basho, played with integrity by another since-neglected actor, Peter Needham. His was a simple and very touching performance, straight down the line – the sort often overlooked. I was the Commodore, loosely based on Admiral Perry and the first of the caricatures I was to impose upon that particular theatre during my stint there, unless of course you begin with Prince Albert, my role in *Early Morning*. As the Commodore, I did rather too much befuddled-Englishman-abroad acting, which I remember at the time thinking pretty funny, but since then I have had the uneasy feeling that I was enjoying myself too much. Making up the trilogy was Edward Bond's earlier and controversial play *Saved*, during which a number of youths stone a baby in a pram, provoking several patrons to contemplate inflicting a similar fate on the author, or even members of the cast who happened to be more readily available. Despite the response to the three plays, which was respectable if not overly respectful, the management was considering an offer from the British Council to tour two of the plays (not *Early Morning*) to Venice, Belgrade, Lublin and Warsaw at the conclusion of the London season.

But one evening, before all this took place, Barry, my agent, brought a pop star to see *Early Morning*. He was a handsome, bearded young man called Cat Stevens. Barry, a social butterfly, dumped him in my dressing room for convenience while he fluttered about the backstage area, getting his face seen. Left on our own, Cat Stevens and I chattered away awkwardly. At least I knew a bit about him, that he'd had a hit with 'Matthew And Son' and recently had been hospitalised with tuberculosis. I felt uneasy calling him 'Cat' but he reassured me by saying that he was known to everyone as 'Steve'. He told me that he was still recovering from the experience of the sanatorium but had been considering writing a stage musical. I asked, 'What sort of subject?' and he replied that he'd been thinking of adapting a Dickens novel. Without bothering to ask which one, I blundered in. 'Oh, you don't want to do that. Lionel Bart's already cornered the market. I'll send you a script in the morning.'

It so happened that, in the extended gaps between jobs, I'd been doing a bit of writing. I'd become fascinated by the Russian Revolution, unfashionably finding the brutal murder of the Royal family deeply affecting, being unable to erase from my mind the poignant photographs of their last few weeks together, the ravishing daughters with their high foreheads, virgin-white frocks and frisbee hats. I'd been going to the huge Reading Room at the British Museum on a regular basis, devouring everything on which I could lay my hands and becoming more and more engrossed by this tale of a privileged family caught up in a rapidly changing world. The title of the script I sent Steve, 'Mind The Steppes', was flippant and deliberately so as, by this stage, I'd removed myself from the epic tragedy of what happened, and had embraced the absurd and farcical side of what I chose to see as the Marx Brothers'-eye view of the Revolution. The chief protagonists, therefore, were Lenno, Stallo and Trotsko, who typically wreaked havoc wherever they interfered. The Margaret Dumont character in the films was the imperious Tsarina, conspiring with the hairy and vile-smelling priest Rasputin to bring about Russia's downfall. The hauntingly beautiful daughters were there, as was Alexis, the haemophiliac heir to the throne, with his minder Derevenko. I didn't know if what I'd accomplished was any good but I found the story fascinating, and a good many times larger than life, so with a 'here goes' sort of gesture, stuffed my manuscript into the letterbox.

To my astonishment, Steve loved it. In a couple of days, he'd rung back saying that he'd like to write the music and the lyrics. It was a project which would occupy the next three years of my life.

Steve would drive to the flat in Notting Hill Gate and wait down below for me. When I joined him, we'd glide off – he at the wheel of his white Mercedes – and while he drove, I'd mull over developments in the text against which he would compose his songs. There was a miniature keyboard casually perched on the front seat and, as I expounded, he'd keep one hand on the driving wheel and, with the other, pick out a tune. If he liked it, there was a tape-recorder in the glove compartment. Although Steve was something like half my age we got along famously. His parents owned a Greek restaurant just behind what is now the Shaftesbury Theatre. If I'd arranged to see him, the routine was that I'd go to the counter, have a word with his mother, who'd yell up the dumb waiter, 'Steve! Friend of yours here!' and I'd go a few yards up the street to the door leading to his studio and wait for him to tumble down the stairs and let me in. Steve was one of the first really famous people I'd known. I must confess to feeling flattered that he should be enthusiastic about my script. He was an extremely nice boy, very warm-hearted and softly-spoken. Our sessions produced something like fifteen songs, one of which, 'Father And Son' (with both roles voiced), reached Number 2 in the charts.

Eventually enthusiasm waned. Steve had found a new audience, and was giving sell-out one-man shows. He felt that he wanted to pursue his concert work rather than getting tied up in all the stresses and strains of putting on a musical which might or might not succeed. I can't say that I minded too much. The whole experience had been enormous fun, and very instructive. It would have been terrific to say that 'Revolussia' was performed and became a huge hit – but it wasn't and didn't, and that was that.

Meanwhile, at the Royal Court I was becoming pally with Edward Bond, who, despite the uncompromising nature of his writing, was splendid company and frequently so outspoken it took your breath away. We set off on our short European tour. 'We open in Venice' goes the song from *Kiss Me Kate* and so it transpired. I shall never forget our arrival on my first visit to this beautiful place which was to become my favourite city in the world. The sun had begun to set as we left the airport and the light from the lamps lining the route was already reflected in the lagoon. As the launch swung into the Grand Canal the entire company rose to its feet as if the Hallelujah Chorus was being sung. We alighted at the Palazzo Grassi, often used as a gallery but now the venue for our performance and where this scruffy band of travellers was to be given a reception. On the landing stage, an imposing woman pushed her way through the crowd of officials and flunkeys and seized me by the hand. 'Welcome to Venice!' she enthused. 'I'm Chaliapin's daughter.' It seemed absolutely appropriate. She led the way into the panelled reception room crammed with distinguished guests, and handed me the first of the glasses of wine I managed to put away that evening.

Edward was there. He rushed over to my old friend and fellow performer Gillian Martell and myself to explain that he'd already been in Venice a day as they'd needed him to do a television interview for which he'd been paid, so that the three of us would be travelling everywhere by gondola. We agreed to meet on dry land at ten o'clock the following morning under the flags in St Mark's Square.

It had been raining during the night and the square was pretty deserted and dotted with huge puddles. Gillian and I were on time but Edward had overslept. Suddenly we spotted him at the far end of the square. He waved energetically, like a survivor sighting rescue and, very much in the manner of the old salt in the advertisement 'Skegness Is SO Bracing', most daintily polka-ed to where we waited, picking his way between the puddles with consummate skill.

After lunch, sightseeing by gondola had to make way for more serious matters. We had been called to rehearse. The 'theatre' turned out to be a large conservatory with a fibreglass roof. Half way through rehearsing *The Narrow Road To The Deep North* it began to rain, gently to begin with, then the heavens opened. The noise of the rain on the roof was deafening and we realised with horror that there was a strong possibility, if it didn't stop in time, that we wouldn't be heard. We experimented with microphones but it was just as bad. I vividly remember playing a scene with actor Peter Sproule. I knew that he was speaking because I could see his lips moving, but couldn't hear a single word. Ten minutes before the play was due to begin, the miracle happened – the rain began to peter out and, by the time the distinguished audience was in its seats, it had stopped altogether and we were able to get on with the show.

In Belgrade, which was next on the itinerary, Edward received his first black mark. It was at a reception at the British Embassy. Neither of us being very good at formal functions, we hid in a corner until we were winkled out by the

Ambassador's wife, who invited us to write something in the visitors' book. Edward was most reluctant, but I coerced him into it, though he insisted I went first. I managed something feeble like 'Best digs in Belgrade' and handed the pen to Edward. He protested that he hadn't a clue what to put. 'Oh,' gushed the Ambassador's wife, 'something from the play.' Edward thought for a second before writing, 'The English always send their bores abroad.' We all crowded round to have a look. I was horrified, but our hostess was absolutely delighted. Laughed like a drain. She wasn't a diplomat's wife for nothing.

Lublin, a gloomy Polish city, was next. We had a hair-raising coach ride from Krakow where we'd landed as the driver, who spoke no English, had obviously been given instructions to get us to the hotel as soon as possible and flatly refused to stop. There was no lavatory on the bus. Some of us had bought duty-free liquor and there was a general consensus that the bottles should be opened and passed round. On our arrival at the hotel in Lublin, I could see a formally-dressed reception committee waiting to greet the company, and in particular the great Mr Edward Bond. Glancing at the seat next to me I saw that the Great One had passed out. As members of the company, in various stages of disarray, tumbled from the bus on to the pavement, I had no alternative but to scoop Edward into my arms, carry him past the open-mouthed local dignitaries, check him into his room, carry him upstairs, undress him and put him to bed.

Warsaw was our final date. It was a pleasant morning so Edward and I strolled to our theatre which was somewhere in the bowels of the grotesquely ugly Palace of Culture, erected during the Stalinist era. In the foyer we met an official from the British Council. I asked what sort of house we might expect that evening. 'Oh,' he replied proudly, 'we're totally sold out.' Both Edward and I were amazed. I remember saying, 'I had no idea so many Polish people spoke English.' Then came the bombshell. 'They don't,' he answered. 'The audience is nearly all English. You know, Embassy staff, British Council people. Expats.' All that way to entertain the bored English! We might just as well have stayed at home.

Some months later, I was doing a season of plays at the old Playhouse Theatre in Sheffield when Colin George, who ran the place, asked whether I would care to do a lunch-time production. Immediately, I thought of Edward and wrote asking his advice. The outcome was his permission to direct *Black Mass*, a short piece, ideal for the slot, and on an anti-apartheid theme which he rightly thought might appeal to me because of my South African background.

It occurred to me that the audience might need a little help understanding the complexities of the apartheid system, so at the box office, without any explanation, we issued two types of tickets, white and coloured – red, green, orange or magenta – whatever we had in stock. After the play had been going for three or four minutes, we slammed on the house lights and two actors dressed as South African policemen strolled on, one of them explaining in a South African accent that it would appear that there were some people sitting in the wrong seats, so would members of the audience kindly hold their tickets aloft for inspection? Students from Sheffield University then infiltrated the house armed with torches to inspect the tickets and finally a decision was made. 'It is against the law for holders of tickets other than those coloured white to be seated anywhere but the last two rows of the theatre. Before the play can continue, would those people in error take their lawful places?'

The audience cooperated like a dream and, after a lot of shunting around with couples being separated and families divided, we lowered the house lights and proceeded with the play. When it came to the interval, another couple of surprises were in store for members of the public. In order to get a drink, they had to present their ticket. If it was a white ticket, they were laughing. The surroundings were tastefully decorated with arrangements of South African flowers and travel posters adorning the bar but, on the other hand, if the tickets were not white but coloured, their holders discovered a partition dividing the bar, the 'coloured' side with old bits of paper scattered on the floor, baked bean tins for ashtrays and their drinks served in paper cups. The lavatories were similarly governed by 'separate development' essentials. No soap or towel or even toilet paper, just small sheets of newspaper held together with string and, when you sought privacy, there was no key, just a photograph of the chief architect of apartheid, Dr Verwoerd, adorning the back of the door and watching your every move. The audience took it all in good part and I think it added to the message of Edward's play rather than detracting from it.

Sadly, our lives drifted apart. Both Edward and his wife Elisabeth corresponded for some years and I still have their letters but gradually we lost touch. It's one of the unhappy facts about our profession. We work together with such intensity over a short period that we seem to be inseparable. But, when we move on to another project, it's hard to keep that momentum going. Edward and I bumped into one another at the National Theatre when I was there with *The Madness Of George III*, just for a few seconds at the stage door. This time, though, it was noticeably awkward. We both did our best, but the flame of the past didn't rekindle. I'm sorry for that as we'd had such good times together over two decades earlier. We shouldn't expect miracles.

The media take a lot of pleasure from time to time in mocking us as 'luvvies' and poking fun at the way we call one another 'darling'. In some instances, this can be written off as envy – we're seen as people who not only enjoy our job but also like the colleagues with whom we work. It's something of a phenomenon in this modern world. Actors mix with a huge number of people during their careers – it would

The Millionairess with Penelope Keith at the Haymarket Theatre 1978

The legendary trio in the series *Yes, Prime Minister*. With Paul Eddington and Derek Fowlds moving into Number 10.

Margaret Thatcher presents 'Her Ministers' of the BBC with an award in 1983.

As C.S. Lewis with Jane Lapotaire in *Shadowlands*, 1989 at the Queen's Theatre.

With Trevor Bentham, partner of 22 years at Radwell Grange in 1992.

Bruce Palmer remained a friend until his death from AIDS in 1992. Here at Radwell Grange in 1988.

As Georgie, with Geraldine McEwan in *Mapp & Lucia*, 1985/86.

'Georgie' dressed as Sir Francis Drake in *Mapp & Lucia*.

Demolition Man with Sylvester Stallone in 1993.

Below: With Sam Goldwyn, producer and friend on the set of *The Madness of King George*.

Left: A first night good luck card for *The Madness of King George III* at the National Theatre, designed by NH in 1991.

MERDE!

As King George III in the 1994 film of Alan Bennett's *The Madness of King George*, for which he received an Oscar nomination.

On location for *King George* with Helen Mirren, Amanda Donohoe, Anthony Calf and Rupert Graves.

Having lunch with Joan Collins and Thelma Holt,
amongst others, following his investiture in 1999.

As Lord Ogleby in the film of *The Clandestine Marriage* with Joan Collins
and Timothy Spall, 1999.

With favourite companions Oscar, Twitch and Bumble.

A reunion with Lena in 1999. She had been maid to the Hawthorne household and has remained a close friend.

Playing tennis aged 70 in 1999.

As King Lear for the RSC in 1999/2000. Mauled by some critics, the production went on to be a huge success with the public.

be impossible to remember everybody's name. So, yes, we do call one another 'darling'. We understand only too well how hurtful it can be if someone who should really know your name forgets it, especially if you happen to have worked together the previous week. 'Darling' therefore is, I suppose, an affectionate cover-up. 'Luvvie', on the other hand, is a word seldom used except by journalists. I don't think we are any less sincere than any other group of people. In fact, even though we're habitually being accused of being bitchy and self-centred, I find journalists, politicians and civil servants rather more culpable, though perhaps, when it comes to accusations of being 'self-centred', as I'm indulging in autobiography, it might be wiser if I didn't pursue the argument.

In early 1970, someone with a Texan accent rang and asked me to play Falstaff in *Henry IV Part One* at Sheffield. When I'd finished laughing – after all, I was only forty years old and twelve and a half stone in weight – I agreed not to reject the idea out of hand but to read the play. Three times I said no, but director Michael Rudman was determined not to let me slip through his fingers and, on the fourth occasion, I agreed. I must have been mad. I was too young, too thin, my voice was too light and there was some appreciable distance between my personality and Sir John's but, if it all had to be applied like the padding and the beard, well, that's what acting is all about. Opposite me as Hal was to be a young actor called Michael Gwilym. He turned out to be a delight. In later years, he was to become a leading actor for the RSC and also one of my closest friends. In many ways he reminded me of Jobie Stewart, who had so enriched my student days. A wonderful sense of humour, an exuberant talent, yet there was also a kindness, a selflessness about him. He's left the profession and now lives in Spain. We've not seen one another for years but recently exchanged letters. It was good to catch up after so long a silence. It was his performance as the Prince which gave me the courage to risk as I had never risked before, and were I to be asked which productions in my career gave me a feeling of achievement, this would be high on the list.

There was still no one in my life. I was leaving it a bit late. Bruce was ensconced at base to welcome me when I had days off and came back to London, but we both knew that after over fifteen years there was never going to be more to our relationship than there was at the moment. Although he was possessive and liable to go into a paddy if I saw anyone more than once, he took no exception to my seeing a lot of Mike. He guessed there was no threat.

I was to see even more of him. Rudman had moved to Edinburgh to take over the Traverse Theatre in the Grassmarket and wrote suggesting that Mike and I devise an entertainment, for presentation immediately before the Festival, based on *Chimes At Midnight*, the compilation from the two parts of Shakespeare's *Henry IV* which Orson Welles made into a film. *Stand For My Father* we called it, writing under assumed names. Sacrilege to the dedicated scholar, we jettisoned a lot of the political stuff and knocked together all the scenes involving the father (Henry) and the father-image (Sir John Falstaff) while, greatly daring, I undertook to play both roles. It involved the assuming or discarding of a beard and wig and a light wooden frame which suggested the Knight's avoirdupois and probably was just as hard work for the audience as it was for us. The bonus was that Rudman had it in mind to cast my old schoolfriend Jobie Stewart. He was told that he'd be expected to double the roles of Justice Shallow and Mistress Quickly. Without turning a hair he accepted. All my Christmases had come at once.

Our audiences were curious rather than enthusiastic and, perhaps not totally surprisingly, numbers were a bit thin, but we enjoyed it – and particularly one another's company. During the run, Michael Rudman had asked me to rummage through a pile of scripts in his office where I uncovered a play called *Curtains* by Tom Mallin to which he gave a season at the Traverse where it was liked enough to give it a brief London airing at the Open Space, a studio theatre in Tottenham Court Road which used to be run by director Charles Marowitz and my old friend Thelma Holt. What a meeting of familiar faces this was turning out to be!

My mother had arrived from Cape Town for a short visit and insisted on coming to see the play while it was still in Edinburgh, despite repeated warnings that it might not be her cup of tea. At one point, for example, my character, immediately prior to a business trip, brings back a young lady (Ursula Smith) to keep his wife (Antonia Pemberton) company while he's away. When he gets home again, the two women have redecorated the flat and moved in together. The husband's clothes have been stuffed into suitcases and are waiting for him near the front door. The two women take their revenge on men in general by obliging the wretched and solitary man to respond like their pet dog, forcing me on to my knees and dragging me around the sitting room by my tie – in their eyes the ultimate humiliation.

My mother was sitting uncomfortably close, having nabbed a seat in the front row, and I can still hear her little whimpers of pain as I was repeatedly yanked past within a few inches of her shoes. She must have wondered then, if not before, what demon had persuaded her son to join this peculiar world of theatre she neither understood nor really liked. For so many years she had endured his self-imposed exile, doing her utmost to lend support when the going was rough. Was this to be her reward? Degradation in front of a packed audience . . . And was this seriously what he wanted to do with his life? Scrape some sort of living by appearing publicly in sordid little domestic tangles involving sadism and perhaps even lesbianism? If he was going to dedicate his life to this world of theatre (I'd constantly professed to her how much I loved it) why, oh why, couldn't his choices be more, well – more dignified? Why couldn't he aim to stand tall alongside the likes of Alec Guinness, Alastair Sim or that nice Cecil Parker?

She must have sat there torn between her undying loyalty to me and her deep disappointment at the direction I appeared to be pursuing, weighing her experience that evening against what I had sacrificed in order to achieve it – the sun, the beaches, the magnificent scenery of the Cape but, above all, and the thing which hurt the most, was that I'd walked out on her and the rest of the family. She said as much, though not as bluntly. I can't speculate about how much she might have wanted to know about the world I'd chosen to inhabit, though I suspect she thought it better not to ask too many questions. It wasn't as though she thought all theatre a den of iniquity, just some of it. And the areas I had chosen, and particularly recently, did nothing to gladden her heart. She wanted to be able to turn proudly to the person next to her and whisper, 'That's my son.' That evening certainly she couldn't bring herself to do that.

West Of Suez was John Osborne's new play. It was to be presented at the Royal Court with Anthony Page directing. Lindsay Anderson strolled up to me one day when I happened to be visiting the theatre and drily asked whether I'd like to be in it. When he saw my face light up, he went off to get a script. 'You can play what you like except Wyatt,' he called out over his shoulder. 'Ralph Richardson's doing that. Anyway, see what you think. The parts all look interchangeable to me.' He had a way of letting you into his confidence by allowing you to think you were complicit in mischief. Having read the play in the pub next door, I decided on 'Christopher'. Lindsay raised an eyebrow. 'I don't even remember a "Christopher",' he admitted. 'I'd pick something else if I were you.' But my mind was made up. 'Christopher' was Wyatt's secretary. If I was going to be in the play, I wanted to be as close to Sir Ralph as possible and, in my judgment at least, 'Christopher' was Wyatt's shadow. Sir Ralph, after all, was one of my heroes.

At the first rehearsal, we all waited anxiously on stage for his arrival. It was a large cast and we were spread out like a fan. I happened to be right at the far end. After an anxious quarter of an hour, the great man arrived. The men in their collars and ties, the ladies in their smart frocks were unprepared for his appearance. He appeared to be wearing a long rubber mackintosh and a gold crash helmet. Aware of being the centre of attention, he chattered on robustly about the perils of riding a motor bike in heavy traffic, while allowing the director to steer him around the stage so that he could say a few words to each member of the company in turn. You couldn't help being aware that he would far rather be meeting a group of Harley Davidson fans. They came to me. 'And last but not least this is Nigel who is playing "Christopher,"' announced Tony Page. There was an uncomfortably long silence broken by a deep sigh from Sir Ralph like a wounded animal. It had a despairing note which might have been exhaustion or, horror of horrors, profound disappointment. I felt every eye upon me. I wasn't what Sir Ralph Richardson had in mind. The paranoia common to all actors leapt to the fore and that evening I fully expected a phone call to say there'd been a rethink. It turned out to be just that – paranoia.

Lindsay Anderson, it turned out, had been right. 'Christopher' wasn't much of a part, particularly the way director Anthony Page insisted I play it. I was so insignificant as to be almost non-existent. When I protested that I needed more involvement if I was there to 'nanny' Wyatt and shouldn't there be more contact, Page, in the teacher-to-pupil attitude common to Royal Court directors at the time, ended the discussion: that was the way he wanted it played. So rather than talk myself out of a job, I settled for sitting at the great man's feet – during one of the previews, almost literally.

The play was acted out on a steeply sloping patch of artificial lawn and we were all slumped about in wicker chairs pretending to be hot, wearing sub-tropical linens and brown make-up to suggest suntans. In the middle of a speech Sir Ralph dried. Juliet, the stage manager, gave him the prompt which he didn't take. She repeated the line. Silence. As I was sitting between Juliet and Sir Ralph and partly obscured from the watchful eye of the audience, I whispered the line to Sir Ralph myself. Yet again, he failed to take it up. Another interminable pause measured its length as both the cast and the audience began to communicate their unease. Juliet tried again. All of a sudden, without any warning, Sir Ralph leaned forward and, seizing me by the scruff of the neck, unceremoniously hurled me to the ground. As I lay in a heap at his feet, he swivelled round to face Juliet. (Obviously I'd been blocking his view of her and he'd been unable to hear.) 'WHAT?' he yelled. Yet again came the line. A mischievous twinkle came into Sir Ralph's eye as he chortled with recognition, 'Oh yes!' and continued with the scene, leaving me to struggle back to my seat with as much dignity as I could muster.

The play went well in preview. It was always a treat to watch Sir Ralph at his tricks, even though I was sure he was investing Wyatt with rather more roguish charm than Osborne had intended. Jill Bennett – Osborne's wife – and I had a little scene towards the end of the play. Rather a good one. Throughout the run, without ever discussing it, we would change it. Not the dialogue, for that never would have been tolerated, but the mood, the relationship, the attitudes and sometimes the moves. Neither of us ever had a complaint either from the director or the management, and I could only assume that what we were doing was being sanctioned because it kept the scene fresh. It was a tactic I was to explore a good many times in my career, though not always with such sympathetic results. After the final performance, Jill wrote to me, 'I'm going to miss our scene . . .'

At the final preview, I was on my way down the stairs to catch my train when I bumped straight into Laurence Olivier. He had auditioned me at the Old Vic not very long before and greeted me like an old friend, clasping my hand in a vice-like grip which he didn't release. Other members of the company squeezed by on their way home, calling out their greetings and their goodnights. He waited until all was quiet – almost deliberately, it seemed to me – then whispered, though there was no need, 'Where's Ralphie?' I took him to Sir Ralph's dressing room and left the two war horses together.

The following evening being the opening night, each dressing room was festooned with greetings cards and bouquets of flowers for which there were never enough vases. I went along to Sir Ralph to wish him luck. He sat, surrounded by unopened gifts and cards, his head buried in his hands. Hal, his dresser, looked despairing. I thought he was feeling unwell and asked whether I could do anything to help. The words came out in a rush. 'Larry didn't like it,' he said. 'Told me I should never have done it.' At that moment, Penelope Wilton, who played one of his daughters, tapped at the door. Between us, we tried everything to get Sir Ralph back on course. I remember telling him that Olivier was just a jealous old man and had said it only because he wished he'd played the part himself. It gave Sir Ralph scant comfort. His confidence had been damaged and that performance at least would be played with his old friend's disapproval running through his mind and sapping his concentration. Even so, despite mixed reviews for the play, Sir Ralph's performance was much praised and collectively we could breathe a sigh of relief for our future.

News reached us that we were to transfer to the Cambridge Theatre. Obviously we didn't know the length of the run, but having Sir Ralph's name above the title would mean we could expect a fair crack of the whip – say, six months or so. Then, totally out of the blue, came a windfall, tinged though it was with tragedy. My grandmother's friend from her school days at Bedales, the kind and gentle Marjory, who had chosen to 'adopt' me, had remembered me in her will. By the time the solicitors and the tax people had taken their share, not a great deal remained, but this, together with the little we'd managed to save and now the prospect of a bit of security in the company of Sir Ralph, made one thing very clear. Instead of paying rent, we could afford to buy a house.

Both Bruce and I were aware that it was time to make a change. Our flat in Notting Hill had served us well but we'd outgrown it. Our limit was £8,500. It was 1971, and although the market was gearing itself up to going mad, prices were still sensible. Every morning, I went house hunting, not just in our area but further afield. As the estate agent at Highbury Corner opened its doors one morning, I stepped in to ask what they had on their books. A house near Drayton Park had come on the market at close of play the previous evening, so I turned up at 56, Witherington Road, where the door bell was answered by a Mrs Whittaker. As I had no appointment and she was unprepared, she wouldn't allow me to see three of the main rooms – a distinct disadvantage. Stepping out into the narrow road after my truncated tour of the property, I reflected on the amount of money I would be risking after so cursory a glimpse. I looked up at the building. It was part of a shabby Edwardian terrace, a house of no distinction that the others in the row didn't have but it looked solid enough. No cracks. There was a patch of grass in the front, and a slightly larger one at the rear dotted with dusty shrubs and dominated by a huge sycamore which had been generous with its progeny. Its seeds scattered far and wide, there were baby sycamores of various shapes and sizes in every crevice. Clearly, Mrs Whittaker was no gardener. After phoning Bruce from a call box and getting his sanction sight unseen, I walked back to Highbury Corner and, taking a deep breath, offered the asking price.

As always, it was difficult saying our goodbyes, and we began our packing in the resigned way people do when faced with the emotional upheaval of moving house. The obligatory tea chests arrived and each precious possession, from a spectacle case to a spatula, was painstakingly wrapped in protective paper before being laid to rest. On Sunday morning we waited impatiently for the removal lorry due over an hour earlier. A small, white van drew up outside, the sort used by jobbing builders, and a pair of hippy youths got out, yawned extravagantly and lit up cigarettes. From the upstairs window, we watched in horror. We'd never get all this into that! It took four journeys to Islington and back, and we were paying by the hour. The removal lads were so exhausted after the third trip that Bruce and I took over and let them take a nap. At least that way we could be sure there'd be fewer damages.

Mandy the cat, named for Mandy Rice-Davies of the Profumo scandal, who had lived in Elgin Cresent, was not a good traveller. In the van, I held her firmly in my arms but she squirmed and growled while trying to claw her way out of the window. We were sure she'd be happier in her new home; for one thing it was goodbye to the litter tray. Yet, in what was to be our new sitting room, she skulked behind a packing case and I was unable to persuade her to come out. I couldn't help wondering why she was panting so much when I was the one who was exhausted. Then, unexpectedly she began stumbling about and keeled over, so I had to look up a vet and ask him to come over. She was diabetic, he told us. It must have just happened, the moment she'd set paw inside the new home – she'd been as right as rain back at Notting Hill Gate. Poor Mandy. It seemed like a bad omen. We tried all we could to save her, but her short life was approaching its end. I watched Bruce drive off with the vet to have her put down while I remained among the packing cases and rolled carpets in charge of the shambles that was our move.

Each time Bruce and I changed our home we made our relationship more concrete. We got along fine as long as each allowed the other his space. That's the secret of a partnership. It's certainly more give than take. The mortgage would set us back a bit, and there was the decorating as well as some necessary alterations like double-glazing, though we might be able to get a grant for that. Our combined finances would help ease things a bit – we both had good jobs – but we were locked into a union from which there was no escape. And it was starting to seem likely that neither of us really wanted one.

In 1972 I was asked to join the Young Vic, just across the road from the Old Vic in Waterloo. The theatre itself, being painted red and chocolate brown inside, didn't seem so far a cry from the Royal Court though its attitude both to the actor and the audience was very different, and its director, the jovial but moody Frank Dunlop, had a touch of the Joan Littlewoods about him in that he liked moving things around, and had an in-built antipathy to the reverential. This looked as though it could be fun, I thought. I soon learnt that, with Frank, the first person who came up with an idea generally had it accepted. You had to be on your toes. Playing Face in a modern dress version of *The Alchemist* was a problem. Face was supposed to be the master of disguise – hence the name – but very soon I learnt that practically everybody else had decided to be in disguise and I was the only one who wasn't. They'd got in first. I tried altering my voice – up a bit, down a bit, some dialect perhaps – but the effect wasn't the same.

After London, we took the production to the beautiful city of Ottowa – my first visit to North America – and also to Vienna where, surrounded by Magrittes and Jackson Pollocks, we played in the Modern Art Museum opposite the Südbahnhof. In both cities, the play was pronounced a great success. Less so financially I suspect, as the two dates were rather a long way apart. Then I was scheduled to play Brutus in *Julius Caesar* – the fascist version because, for economic reasons, there was a paucity of actors for the crowd scenes and also because of the effectiveness of a PA system echoing the great speeches around the Roman Forum. Next came Baptista in *The Taming Of The Shrew*, another in my line of befuddled gentry, and then there was a play in the studio theatre for the younger child about the Senses. This gave the impression of being a good deal more significant than it was. At a matinée, I was talking about the sense of smell. 'What,' I asked a full house of these younger children, 'is your favourite smell of all? Is it toffee, is it fried sausages, is it the smell of salt in the sea air . . . ?' I really held the audience in the palm of my hand. 'Dog shit,' came the reply, recovery from which was well nigh impossible, especially as the wretched child had so much success with his response, he threw it in at random for the rest of the performance.

The Young Vic, as its name implies, catered for young people. I knew what I was letting myself in for when I joined, but as any other seasoned veteran will tell you, sometimes youth can be hard work. I began to long for a more sophisticated approach. Because of the shape of our particular auditorium and the demands of our audience, subtlety was seldom in the forefront of our minds. The theatre had what is called a 'thrust' stage, which means that it juts out into the audience so that they can watch you from three sides rather than just the one, as in conventional theatre. It required a massive amount of energy; the larger the cast, the more we all had to scamper about in order to give someone else a chance of being seen, so I can't pretend to feeling totally despondent when Frank Dunlop announced that he'd been asked to direct John Osborne's new play back at the Royal Court and there were parts in it for Jobie Stewart's great friend Denise Coffey and myself, if we'd like to go. I opened my new-minted copy of *A Sense Of Detachment* with huge excitement.

What a let down. The first act was short, I wouldn't have put it above twenty minutes, and nothing happened apart from the fact that half a dozen actors strolled on to the stage, sat themselves on bentwood chairs and insulted the audience. By the end of our first week of performance the pattern was clear. When they returned to their seats after the interval, there was a dangerous mood in the air. They didn't take kindly to being short-changed in the first act. Nightly, just when it seemed as if all hell was about to be let loose, we made matters worse by reciting to them extracts of English poetry most of them had learnt at their mothers' knees, played them recorded snatches of Elgar and Vaughan Williams, showed slides flashing on and off a screen, and they looked suitably aghast as quantities of explicit pornography were read out by an elderly lady (Rachel Kempson), who claimed that the stuff had been pushed through her letter box and what did it all mean? (One evening a helpful lady called out from the audience, 'Perhaps you'd care to demonstrate, Lady Redgrave?') Towards the end of the play they were treated to a lengthy Osborne diatribe decrying the state of the kingdom, delivered by John Standing from a pulpit – but no plot. None at all.

There were people planted in the auditorium and the audience was encouraged to participate. After a week of this, I longed to go back to the 'dog-shit' days of the Young Vic. They were baying for our blood. They threw things. Programmes, coins, Pontefract cakes, boots (from the gallery), umbrellas – in fact any missile which was handy. Each night was a test of our vigilance and strength of character. One evening, at the curtain call, Rachel Kempson had been so infuriated by a couple of jokers endlessly barracking from the stalls that she leapt off the stage and belted them round the ears with her prop handbag. They turned tail under the onslaught and ran for the exit. Their way was barred by members of the public, who – presumably of a similar disposition to Rachel but also very much in the spirit of the evening – took over where she had left off. There were black eyes to show for it. The whole thing was pretty degrading all round and a lot of people walked out but Harold Hobson liked it. Hobson was one of the great critics. He specialised in championing plays the others loathed – including, famously, *Waiting For Godot* – but was eminently capable, as indeed were they, of getting it wrong. On this occasion, his paeans of praise stirred crowds to besiege the box office with requests for seats. Seldom have I wanted a play to close with such passion. Fat chance. In fact the run was extended.

12

More to Life

My experience of films at this mid-stage was minimal. Although
I had gravitated towards the footlights because back in Cape
Town, apart from radio, there was no other outlet, my pipe
dreams were to do with being a screen actor – not, I hasten to
say, in the heroic mould – I only had to glance at the mirror to
know that could never be a reality, but there was a fascinating
breed of character actors who popped up all the time, as
familiar as the stars they supported because they appeared with
such regularity, yet their names were unknown by the general
public. Whenever they came on to the screen we felt we were
in good hands. They gave more or less the same performance
each time, although their disguises were legion. They were the
aloof shop assistants, eccentric butlers, cuckolded husbands,
patriarchs, supercilious major domos, sneery bank managers
and church wardens of the movies. While a part of me wanted
to duck out of the spotlight thanks to the camouflage of a
supporting role, there was another side of me which whispered,
'Charles Laughton became a star. Nobody could accuse him of
being good looking.'

It wasn't much help being without an agent. Barry had gone
to Los Angeles to work and he went on to become highly successful there. Like a ship without a rudder, I floundered about
for a while with an assortment of reputable but unadventurous
representatives to find that, like most other actors, they rarely
got me any work. The plain truth of the matter is that no agent
can get his clients work. He can put forward their names but
the decisions will not be his. I rather wished I'd had the nerve
to frequent restaurants, bars and other haunts of the influential

but, besides not knowing what I'd have done about it when I got there, I concluded rather feebly that such behaviour wasn't the right way to go about things and that, were I to persevere, somehow, some day my luck would change.

I heard that Richard Attenborough was to direct a film called *The Young Winston*. Knowing that Churchill had fought in South Africa as a young man, and learning that two Boer soldiers were required for the scene where he was under detention, I applied for an interview. 'Are you a bore?' asked American producer/writer Carl Foreman. 'I hope not!' I replied cheerfully, then noticing a cloud of irritation sweep across his face, hurriedly pressed on, 'Ah! I think you meant "Boer" rather than "bore". That's the way it's pronounced over there.' I had supplied my own shovel and my grave was almost dug. Foreman turned abruptly away to snap a command. 'Get me someone with a beard!' Miriam Brickman, the casting director, reached for a pencil. 'Stick one on,' I suggested brightly. They both looked at me as though I was mad. It was then that I remembered that in the current edition of *The Spotlight*, the actors' casting directory, there was a photograph of me wearing a moustache. Carl Foreman turned me up. 'Oh my God!' he exploded. 'You're with that ghastly woman!' He was referring to my current agent. 'I'm sorry, I know she's your agent but . . . oh, my God!' He slammed shut the volume with a terrible finality and put it to one side. Things were not looking good.

This was totally crazy, I thought, as I made my way down the stairs from his office, back to the Underground. The part was only two or three lines – it wasn't exactly the lead, but it was custom-made for me, I could do it standing on my head. I had been brought up in South Africa so the accent would be second nature. If it was for the sake of a silly beard . . . Back home in Islington, I telephoned Rafael, a photographer friend of mine who lived in the Charing Cross Road. 'I need a ten by eight of me in a beard to have on Carl Foreman's desk first thing on Monday morning. Can you do it?' He didn't hesitate. 'If you can supply the beard,' he said.

By then, it was after six on a Friday evening and all the wig people had gone home for the weekend. I dug out my make-up box. At one time, these were part of every actor's equipment. They went everywhere with us. They were often old cigar boxes or workmen's lunch boxes made of tin. Inside, resting on the upper tray, was an assortment of sticks of greasepaint of various shapes and sizes, all the colours of the rainbow, rather grubby and well-used. Crammed beneath the tray was a jar of removal cream, powder to eliminate shine, tissues, a hair brush and comb, a tube of toothpaste, a pair of scissors and a nail file, a wad of cotton wool, toothpicks, lucky mascots, packets of throat lozenges, odd bits of soap nicked from bathrooms through the years, a powder puff, spare shirt buttons with a pre-threaded needle and, the vital thing for which I was searching, crepe hair. This came by the yard and was plaited. Before it could be used, you'd have to wind it round a bottle, secure it with a safety pin, dampen it, then leave it to dry. This procedure would take out the crinkle and make the hair look more realistic – in theory. The following morning I turned up at Rafael's flat wearing a military-style khaki shirt and holding a carrier bag containing the unravelled crepe hair, a small bottle of Boots' spirit gum, a towel and an old toupee I'd invested in years previously when I thought I was going bald. Mary Millar, his actress wife, was out so I sat at her make-up mirror and got to work.

I felt pretty foolish traipsing through the West End dressed like someone out of Gunga Din and wearing a stuck-on beard. It itched. It felt ten times its actual size. Being a Saturday, the pavements were jammed with people. Rafael and I threaded our way among them up Long Acre, in the general direction of Covent Garden, on the lookout for a piece of waste land which, rather optimistically, we hoped might suggest the high veld around Pretoria. Because I'd prepared in such a hurry so as not to keep Rafael waiting, bits of hair kept peeling off and floating away. Surprisingly, the toupee had come in handy for the chin section. Having tried a number of variations, I discovered it was best when inverted, coated with spirit gum on the underside, and pressed firmly down beneath my lower lip. I had then simply filled in the remaining gaps with crepe hair. The following morning, greatly excited, I went in to Rafael to collect the prints.

I looked a right mess. Even to the unpractised eye there was no doubt whatsoever that the beard was a botched job. It gave the impression that I was suffering from an advanced form of alopecia, and the false hair looked even more false because it hung so unnaturally straight. We filled in the gaps with Biro as best we could but if you tilted the photo in either direction it caught the light so that you could clearly see where we'd been at work with the pen. Nothing daunted, I went along to Carl Foreman's office with the photograph in an envelope and inside a sheet of notepaper stating quite simply, 'Dear Mr Foreman, don't laugh – but this is me in a beard.' To my astonishment, I got the job. I can't truthfully claim it was worth all the trouble. It was only a few hours' work one evening at Shepperton Studios and I got back home nearer dawn than not, but, wonder of wonders – I'd made it to the movies!

Touchstone in *As You Like It* is just about unplayable. Cruelly the programme lists him as 'Touchstone, a clown' and the actor is left with the fearful responsibility of making him funny, if possible without cheating. The trouble is that the lines are little or no help, laced as they are with jokes which may have had them rolling in the aisles in Shakespeare's day, but now fall flatter than pancakes on Shrove Tuesday. Clifford Williams was to re-create his famous National Theatre production of some years earlier, known as the 'all-male' production because that is what it was. It was scheduled to tour the United

States from San Francisco on the west coast to Broadway on the east. Touchstone, eh? I had a think. I was eager to visit the States and six months' work would come in very handy, but try as I could I was unable to find Touchstone anything but deeply unfunny, particularly all that stuff at the end about 'the lie circumstantial and the lie direct'.

Derek Jacobi, who had appeared in Clifford Williams's original production in the role, had impersonated Frankie Howerd, I was told. 'That's cheating!' I cried. 'It was very funny,' I was told. That stopped me in my tracks. Funny was vital. But, Frankie Howerd? No one in the States would know how he sounded or, even more importantly, what it was about him that made him funny. I pondered a while and came up with a brainwave; W.C. Fields! It was the perfect substitute. A rude, intolerant loner who loved words, had an idiosyncratic way of speaking – perhaps I could introduce a bottle, implying a secret vice? For weeks I studied recordings and watched old films until you could hardly tell us apart. Clifford was abroad, so I had no opportunity of discussing the idea with him, but I made up my mind to turn up at the 'get-together' a few weeks later as prepared as I could be. What I hadn't been prepared for was Clifford announcing on the spur of the moment that it might be a good idea if we all sat round the table and read the play. I still hadn't spoken to him about my impersonation of W.C. Fields. As the cast began the first scene in the orchard, I was faced with two options. Read it straight and talk about it later to Clifford – or do it without telling him. Dive in head first. Which, being me, is what I did. After the reading, we all sat round talking about the small details of touring – visas and hotels and the various practical problems surrounding a long engagement away from home. At no stage was any mention made of my W.C Fields impression. The next morning at rehearsal, I got cold feet and decided to abandon the idea and just play it straight, off the top of my head, relying, as usual, on my instinct to guide me step by step. To this day not one single person, including our director, has ever asked me, 'What happened to W.C. Fields?' It's as though it never happened.

Gorden Kaye, later to become a celebrity because of *'Allo 'Allo*, was to be my Audrey – played first time round by Anthony Hopkins – and nightly I would metaphorically sink to my knees in gratitude to the casting director for suggesting him. I have treasured memories of Gorden in a three-quarter length white plastic frock stiff with fringes and wearing long, yellow plaits. He was so funny that, by association, he almost made me funny. In reality, I was so deeply unamusing that even I wouldn't have cracked a smile. My performance had no dimension. It wasn't entirely my fault. I had been through the text with a fine-tooth comb, searching for complexities and redeeming depths, but none could I find. Well, I'd done all I could. At least I was going to enjoy being in America. And I did. Enormously.

Though it did put me off eating meat for life. Each place we visited had its steak house or hamburger joint within walking distance of the hotel. Why look further? If you tired of steak and French fries there was chicken and French fries. If you got sick of eating chicken and French fries, you could always go back to steak and French fries or hamburger and French fries. It was only after I'd got back to England and thought, 'There must be more to life than this' that I stopped eating first red meat, then white meat and finally the French fries, starting afresh with some fish, some pasta, a slice of quiche and a tentative flirtation with nut rissoles.

America was an eye-opener after England. I found the people less remote, more like the people I'd grown up amongst in South Africa. You could just drop in on them at home without first making an appointment. You were received with open arms. In addition, they seemed less brash on their own patch than they are when they're abroad. Their friendliness and hospitality were a tonic. When I'd arrived in England in the early Fifties, it was still recovering from having been at the centre of not one but two horrendous wars, and the people had become accustomed to tightening their belts. Vital during war time, what started as an emergency measure seemed to have come to stay, making everything about them wary and less inclined to be generous. I know that I'm speaking generally, but I hadn't been aware of the contrast until I got to the States.

Here, at the start of our tour, it was 1974 and the tail end of the hippie revolution – though the flares had yet to be quenched. I wore them myself, you could hardly see my shoes, grew a Viva Zapata moustache and packed some frilly shirts – we were going to San Francisco, after all. We arrived to rejuvenating sunshine, cable cars clanging up and down the hills, the whiff of marijuana on every street corner, sexual extremists in studded leather caps and pierced nipples, but like all tourists we made a bee-line for Fisherman's Wharf to sample the lobster and, screwing up our eyes in the glare, looked out across the bay to Angel Island, that blessed sanctuary we could reach on the Red and White ferry (which took you as far as the Golden Gate bridge, past Alcatraz and dropped you off at the jetty). We could hire bicycles there or just stretch out on the grassy slopes, sampling our sandwiches and cheap Californian wine, gazing at the city across the turbulent water and barely able to believe our luck.

The Greek Theatre in Los Angeles, our next date, is normally reserved for concerts. Pop groups play the Greek. In this huge venue, we had to contend with the local coyotes and the indifference of spoilt and swanky Californians who had spent too much time in the sun. We were amplified, or nobody would have been heard, and as a result the voices sounded tinny and similar. I found, too (because we were somewhere way down there if you happened to be unlucky enough to have a seat more than a few rows from the front), that Sir Ralph's trick of drawing attention – tip a hat, cross a leg – came in very handy. The production was greeted with respectful and, I suspect, bewildered silence. Throughout our tour I would be asked, 'Why are the women's roles played by men?' yet, though I'd waffle on about purity and clarity, I was never able to persuade them that it was anything other than a gimmick. We know that female roles were played by boys in Shakespeare's time, but to have a man with five o'clock shadow striding about pretending to be Rosalind or Phoebe and talking in a rich baritone must have been, to the average man in the street, somewhat disconcerting. We carried on across the vast continent, travelling mostly by air or by coach for the shorter hops, through the mid-west (a lot of disconcerted people there), up into Canada, then down as far as Atlanta, Georgia (even more here). And the theatres didn't get any smaller.

By the time we reached New York just before Christmas, our performances had become so inflated to accommodate the venues that we could have played Wembley Stadium without mikes. Clifford Williams was unable to scale them down in time for the opening. Also it was noted that, although we were billed as 'The National Theatre of Great Britain', only one member of the company had ever played there. After we had all taken our bows, we retired to Sardi's to party in the true Broadway tradition, but when the reviews came out and were spread across the tables for all to see, Sardi's emptied like sand trickling through fingers. Not to be successful was bad news. Nobody wanted anything to do with us. Contemptuously, they flung our salary packets across the desk to us as though we were the lowest of the low. Failure in the West End can be extremely unpleasant, but there's nothing quite as humiliating as 'bombing' on Broadway. We eked out five miserable, hostile performances and came back early to England, our tails between our legs. But, despite the punishing schedule of the past five months and the shattering disappointment at the end, it's an experience I wouldn't have missed for the world.

On my return, the Mermaid Theatre was in touch to offer me Cutler Walpole in *The Doctor's Dilemma* by Bernard Shaw. I wasn't keen and said so over the phone. It's very restricting playing Shaw. He leaves so little room for the actor to manoeuvre, and has laid down what to do and how to do it. Every comma has its purpose, every intake of breath should be where he has indicated. Furthermore, if you try to go your own sweet way, you're wrong. His way is best. Bob Chetwyn, who was to direct, came on the line and asked me to pop over to the Mermaid Theatre office for tea, 'just to say hello' as we'd never met, swearing blind that he wouldn't talk me into changing my mind.

Tea was very pleasant, as tea can be, and particularly so as Bob kept his word and *The Doctor's Dilemma* was never mentioned. He knew that I was adamant. We chattered on about everything under the sun and eventually I stood up to leave. It was as though this simple movement had triggered a signal. The doors of the office burst open, frightening the life out of me, and the one and only Bernard Miles, who ran the theatre, charged into the room in full flood, declaiming a mixed bag of Cutler Walpole's speeches which presumably he had committed to memory especially for the occasion. Round and round the tiny office he stormed in the grand manner, gesticulating to left and right, his voice at full throttle, pausing only to see the effect it was having on me, while I in turn, recoiling under the onslaught, desperately tried to keep a straight face. Finally, he reached a climax, jabbing at the ceiling with his index finger, and then leaning to within an inch of my nose he brought down his fist with a wallop, thumping the table in front of me and rattling the tea cups. 'NOW,' he roared, 'NOW tell me you don't want to play Cutler Walpole!'

The play was well received by the critics and I'm delighted to be able to report that the run was most pleasing after all, and I thoroughly enjoyed myself. I was captivated by the Mermaid.

In those days, it looked over the Thames so the clientele of the restaurant could watch the water traffic passing by. Puddle Dock ran alongside; a ship's bell was rung to let the audience know the play was about to begin, while the warehouse style of the auditorium with its brickwork, comfortable seats and excellent sightlines surely makes it the most attractive and atmospheric venue in London. I should have put that into the past tense for theatregoers don't frequent the Mermaid these days. It's used mainly for conferences. After the developers had done their work, burying the theatre in a jungle of concrete, tourists in search of entertainment were frequently unable to find the place, returning to their hotels bewildered and disappointed. Poor, dear old Bernard, who had put so much of his heart into the birth of the Mermaid, so much adroit manipulation to persuade the City fathers to invest in it, so much gentle persuasion to seduce the public into playing a part in his dream. Well, things have to change. Dreams end. Fashions come and go. The Mermaid had a short life in theatrical terms but a very special one. It's sad to see what it's become. Lord Miles, the old rogue of Puddle Dock, must be writhing in his grave.

As one whose enthusiasms don't extend to the game of cricket, I would never qualify as Harold Pinter's best friend, yet I admire him tremendously both as a writer and as a director. He cast me as Alan Bates's elder brother in Simon Gray's new play *Otherwise Engaged*, which happily occupied me for a year at the Queen's Theatre in Shaftesbury Avenue. Half way through the run, Alan, who had signed for six months, was replaced by Michael Gambon, eleven years my junior, in one of his first leading roles in London, and tucked in amongst the rest the brilliant and witty Ian Charleson, who was to die of Aids at a tragically young age.

Pinter's way of directing was to allow the actors free rein, encourage them to explore the horizons and then, during the final week of rehearsals, to pull it all together. I found it the perfect way of working. Because he was an actor himself, he knew how we needed to investigate the ins and outs, understood that we had to be given time to absorb details and weren't necessarily able to deliver the goods first time round, realised that there may well be a hundred ways to get a laugh but only one way which suits the particular individual. Each actor has to find his own way. He allowed us the time to make these discoveries, then got rid of anything which was extraneous.

As a company we all got along extremely well, Alan being delightful and the supreme professional at all times, as, indeed, was Michael Gambon, though he had a wickedly playful streak which very often threatened to make mincemeat of almost all of my theories about being well-behaved on matinée days. As I grew older I used to rest between shows. Sometimes I'd have a massage and then sleep for an hour or so to recharge my batteries, but in those days we went out to tea. Cranks, a vegetarian restaurant just off Carnaby Street, was favourite. Alan was a 'veggie' and I increasingly so. Trevor Bentham was working down the road from us at the Lyric Theatre where he was the company manager and he used to join us most weeks. We hadn't seen much of each other since the Royal Court days. Like the title of Simon Gray's play, we had been otherwise engaged. He had been living with Kevin Lindsay, an Australian actor who had died the year before from a coronary, leaving Trevor inevitably sadder and wiser. The seven years since we had worked together on the original *Early Morning* had turned him into a good-looking thirty-two-year-old – but still mercifully blessed with the same sense of humour. I began to look forward to those teas, and can still remember to this day the disappointment if Trevor didn't turn up – or worse, had someone else with him.

At the end of 1976, I took myself off to Malvern for a few days. I was tired and needed to clear my head. It was late autumn and the little town was sleepy, which suited my mood, but the hills I walked every day soon became depressing. There was damp in the air, the leaves had gone or were going from the trees and there was no one to whom I could talk. I remembered that my old friend Mike Gwilym was not far away at Stratford, and was always saying that I had an open invitation to visit him. There was a spare room in the cottage he rented from the RSC, and plenty of actors in the company I knew, so I rang him and asked myself over. I then took the precaution of phoning my agent, Ken McReddie, to tell him where I was going in the unlikely event that anything should come up.

'I'm not speaking to you!' Mike said when he opened the door to me. 'Not one script has arrived for you, but two!' One was from the Royal Shakespeare Company and the other from the National Theatre. It was the first time in living memory that there'd been a battle for my services, and also the first time I had been offered anything at all by either of these two companies. *Bedroom Farce* by Alan Ayckbourn was supremely funny. I had always admired his skill. He was the master of situation comedy, and the role I was offered was right up my street. The other play was by Peter Nichols and called *Privates On Parade*, a rude, rambling semi-musical with a wonderful leading role and a very funny supporting part, Major Flack, which seemed to me to err on the side of caricature. I chose to do the Ayckbourn and told Mike of my decision. At breakfast the following morning, I was confronted by surprise visitors – Ian McKellen and Judi Dench, who were enjoying a triumph in Trevor Nunn's 'chamber' production of *Macbeth*. I suspected that they were there at Mike's instigation. They all protested that they wouldn't hear of my joining the National, and between them, over the toast and marmalade, succeeded in persuading me to change my mind. I was flattered that they should be so eager for me to join their company, yet was seriously worried, by the time they left, that I was making the wrong decision.

Rehearsals began in London. *Privates On Parade* was about a military entertainment unit in the Malayan jungle, based on Peter Nichols' own experience. Denis Quilley was playing the part of drag queen Terri Denis and had us all helpless with his impersonations of Carmen Miranda and Vera Lynn. An easy-going and popular man, there was no doubt right from the beginning that he was going to have a personal triumph. I, on the other hand, limped uneasily along, feeling very out of place. There was a plethora of big personalities in the company and I shrank into my shell and wouldn't come out. Cicely Berry, the RSC voice coach, offered to take me through my long speeches, but I kept putting her off, having discovered what I was sure was a fascinating character peculiarity in Major Flack. This was due entirely to a couple of typing errors in the script, and I feared her deflecting me from developing it. As it transpired, it was these errors which gave me the clue to the whacky major, but at that early stage, I had absolutely no idea what a stroke of luck it was.

The speech came from the scene involving a church parade. Major Flack addresses the men: 'We mourn the loss of our comrade-in-arms. Both as a man and a Company Sergeant Major, Mr Drummond deserved the admiration of us all. Not least in his attention to detail . . .' and so on. In the rehearsal script I was given, the difference was slight but significant: 'We mourn the loss off our comrade in arms both as a man and a Company Sergeant Major. Mr Drummond deserved the admiration of us all, not least . . . in his attention to detail . . .' When I worked at home on the text, this is how it appeared. Peter Nichols at rehearsal, however, pointed out the punctuation mistake.

That evening, after rehearsal had ended, I wondered whether Major Flack might have a habit of running things together and pausing suddenly and for no reason in unexpected places: 'We mourn the loss of our comrade in arms (deep breath). Both as a man and a Company Sergeant Major, Mr Drummond deserved the admiration of us all not least . . . (a long silence, knowing he has the full attention of the platoon – choosing his moment) in his attention to detail.' On paper it seems a tiny point, but this particular attention to detail opened the way to a quirky mannerism which I used throughout the play. It proved to be both effective and funny. The evening was a hoot. There were full houses and cheers. Denis Quilley and I were given awards, the first I had ever won – it would have pleased my Dad had he been alive. In those days, they were called the SWET Awards (The Society Of West End Theatres). It was with a sigh of relief all round that these were later renamed the Oliviers.

I had now, to all intents and purposes, justified – to myself, at least – my choice of career. But an actor can be only an interpreter. He has to hang around waiting for people to put him into plays, he learns lines which he hasn't written himself and scoops up all the plaudits, as well as the brickbats. Did all that make me a success? They say that, in Hollywood, you're as successful as your last film. Was it to be the same in the theatre? Would I go back to where I'd been or keep going forward? And where was all this leading? What did it amount to, this sequence of, for the most part, trivial adventures in Wonderland? Was that all I wanted to do with my life? Are we obliged to do something dynamic during the short time allotted to us – and what did it all matter when I had no one with whom I could share it? I knew precious little about what was going on in the big, wide world because the theatre is a cosseted, parochial environment, despite its capacity to present to the public every subject under the sun. Theatre people are inclined to talk theatre talk. The people who work in it seem to have more than enough to absorb their interests and not many of them look outside unless they have political aspirations. But in some ways I was an outsider. I hadn't married and had no family of my own. I shared a house but not a life, not in the real sense.

One evening after the show, a man and woman stopped me in the street. 'Thank you,' said the man, 'for all the pleasure you've given us.' They really meant it. They were shy people and it must have taken courage for them to have approached me. We shook hands warmly and, as they turned and walked away, I knew – perhaps for the first time – that I was on to a good thing.

Apart from school cadets, *Privates On Parade* was probably the nearest I got to a war. The delightful Michael Blakemore was the director, but had been ill during the rehearsal period and conducted proceedings from a chaise longue from which he seldom rose. His inertia didn't act as a deterrent to the rebellious elements in the cast, and there were several; indeed very often it was difficult to establish order. I know that I was very shocked by this anarchy. In a way, I believe it helped the spirit of the show because it was contagious, added a masculine challenge to the behaviour of the characters, but I do know that I found it difficult to operate under such conditions, despite my experience with Theatre Workshop. I had another problem with the character I was playing. Major Flack was a loner who made precious little contact with his men – when he did he was often clumsy and absurd – and the isolation of the character affected me as a person, setting me further and further apart from the others.

Trevor Nunn was in one night and, after the show when my dressing room was crowded with friends, threw his arms round me saying, 'Promise me. Promise me you'll come to Stratford!' I muttered my thanks, and after he'd gone a buzz went up in the room. 'Did you hear that? He wants you to go to Stratford! Isn't that wonderful?' They were quite astonished by my anger. 'I've been trying to get to bloody Stratford since 1951! NOW he wants me!' I'd gone to annual auditions, held in theatres throughout the West End, where you did two pieces in front of the team who were running the season. I'd never had a recall. Nobody had ever shown the slightest interest – until now.

Less than a year later, it was decided to transfer the production to the enormous and draughty Piccadilly Theatre. When the RSC rang and asked whether I'd be interested in continuing, I have to say that I was extremely reluctant in the light of the disruption which had so affected me in the original production at the Aldwych. I asked for time to consider. One afternoon, the telephone rang. To my surprise it was Trevor Bentham, who was now working for Eddie Kulukundis, the producer responsible for transferring the show. Eddie had asked if he would consider being company manager; did I think he should do it? I told him that I was very uncertain as to whether or not I would be doing the transfer and we ended up saying, 'I'll do it if you do it.' I wasn't to know at the time, but this indecision was to change the whole course of my life.

Bruce and I had moved the previous year to a larger house in Ockendon Road, just off the Essex Road in Islington. It had a hundred-foot garden and I was able to occupy the ground floor while Bruce had his bedroom on the one above. It gave us an opportunity to be independent of one another which before that time had been impossible. It was a bit of a walk to the Underground, but there was a good bus service and we thought we'd like it there. Bruce elected to paint the hallway in a deep maroon which never failed to throw me into a gloom when I came home but, in the basement, he painted a mural which was much admired. In a short space of time, we'd made friends locally and I settled down to a new life. Trevor lived in Southgate on the outskirts of London. He had to pass through Islington on his way home and, as I still hadn't learned to drive, he'd often give me a lift. It gave us both a chance to unwind after the show. It also began to draw us closer than we were prepared to admit.

Laurence Olivier came to see the show one night accompanied by the owner of the theatre, Ian Albery, and I was summoned to say hello. 'There, Larry. Doesn't Nigel remind you of yourself as a younger actor?' he asked. I wish I could say that I noted Sir Laurence's reaction. I'm afraid I looked away. Knowing that the mighty man would loathe having another actor compared with him, I was deeply embarrassed. Lauren Bacall was another visitor. 'I've been in love with you for as long as I can remember!' I gushed. 'Well, don't just stand there!' she replied. 'Do something about it!' Several times a week somebody famous would visit the show and come backstage to be introduced. I would like to be able to report that we were a huge success but we did only moderately well. The run began well enough, but there was some outrage at the bad language and that seemed to be instrumental in business tailing off until finally the notice went up that we were to close.

One evening as Trevor drove me back to Islington after the performance, I suggested to him that, as we were both lonely and unhappy, it might be a good idea if we went out together to one of the clubs on the off-chance that we might meet someone. We settled on the following Friday. On our way to the club, we stopped at some traffic lights. I remember turning to Trevor and saying, 'Why do we need to go to a club?' That moment was the beginning of my happiness, as well as his, and a relationship that, as I write, has survived twenty-two years and will end only when one of us dies. Most people think of homosexuals as incapable of fidelity. While it is true that a good many gays, like heterosexuals, *are* promiscuous, there are, nevertheless, those of us who crave nothing more than a long and secure relationship. But, as ever in my life, there was one stumbling block. His name was Bruce.

While I was appearing in *Privates On Parade*, I took on another job with the agreement that I should be released early on matinée days. It was the television miniseries *Edward And Mrs Simpson* in which I was to play Walter Monckton, legal adviser and close friend of the King. It was the most fascinating story done with taste and attention to detail. Edward Fox was perfectly cast as Edward, while to play Mrs Simpson, Thames Television brought over from New York a wonderful actress, Cynthia Harris, who played her to perfection. Peggy Ashcroft as Queen Mary headed the remainder of an impressive cast which read like a page from *Who's Who*. Some of the filming was done at Fort Belvedere near Virginia Water, a large and rather unimpressive house which, for a while, became Prince Edward's home. It looked out over what estate agents delight in calling 'superb views of rolling countryside'. Empty while we were there, I was told later it had been acquired by an Arab millionaire who planned to turn it into a casino. On the spiral staircase leading to the bedrooms I noticed that a small stained-glass window had been inserted dedicated to the Duchess while, on the ground floor, Edward's very masculine bathroom with its huge taps and marble surrounds alone made the visit worthwhile.

The moment the series was over, Trevor and I had planned a holiday on the Greek island of Paros in the Cyclades. Surprisingly, Bruce showed an unusual acceptance of my new situation – probably for the first time since we had met in Northampton. He genuinely liked Trevor, and as Trevor owned his own home and had a successful career he saw him as no major threat to his own domestic security. Besides, Bruce's own life was becoming increasingly promiscuous and, with hindsight, I suspect that he was quite grateful to have me off his hands for a while.

Thames Television, however, declined to commit themselves to the date on which I would be released. The night before our flight, I was filming in Portsmouth – Edward and Wallis were going off into exile and Monckton had come to wave goodbye. It was touch and go whether or not I'd finish or be held over for another day. Trevor had arranged to meet me at Heathrow with all our luggage at 7.30 the following morning. At 2.15 a.m. I was told I was cleared. A car dropped me off at the airport where I curled up on one of the benches and tried to catch some sleep. Trevor arrived at the appointed time and we trotted along to the check-in desk in great anticipation. We needn't have bothered. Our flight was delayed for eight hours.

We managed to miss all our connections but, at long last, were stretched out on the upper deck of the ferry from Piraeus under a glowering sky. My face was as grey as the clouds above through exhaustion and I woke with a start every time the ship's hooter heralded our arrival at a new port of call. As we set foot on Paros the heavens opened. A taxi drove us to the seaside village of Naoussa where we'd reserved a room in a small hotel. We sat on the bed looking dejectedly out at the rain splashing on to the refuse bins in the area below. It was a bad beginning. 'Let's go for a swim,' I suggested. 'In the pouring rain?' asked Trevor. 'Why not?' I replied.

As is often the case when it rains, the sea was as warm as toast and we managed to avoid being stung by jellyfish. It was still throwing it down as we emerged invigorated from the surf but there in front of us on a small promontory was a simple, concrete bungalow. Painted on the wall in large letters was a single word, 'ROOMS'.

They weren't at all happy when we cancelled our booking at the hotel, but we would not be deterred. 'ROOMS' had our vote. The shower was cold, the beds narrow, too short and as hard as concrete, and there were no rugs on the tiled floor but, when we woke the following morning, the sun was out and it remained that way for the whole of our stay. Had we been a married couple, this would have been our honeymoon, I suppose. As Trevor is fourteen years younger than I most people assumed that he was my son, so there were no odd looks when we appeared together. Like the beginnings of most relationships, it took time for us to adjust. At first it was far from easy. We both had our own way of doing things and moved at a different pace. I don't remember what we argued about but occasionally there was a spat. We weren't used to one another. And matters certainly weren't improved when one day I told Trevor that I could never leave Bruce. To be fair, Trevor had never asked me to, having seen Bruce's dependence with his own eyes, but I admit my timing could have been better. That and several other moments aside, it was the happiest two weeks I'd ever spent in my life. When we were there, nearly a quarter of a century ago, it was still unspoilt. There was little to do but eat, sleep, walk, swim or talk, but we both needed a healing break so we couldn't have made a better choice. And I knew for the first time in my life that I had fallen sensibly in love.

We returned to the UK to confront the daunting prospect of having to buckle down to work. Trevor was to be company manager on *Deathtrap*, once again with Michael Blakemore and Denis Quilley. It was an American comedy-thriller which enjoyed an excellent run at the Garrick. I'd agreed to be in Shaw's *The Millionairess* which was going into the Haymarket, and starred Penelope Keith, then at the height of her considerable popularity. We were sold out for the entire run, not, I hasten to add, on the strength of my name or Mr Shaw's, but hers. Penny's and my acting styles were diametrically opposed. Her technique is sharp and incisive, like a diamond, each performance as perfect as the last. My approach is more hit and miss, emotionally varied and subject to change. It was not a happy coupling. Not that it really mattered; Penny was the leading lady and Sagamore, the character I played, was little competition in the popularity stakes. While it was wonderful to play to full and enthusiastic houses, I had a miserable time and could hardly wait for the season to come to an end.

A similar fate was hovering over my private life. Having convinced both Trevor and myself that my relationship with Bruce was a permanent one and that I would never leave him,

Trevor and I did our best to pick through the threads of our own relationship. He was still scarred and vulnerable from Kevin's death, and a period of nearly eighteen months as 'gentleman caller' had certainly not helped him. The snatched moments began to prove unsatisfactory, and we started to bicker. Bruce was fully aware of the situation, and clearly revelled in the power it gave him. He would organise theatre and dinner dates for the two of us or with friends as though Trevor didn't exist and nothing at all had changed. I made a trip to Bath, where Trevor was touring with a new show, and walking along the banks of the Avon we decided for all our sakes to split up.

For the next three weeks I was like a bear with a sore head. My whole world seemed to be collapsing around me. Then one day, totally out of the blue, Bruce said something I would never have expected: 'If you want to go and live with Trevor, then why the hell don't you go?'

13

Hello, Humphrey

Trevor's house was charming, but small, a Victorian semi in Avenue Road, Southgate, which he had bought some years earlier with his partner Kevin. Not that there were ghosts remaining, but neither was there much room for me. Poor Trevor; I think my moving in came as a bit of a shock. After all, I had firmly planted the idea that this could never happen, so my arrival with a suitcase was bound to put him on the spot. He coped, as he coped for ever after, with good grace and humour.

It's not every day that a script as good as *Yes, Minister* comes through the letterbox. I was immediately struck by the brilliance of the dialogue, even though the central, complex relationship between the elected Minister and the senior civil servant which provided much of the comedy was not something with which I was familiar. Thus far, in the light entertainment field, my experience had been of contrived situations, feeble jokes and far too much padding. It was up to the star to make the thing work. Here, the opposite was the case. Paul Eddington I knew as a fine actor and one of the principals in *The Good Life*, but in those days I wouldn't have labelled him a 'star'. Nor Derek Fowlds, whom I had remembered chatting to a fox called Basil Brush. Our star was the script. Throughout the ten years we were involved, I never encountered a duff one. Each had its own distinction. The language was crisp, pertinent and witty and the situations extremely funny. I recognised the potential in Sir Humphrey the moment I'd reached the end of the first page and, long before finishing the last, had decided to do the job.

Our director was to be Stuart Allen, well known for *On The Buses* which, although rather a different kettle of fish, had enjoyed an enormous success over a long period. The delightful Diana Hoddinott was playing Jim Hacker's wife and we were promised the cream of English character actors to play the supporting roles. It all seemed too good to be true. As had been my custom, I learnt my lines well in advance and was extremely grateful that I had, as we had been threatened with a studio audience, and their reactions could be both unexpected and unsettling. In every episode (we had only two script writers, Antony Jay and Jonathan Lynn) there was a special tongue-twister for Sir Humphrey. It was never easy to learn because it had to be delivered with assurance, but each had its logic and, once I discovered that, it was like being in Restoration comedy. You started at the beginning and thought your way through to the end.

Two significant things happened during the rehearsals of that first pilot programme. Paul and I were watching Stuart Allen direct Diana Hoddinott. She was crawling about on her hands and knees searching for cuff-links or ear rings. Stuart was encouraging her to waggle her bottom in the air. 'It's all dialogue, we've got to get in some visuals,' I heard him say. I remember going over to Paul whom, at that stage, I barely knew and saying, 'Surely the script's funny enough in itself, we don't have to try to make it funny?' We solemnly agreed then and there that, come what may, we would play it for real – with a comic awareness of course – but vowed never to be tempted to resort to anything cheap.

The second instance involved the credits which were embellished with 'political' caricatures of the chief protagonists. These alarmed me because they were so crudely executed. In any case, they didn't look like us. I registered my concern, and a round-table discussion was held during which I was asked who my choice would be. 'There is only one, and that's Gerald Scarfe.' And so it turned out. Now, with the parameters solidly established and our five and a half short days' rehearsal seeming alarmingly inadequate, we pitched up on the Sunday morning at the Television Centre in Wood Green to begin our camera rehearsal. With the news under our belts that the BBC had commissioned a series, we were on our way.

With the blithe tactlessness peculiar to the BBC, it had been decreed that the studio audience form a queue immediately outside our dressing-room windows on the ground floor before being admitted. Judging from the snatches of their conversation which drifted up as we tried to assemble our thoughts before the recording, many of them would have preferred to be coming to *George And Mildred*. A warm-up comic named Felix had been engaged to get the audience going when they had settled in their seats. I came out of the make-up room to hear gales of laughter rocking the studio. It was only when I stayed to listen that I realised a lot of the jokes were decidedly blue, and that Felix was gearing up the audience to expect a very different show from the one which we were to present. That was another thing which would have to be sorted out if we were to do a series.

I had made the mistake of appearing in a stage play at the same time as rehearsing the episode. The play was one I was very keen to do, but the timing was unfortunate due to circumstances beyond my control. I'd met Nancy Meckler and her husband David Aukin at a dinner party during which Nancy had asked whether I'd ever played Uncle Vanya. On hearing that I hadn't, David told me that he would arrange a production at the Hampstead Theatre Club which he ran. Nancy, his wife, would direct, and asked whom I would like as the country doctor, Astrov, I immediately said, 'Ian Holm. But you'll never get him.' Ian's last stage performance had been as Hickey in *The Iceman Cometh* at the Aldwych, but horrifically at one of the previews his nerve deserted him and he was incapable of completing the performance. To my astonishment, Ian accepted without hesitation, and Nancy assembled around us an extremely impressive cast, the play running to capacity at Hampstead after glowing reviews. At the end of each *Yes, Minister* rehearsal, I'd return to Hampstead for the Chekhov, a routine which I found exhausting and swore never to attempt again.

Back at the BBC all was going swimmingly. The new language of the show was creating a buzz which even the studio audience seemed to catch on to. There was a growing feeling of assurance that was both exciting and stimulating. Paul, Derek and I got on very well and I don't remember a harsh word from start to finish. The 'boys', as we called the writers (or sometimes the 'vultures' because they were prone to hover), had a very good arrangement with the Beeb which didn't hold them to contributing a series every year. Instead, they were told that, when they found they had something to say, all they had to do was pick up the phone and wheels would be set in motion. This allowed everyone breathing space and the actors had licence to find other work during the interim periods if they wanted.

Through the months that followed, Trevor and I became increasingly fond of each other. We regained our ability to laugh which was only natural, I suppose, as we were so happy. I was very nearly fifty and could hardly believe my luck. I spoke regularly to Bruce though it was seldom that he rang me. These conversations were something of an ordeal. I think that the poor man had assumed that by playing into our hands I would soon get disenchanted and go back to him. As this was not to be the case, he seemed determined to punish me by making things as difficult as possible. My bedroom and office back in Islington had been converted into a shrine worthy of Miss Havisham – though without the cobwebs. Whenever I went back to collect something I needed, an article of clothing or a book, I couldn't help but be aware that everything remained exactly as it was when last I'd been there. And the time before that. The magazines on the coffee table, cushions, letters and ornaments were in precisely the same places as on the day I'd left. Eileen, his cleaning lady, must have been told to work round them. On those visiting days, Bruce was unyielding, unfriendly, unforgiving. For my part, I suppose I tried too hard to compensate, feeling that I needed to please him in order to make things better. The harder I tried, the cooler he became.

Always having operated on a fifty-fifty basis, half the house was mine. But, with four floors, it was far too spacious for one person. Yet I knew that I'd have to let him rattle around in it until he was ready to sell up and move to somewhere more suitable. It had to be Bruce's decision. If I attempted to influence it, he'd merely prolong the agony. Trevor, who had done no wrong, was *persona non grata* and Bruce chose to spread it round to our friends that he had spirited me away. It was very far from what happened, of course, but, needing their support and the continuation of their friendship, Bruce reckoned that by being economical with the truth, he would save face.

All this was to make me feel guilty, of course – which, to a huge extent, it did. I was genuinely sorry for causing his loneliness, that I had led him to believe that we would never split up, but being away from him gave me a freedom that I hadn't known in decades. And in that freedom, I fervently hoped that he and I would one day come to like each other again.

In order to distract himself, Bruce took to going on holidays with friends whenever he could afford it. While he was away, I would pop in from time to time to see that all the plants were watered. On one of these visits, stepping out into the hundred-foot garden at the rear of the house, I was horrified to see what I can only describe as a plantation of flourishing,

shoulder-high marijuana plants. Any fool with passable eye-
sight could have identified them and not all our neighbours
could be described as bosom pals. I waited until dark, slashed
them down to ground height with a scythe, hung them upside
down in the garden shed and padlocked the door. I knew that
I'd committed an appalling act of vandalism, but when Bruce
got back he seemed surprisingly grateful. For once I'd done
the right thing and he had a wonderful crop to enjoy at his
leisure.

The impasse between us was solved once and for all on
another of Bruce's trips, this time to New York. He phoned
Southgate in panic, to ask me to fetch him from the airport
because he was having some internal bleeding as a result of a
suspected ulcer. I was away, and Trevor answered. Without
hesitation, he rushed to Bruce's aid, escorted him to doctors
and hospitals, and looked after him so well that Bruce, quite
literally, threw all his prejudices away. From that moment,
Trevor could do no wrong.

Yes, Minister meanwhile had turned into an international
success being sold to forty-eight countries. Margaret Thatcher
had given it her seal of approval, even going so far as to
declare it her favourite programme, and I was having the
novel experience of being stopped in the street and asked
for my autograph. Paul and I were invited to Downing Street
and it seemed as though everyone wanted to shake us by the
hand. Stuart Allen had been replaced by the highly experienced
Sydney Lotterby, and by the estimable and rather military
Peter Whitmore when Syd was unavailable. Both handled the
material and the actors with expertise and tact.

In 1982, I was nominated for a BAFTA award. That year
the ceremony was being held at the Talk Of The Town. As
my category – Best Light Entertainment Performance – got
nearer and nearer, I grew increasingly nervous. Nominees are
not notified in advance whether or not they've won, so you

have to have some sort of speech of thanks up your sleeve and pray to all the powers that be that you'll remember everyone's name. My bladder was giving notice, so I slipped away from the table where I was positioned and made my way down a steep flight of stairs to the Gents. Coming out of the door was another of the nominees, Stanley Baxter, the brilliant comedian whom I had always admired. Next to his, my talent felt very small beer. As we passed on the stairs, he reached out to touch me on the arm. 'I hope you win,' he said. It was just about the kindest and most generous thing anybody had ever said to me.

It so happened that I did. Paul had been nominated too. It was unfortunate that we should both have been selected for the same category; we were a team and should never have been put in competition. I won four times for Sir Humphrey, and each time it was against Paul. I knew how desperate he was to get the award so it became increasingly difficult to know what to say to him. He told me once that he'd been in Australia on the night of the awards attending another function, when someone raced in calling out, 'You've won! You've won!' Paul told me with a wry smile that he'd promptly bought champagne for the whole assembly, only to be told twenty minutes later, 'I'm sorry, mate. It was the other one.' Paul was very good at telling jokes against himself. He was once cutting the hedge outside his home in Muswell Hill, when a lady stopped to congratulate him on the performance he'd given in a play shown on television the previous evening. 'You were wonderful!' she told him. Paul told me that he'd glowed, thanked her profusely and was about to continue with the hedge when she added, 'You're usually so wooden.'

Paul and I were very friendly but I wouldn't have said we were great friends. I used to get the feeling that he never thought that either Derek or I were quite up to it. I'm not suggesting that he thought he was better, just that his support could have been more classy. But there were no arguments or tantrums, there just wasn't time for anything like that. He was extremely interested in politics; touchingly vain, he loved being seen in public and was very proud of his membership of the Garrick Club. When abroad, he'd be treated as if he were the real thing and revelled in it. I led a far more mundane life, growing to love the countryside, having a circle of friends who, more often than not, had nothing to do with things theatrical – and certainly not matters political – becoming more and more insular because of my deep involvement with Trevor, preferring above everything to be in his company. While we were escaping from suburbia and into the Hertfordshire countryside, Paul and Trisha his wife were moving from suburbia to a converted warehouse on the Thames. He was a man of tremendously strong principles, a Quaker, a pacifist, and opposed smoking. I greatly admired the stands he took, though I couldn't share his love for the bustle of London which, for us at least, was rapidly losing its charm. Neither Trevor nor I sought the bright lights. We glimpsed them and then got out fast. Away from the city smells, we opted for creating a garden and involving ourselves in charity work within the county, supporting local events rather than the big-time celebrity stuff up West.

Derek Fowlds was a delight, seldom taking anything very seriously unless it involved Chelsea Football Club, of which he remains a loyal supporter. Although Paul disapproved of Derek's lighthearted approach, particularly where his work was concerned, as a pair they got on extremely well and I know that Derek admired him as much as I did. It is impossible not to like Derek, and he and his partner Jo have remained our good friends ever since.

In 1982, I returned to the Young Vic to do three plays by John Mortimer, the central piece being *The Dock Brief*, a minor classic. The first of the short plays alarmingly had yet to be written, but was to do with medicine we were told, the third being *The Prince Of Darkness* on the subject of religion. In other words the evening concerned three professions, medicine, law and the church. I was in Cape Town visiting my family with Trevor when the offer arrived and we agreed that the combination of Mortimer, that splendid actor John Alderton and my old friend Denise Coffey as director sounded very promising. So I telephoned my agreement, basing my decision on Mortimer's reputation rather than the plays which, apart from *The Dock Brief*, I hadn't read. It was a reckless decision as it turned out, though it seemed like a good idea at the time.

The first draft of the new play rambled all over the place so John Mortimer offered to rewrite it. And again. He just couldn't make it work. And time was running short. The weekend before our previews Denise, together with Frank Dunlop, who ran the theatre, agreed to go over to John Mortimer's home, promising to return on the Monday morning with a new and workable version. It proved to be a good deal thicker than any of the previous drafts, and John Alderton and I looked at one another with considerable apprehension. The first preview, after all, was the following night. We sat round the table and read it aloud.

I looked at John. John looked at me. 'Well,' I said, 'that doesn't work either.' The atmosphere in the rehearsal room was as if the *Titanic*'s sister ship had just gone down. John and I withdrew from the tense scene, sidled over to the trestle table and helped ourselves to a coffee. After a long while, John Mortimer joined us, taking me to one side. 'There's only one thing that will save the show,' he told me, more serious than I had ever known him. 'Instead of playing a doctor . . .' he hesitated before dropping the bombshell, 'you're a matron.' There was a moment of stunned silence. I couldn't believe I'd heard correctly. 'DRAG?' I blustered. John Mortimer was sympathetic but firm. 'It's the only thing which will work.' I was hauled off to the costumiers and togged out with a blue uniform complete with a generously padded bosom, a frilly cap with streamers, an apron and high heeled shoes, then to the wig makers for an Elsie Tanner look-alike. We tried it all out at the dress rehearsal the following afternoon. It was pronounced a huge success. I felt – well, emasculated, panic-stricken and completely out of my depth. My first entrance involved this wretched matron racing ferociously around the stage at great speed, not easy in high heels, spraying the audience with insecticide as they do sometimes on flights. Following this, a long monologue to the audience before John Alderton came to my rescue as the patient, and I could catch my breath.

That night, as the audience took its seats, I hovered in the wings, aerosols at the ready. I had seldom been more nervous. The well-meaning assistant stage manager came over to wish me luck. Just before leaving she whispered, 'Laurence Olivier's in the front row.' Nor was she lying. I learnt afterwards that Olivier had recently completed filming Mortimer's *Voyage Round My Father* at his home in the country. An invitation had been extended and he'd brought the whole family to see the first preview. The house lights were lowered, the stage lights came up and I was on. As I teetered around the stage spraying and praying for all I was worth, one thing was uppermost in my mind. 'Whatever you do, never for one solitary second let your eyes settle.' I knew that were they to meet the reptilian gaze of the man acknowledged to be the greatest actor in the world, I wouldn't even finish the play. I'd just leave the stage, jump on the first available means of transport, emigrate to somewhere they'd never heard of theatre and become a Trappist monk.

By the end of the evening, I was in a lather. We had been invited to a reception in the studio theatre after the performance, and it was with profound embarrassment that I stood barely inside the door nursing a much-needed drink. Only a yard or two away, I could see Olivier and Joan Plowright with their family. Olivier's jacket was accidentally turned up at the collar, making him look rather seedy – less great actor, more Archie Rice. Frank Dunlop came over to say that he had asked for me. Knowing how critical he could be of other actors, and remembering in particular Sir Ralph's experience after the preview of *West Of Suez*, it was with trepidation that I allowed Frank to steer me in Olivier's direction. You could have knocked me down with a handbag. He couldn't have been kinder, more friendly or more generous if he'd tried. Unless he was the most terrible liar, he had thoroughly enjoyed the evening, and even been delighted by my drag act at the beginning. Unfortunately, the critics didn't share Oliver's enthusiasm, but the run passed pleasantly enough. The episode, absurd though it may seem, helped crystallise a thought which had been buzzing round my head for some time. I no longer enjoyed theatre as much as I did. I was losing my faith.

I suspect that there isn't an actor unhung who hasn't been faced with this realisation at one time or other, each of us knowing that it amounted to treason. Many of us in middle life are faced with a similar crisis. Tony Holbery, my old University friend from Cape Town, had entered the Church to become a Roman Catholic priest, only to discover when he was nearly fifty that he had lost his faith. We had spoken of his dilemma on a number of occasions, and I had done my best to be of help. In his heart of hearts, he knew he would have to get out or spend the rest of his life living a lie. He had no qualifications other than those which equipped him for the Church. But he was an exceptionally brave and honest man. He made his decision and got out.

Naturally, my choice was as nothing when compared with his. Bravery didn't come into it. Having established myself to a degree, I could fall back on television or do the odd film, if anyone would have me. Poor Ant stuck to his guns, though understandably the early years were an emotional upheaval. Now he makes a modest living and enjoys peace of mind. Trevor, too, had made a change. I had persuaded him to give up the theatre. The work he was doing in management was giving him very little satisfaction, the pay was inadequate and the hours long. He'd always wanted to write, and his work was wonderfully skilful and full of brilliant observation, so I encouraged him to hand in his notice, explaining that until he began to be successful, I was making enough to ensure that we lived in some degree of comfort. Ours was, after all, a partnership.

We had moved from Trevor's house in Southgate to Crew's Hill, outside Enfield, where it was almost countryside but not quite, as if we were dipping our toes in the water to test it, finding it passable but short of ideal. The area is noted for its garden centres, there's one whichever direction you turn, so it would be true to say that it was here that we began our serious interest in plants.

At Crew's Hill the main problem was neighbours, be they academics who noisily scorned my rendition of Archdeacon Grantley in *The Barchester Chronicles* and Orgon in *Tartuffe* at the RSC or the family next door who built a viewing platform so they could look into our garden at all times. The price of new-found celebrity was becoming ominously high. I was either up for the pillory or for peering at. When a fibreglass factory opened on the adjacent property, we knew it was time to reluctantly make another move.

Each weekend we'd drive around looking at likely areas. We liked Hertfordshire. It was handy for London and parts of it were extremely pretty. On Trevor's insistence, I had learned to drive, passing first time – which never ceases to astonish me (or him!) – so we could come and go as we pleased. Right up in the northern part of the county, outside the attractive market town of Baldock with its wide and handsome main street and impressive collection of inns, we found a four-hundred-year-old farmhouse with high brick chimneys and splendid views. We brought along Bertie the cat and Oscar, our gentle, puzzled and totally irreplaceable rescue dog who had a spastic tongue which meant that he couldn't drink water – he had to eat it. Later, we got him three bitches for company, Twitch, a kind of terrier, good-natured and sensible, Bumble, a delightfully dotty Irish Setter, and Havoc, a Ruby Cavalier.

The previous owners hadn't been there very long. For some time, the house had been derelict and was in poor condition but, by the time they'd restored it, the husband was made redundant so it was put back on the market and we were given the opportunity of buying it. It meant that we were able to build our garden from scratch – most gardeners' dream. We had become increasingly fond of the hobby, indeed a whole section of our library was given over to books on the subject, getting to know the names of the species, learning about propagation and when or when not to prune. We loved England and its muted light, and felt that a garden should reflect the tranquillity this suggested, peace away from professional life. We tried to ensure that the colours in the flowerbeds were harmonious, packed with old roses, shrubs and perennials.

Meanwhile, with the *Yes, Minister* series developing into *Yes, Prime Minister*, I was finding myself drawn more and more into community life – asked to open fêtes, start marathons and become patron of this and that.

Vaclav Havel had written an intriguing two-hander about dishonesty called *The Petition*, which the BBC were proposing to televise. It was to be produced by Innes Lloyd, and I had been invited to play the part of a successful playwright. This eminent man's willingness to toe the Party line had ensured him a life of some considerable comfort in Prague which, understandably, he is anxious to retain. Visiting him that day is the other character in the play – himself a writer who, having spoken out against the authorities, has recently been released from prison. He brings with him a petition pleading for freedom of speech and the lifting of censorship on artists which he would dearly like his eminent colleague to sign. It takes my character the entire play to talk his way out of doing so, realising that if he did he might easily forfeit his lifestyle or, indeed, be sent to prison.

I was asked to help with the casting of Character B and, going to the Television Centre one day, hit upon an idea. As Character B had been sent to prison for being honest, so Character A was dishonest – hanging on to an easy life by refusing to sign a document he knew to be right. Surely, it was two sides of the same man? I suggested that I should play both roles, and this is where the trouble all began.

Disguise wouldn't be a problem. As Character A I would wear a short, rather trendy beard, while Character B would have a long, unkempt wig. The Beeb engaged an actor called Guy as my stand-in, explaining to him that only the tip of his shoulder, perhaps his arm and the back of his head would be seen and that he wouldn't have to learn any lines as I would be doing both parts. Guy seemed to understand the situation. Shooting was confined to two days. Character A the first day, Character B the second.

The rehearsals went well. People liked the unusual approach and were fascinated by the technical demands thrown up by the split-screen technique. When we came to our two recording days in the studio, however, two problems emerged: Guy decided it was his big chance and the director had never used this technique before.

Day one in the studio was tense. Guy kept stopping the recording to complain that he'd got a word wrong, or simply just wasn't satisfied with the way he'd played the scene. We reshot page after page for his benefit, doing our utmost to get him to understand that he was only doubling for me, that there would be just glimpses of him, usually from behind his ear, his thumb, his knee, and that the audience wouldn't hear his voice at any time, only mine, and these were the scenes we would be shooting the following day. But Guy was insistent.

'I'm a professional,' he kept saying. 'I didn't feel right. I'd like to do it again.'

The following day, when I was Character B, the same thing happened in reverse. Added to which, the director – having scraped through the first day and now faced with Character A and Character B (both played by the same actor) having to talk to one another – panicked.

I invited Trevor to the second day's recording, and he watched from the control room. At one point, Innes became so depressed that he curled up on a large settee and fell sound asleep, waking only when the director, in a state of extreme agitation, yelled at the top of his voice, 'Is there an expert in the building?' As it happened, there wasn't. Throughout the debacle I remained worryingly calm, nobody quite understanding why I hadn't blown my top. I suppose I must have felt there was quite enough going on as it was.

The Petition went out the same evening as an episode of *Yes, Minister*, with just the News in-between. I rather hoped that with such a surfeit of Hawthorne, people would just switch off and go to bed. But I think I did learn one thing from the experience – wherever possible to keep my big mouth shut.

Only two years after we'd moved to our beautiful new home, I was sent a script for a stage play – something which, because of my new-found contentment, used to make my heart sink as I knew it would take me away. Called *Across From The Garden Of Allah*, it had been written by Charles Wood in semi-blank verse for two people and a bellhop. Glenda Jackson had specifically asked for me to play opposite her so, despite my feelings about giving up the theatre, and working exclusively for the camera, I found the job impossible to refuse. The play was set in Hollywood where a middle-aged writer has taken his wife while working on a film script. Although the situation was very close to Charles Wood's heart, the play didn't work and Glenda took to racing through it at breakneck speed so that she could get home as quickly as possible. We eked out our poorly attended run at the Comedy Theatre with stoicism.

One evening my old friend, the director Michael Rudman, came backstage. We embraced warmly as it had been a long time since we'd met, and had plenty of stories to tell – mostly his, I have to say, as he is a brilliant raconteur. He'd been asked to go to the National Theatre to direct Pinero's *The Magistrate* and wanted me to play the lead. Yet again, my plans to retire from the boards had been thwarted. The part suited me perfectly, being emotional comedy, and, by accepting his offer, once again – though I didn't know it at the time – my whole life was about to change. Throughout the run, you couldn't get a seat. It was exhilarating hearing the gales of laughter from the Lyttelton Theatre audience, especially after the dribs and drabs we had managed to attract at the Comedy Theatre. Between them, the plays had yanked me back into the theatre with a vengeance.

Half way through the run at the National, I had a totally unexpected surprise. An official letter arrived from Downing Street asking whether I'd accept the CBE. Paul Eddington had received one too. My sister Sheila made the trip from Cape Town, and Trevor, she and I wore our very best to the Palace – though mine, of necessity more formal, was on hire from 'Suits You' of Hatfield. We were separated at the entrance to the Palace, and Trevor and Sheila were directed towards the throne room where the band of Her Majesty's Coldstream Guards was providing a curious medley of tunes from the shows, including 'Gonna Wash That Man Right Outta My Hair' and 'I'm Just A Girl Who Can't Say No'. Meanwhile, in an ante-room stuffed with Van Dycks and Rubens, those being honoured with CBEs were cordoned off like sheep to keep us well away from those awful Knights Bachelor, the MBEs and OBEs.

A friendly lady from the Milk Marketing Board asked me if I thought the Queen would object if she wore her elbow length gloves throughout the investiture, as she'd been creosoting the shed. Though in no way qualified to speak on Her Majesty's behalf, and mindful of the bizarre outfits around us, I assured her the Queen wouldn't have cared if she'd pitched up in her jeans.

The following year, 1988, I had a distressing telephone call from Bruce. I don't remember too much about what was said, though I remember how emotional it was. He told me he'd just come from the doctor and that he was diagnosed HIV positive. It was at a time when the disease was at its most rampant and, because of the promiscuous lifestyle of many homosexuals, of all groups we were the most vulnerable. Nobody quite knew how easily it could be transmitted, and I think it's true to record that for a while homosexuals were ostracised by the heterosexual community for fear of contamination. From our home in the country, both Trevor and I were aware of a slackening-off of invitations and, if we did go out to tea, we were convinced that, after we'd gone, the tea cups and spoons would be given a second go in the dishwasher. Bruce was in a terrible state. There is nothing quite as lonely as illness, so I dropped whatever it was I was doing to go round to him to try and talk it through. There was no point in retracing steps to find out how, why or when he might have been infected, the fact remained that he'd got it and it was a time for us all to rally round. He became a constant visitor to our home.

I went into *Hapgood*, a mystery play about physicists. Its meaning remains a mystery to this day. The part was cerebral, and perhaps I had only agreed to do it because it was written by the brilliant Tom Stoppard, a gentle, warm-hearted, chain-smoking delight, but, rather disappointingly, it returned me to the Sir Humphrey image of smooth men in ties which I had been hoping to escape. The play was one of Tom's least successful, though it went down very well in America. I think we puzzled more people than we entertained.

What I didn't realise at that stage was that the emotional strength I had unlocked in *The Magistrate* (even though it was a farce) had been noticed, and one day I was sent another new play. It was called *Shadowlands*, written by William Nicholson about the Oxford don C.S. Lewis and his love for Joy Davidman, an American groupie. A quantum leap for me as an actor – but it was one that I felt ready to take.

Yet, perhaps it was not I who was making the leap but Elijah Mojinsky, the director, and Brian Eastman, the producer. When you happen to have been associated with a specific type of role, it is often very difficult for people to see you as anything else. We call it type-casting. Critics often seem to have the problem. An actor is a stage actor, a film actor or a television actor. He can't be all three. In the critics' case it can amount sometimes to snobbism: if an actor has devoted his life to the theatre, then that is where his loyalty lies, he shouldn't squander his talent experimenting in other fields, and Richard Burton's case is aired yet again. If an actor is seen to play comedy for preference, that is the style to which he is suited. If he is at ease in straight drama, then, by definition, he must be ill at ease in farce. It is an opinion widely held but, of course, total rubbish. I believe that an actor's frontiers should be open and that all challenges should be met face-on. If someone associated with the arts declines to take risks or is discouraged from so doing, he is bound to be less interesting because he has nowhere new to go. In any case, his experience in a different field can only enrich the one in which he is working.

With me in *Shadowlands* was to be my old friend Jane Lapotaire. We had first met when we'd played opposite one another in *Marie Curie* in 1977 for the BBC and had always found pleasure in one another's company. We were all dispatched to Plymouth where the production was to open and, once there, tried to come to terms with Bill Nicholson's sprawling script. I'd been reading everything on which I could lay my hands to prepare me for the role, from the

Narnia stories to *A Grief Observed*. I realised that, as a man, I hadn't a great deal in common with Lewis, apart from the fact that by late middle-age we were both still bachelors. He was an academic able to sublimate his emotions behind a cloud of pipe smoke and Christian debate. There was no evidence that he'd had a relationship with a woman before.

A married woman with two sons, Joy Davidman begins a correspondence with him from America. Lewis is warned by his colleagues that she has ulterior motives and is probably after his body. Joy arrives in Oxford, which is more or less when the play begins, and friendship blossoms into love. Joy gets cancer. Lewis marries her in hospital. She has a remission during which they visit the Greek islands, returning to England where she dies. One can appreciate why Nicholson had difficulty condensing the story into a manageable stage play. Mojinsky worked wonders with designer Mark Thompson, combining the magic of Narnia with the male world of the academic and the various worlds at home and abroad in which the unlikely lovers found themselves.

If Mark, Elijah and Bill Nicholson had their problems they weren't alone. Like the best theatre, it is left to the audience to fill in the gaps with their imagination. As a woman bursting with life and good humour, Jane had to disintegrate to a bedridden invalid. After she dies, the son (Bill reduced the number of boys for simplicity) is required to approach Lewis, his adopted father, and, as the two embrace, the die-hard Lewis, who has never shown a whisker of emotion, explodes with grief.

As we approached the end of the play at the final rehearsal in Plymouth, I started to panic. So far, I had managed to stave off any display of grief by 'marking' it. In other words, when we got to the point I'd say something like, 'Okay. This is where he cries, et cetera, et cetera', perfectly well aware that sooner or later I was going to have to commit myself but simply putting off the evil moment out of cowardice. We came to the moment where Joy has died and there is a short scene with the boy, at the end of which he runs towards Lewis and flings his arms around him. I hadn't worked out anything. Something had to happen or I would be leaving it too late. But I had no idea what it would be. The boy came to me and wrapped his arms about me. From somewhere deep inside me, something began to happen over which I had no control. All the turbulence and frustration I had been storing away since I was a child erupted from me. It was embarrassingly loud, it was certainly unmanly, but I didn't care. I had no choice in the matter. I couldn't stop it, nor did I want to. I remember hearing Elijah, not quite knowing how to cope, muttering things like 'Let's finish the play, shall we?' and clearing his throat. Nothing he could have said would have made any difference. I had to cry myself out and I did. Jane Lapotaire took me in her arms and comforted me. Instinctively, she was aware that it was a significant moment in my life. I must have cried for twenty minutes, the actor in me constantly stepping outside himself. I kept trying to remember how I was doing it – noticing that the tears came in surges, how just when you thought that they'd stopped, off they'd go again – what I was doing with my hands. I remembered, in particular, that I put them on top of my head as though there was an open gash and I was trying to stop my grief from escaping. Actors are accustomed to using their own experiences and very little is wasted. I knew I was going to have to reproduce the moment each night – probably for a long time to come.

The critics sniffed rather when we reached London though by this time I had given up reading them for some years. Besides constantly finding their judgment unreliable, I noticed they'd influence what I was doing – depress me if they didn't like it, make me tinker about with it by embroidering details they'd picked out as being praiseworthy. So I thought it a much better idea to let the audience point the way, a system to which I have adhered ever since. I had never before been in a play like *Shadowlands*, where the audience was so emotionally involved. Because the story touched so many lives, people began to write to me. Not just one or two letters, I have files stuffed with them, very often thanking me for releasing pent-up emotions in themselves, telling me in detail about their own relationships, how they'd reacted when their partner had died, and how long it had taken them to adjust to being on their own. I felt enormously privileged to have been the indirect catalyst in liberating so many people, and aware that I had a particular responsibility – I could never allow myself to cheat on the emotion. If it meant so much, then I'd have to give it all I'd got; each and every time it had to be as exposed and painful as it had been that afternoon in Plymouth.

By the time we had opened in London and were settling down to being a modest success, the subject matter of the play, which those scared of sentiment were inclined to write off as morbid, had gripped the attention of the public. The audience seemed determined to make the play its own. Each night, long after the show had ended, little pockets of people, largely female, could be seen dotted about the auditorium or huddled in corners, until the theatre staff came round to make it quite clear that it was well past the time for them to lock up so would they please go?

Bruce was beginning to be confined for long periods in the Broddrip Ward at the Middlesex Hospital where a lot of the male HIV/Aids patients were housed, so on my way to the theatre each evening, I'd go in early to visit him. It was an odd sensation, holding the hand of a slowly dying man before going down to my place of work, the Queen's Theatre in Shaftesbury Avenue, where I was to play tender, bedside scenes with a 'dying' woman, both of them attended by nursing staff, one lot real, the other not, both propped up against steep steps of snow-white pillows. It became increasingly difficult to separate the real from the fake. Emotionally, too, it was very draining. I can't praise the nursing staff at the Middlesex too highly. Nothing was ever too much trouble. They listened and they joked though, in the majority of cases, they must have known that any vestige of hope was unrealistic. Distressing though it was for me to come into a ward crammed with emaciated men, some surrounded by members of their families, others encircled by screens, some merely lying there staring into space, it was hard not to experience an immense feeling of relief as I sat in the visitor's chair, feeling uncomfortably fit and constantly reminding myself, 'There, but for the grace of God, go I.'

When Christmas came around, it was customary to discharge as many of the patients as was possible, so that they could spend the time at home with their families. Having no family but Trevor and me, Bruce chose to spend the time with us. Two Christmases in succession, we had to take Bruce back to the hospital on the day itself as he was just too ill for us to handle. He had little enthusiasm for anything because of his condition, but would rest quietly on the settee wrapped in a duvet, not speaking or sleeping, but allowing his haunted eyes to become absorbed with what we were preparing in the way of meals, and then eating what was put before him while insisting point-blank that he had no appetite. I remember well one Christmas Day when Trevor and I were returning Bruce to the Middlesex. I had gone inside the hospital to get a wheelchair, leaving the car parked in a side street. Trevor realised that, in my haste, I'd gone off with the keys, having absent-mindedly locked the car, thereby switching on the burglar alarm. Trevor's worst hopes were realised when Bruce suddenly announced, 'I need a pee!' Without pausing, he opened the door and, clad in nothing but pyjamas, headed for the nearest gutter, while the car alarm screamed for attention, lights flashed, windows opened up and down the street, and the situation was only narrowly saved by my reappearance with a wheelchair.

At the end of the London run of *Shadowlands*, I realised that it would be some time before I saw Bruce again. The play was going to Broadway. Sadly, Equity wouldn't agree to Jane Lapotaire taking the part of Joy to New York (in fact, I was the only member of our company they would allow) and a much admired American actress, Jane Alexander, was engaged as substitute for her. Their acting styles were very different, but the management had invited Jane Alexander to play the final six weeks in London and the audience reaction had been every bit as intense and exciting.

It was Bruce's ambition – whatever his state of health – to fly over to New York to see *Shadowlands* but my rented apartment had only one bedroom and I realised that to have him stay would have been exhausting, especially as he was so ill. Mercifully, at the last moment he agreed to stay with a friend. He managed to see the play but shortly afterwards had to fly back to Britain as he'd become so ill. During the six-month Broadway run, I made sure Trevor would fly over at least once a month by having a clause in my contract which guaranteed that. It was the year of the Gulf War, so planes were all over the place, nothing arriving on time, and long-distance passengers had to check in three hours before the flight. It was wonderful to see him each time, even though he barely got over his jet-lag before returning to England.

The run was hugely successful despite a carp or two from Frank Rich, the notoriously hard-to-please critic of the *New York Times*, and it was rumoured that I might win the coveted Tony Award. As luck would have it, the run ended before the nominations were announced and I had flown back to England before I was notified that I had indeed been nominated and was invited back to New York for the ceremony.

There seemed to be far more rivalry at the Tony Awards than at any of the counterparts I had attended in England. Heaven knows, our ceremonies are interminable affairs crammed with over-long embarrassing speeches, but we don't have the same barracking, we're not partisan, but more reserved and tend to be more generously disposed to each other than they are in the States. It so happened that I did win, and was handed my award by an actor I much admire, Denzel Washington.

Much as I love America and its people, it's always England that will hold pride of place. Often, it's quite hard to explain my attachment but despite the grey skies which greet the touch-down, its lack of courtesy, its selfishness and its laziness, England has it for me over any other country in the world and it's always a pleasure to return to it.

During the Broadway run of *Shadowlands*, Nicholas Hytner, who had been there preparing for the opening of *Miss Saigon*, the musical he had directed in London, came to see the play. Not long after my return I had an offer from him to play the leading role in Alan Bennett's new play which was to be presented at the National Theatre. The script was thick and richly detailed. It dealt with the illness of one of our monarchs, and was called *The Madness Of George III*.

14

The Queen and Mr King

I'm sure we all hope, when things start to go wrong – when what we used to be able to do is no longer possible, or we've contracted some dreaded malady and we need help every inch of the way – that the person at hand will be not just a detached agency nurse who goes off at 7.30 on a Tuesday and there's fat chance of seeing her again until the following Sunday evening, but someone who knows you and loves you and who supports you because it's what he or she wants to do. Such beings are like gold dust.

Friends of mine will understand what I'm saying as I have been blessed by just such a person. Always there, at my side, giving strength when it's needed, taking my hand and guiding me through those moments of private despair when I think I can no longer cope, easing me back on to the rails. A good deal of the work rests upon my own shoulders, of course, the will to persevere, however unequal the odds, but at least I am assured that shoulder to shoulder with me is a partner – I think it's a good word – who wants what I want, as clearly and as wholeheartedly, who will remove from my hands the responsibility of when to do what and how often – crucial as I'm the one who's ill and on the drugs – and who'll stand by me whatever happens. We've never questioned one another's attitude, there doesn't seem to have been any need.

This is where all those depressingly archaic theories pontificated by bigots fall apart. Two people of the same sex living together who give one another enduring support, comfort and companionship surely have an honourable place in society, and their presence in it should be acknowledged. It's nothing to do with religion. Given a parallel set of circumstances, two deeply religious people who slavishly live by The Book don't necessarily lead a happier life. It is possible that by their standards the way Trevor and I conduct our lives is wrong, even sinful, despite the fact that in the eyes of society we break none of the rules. There is a built-in assumption that because we have drifted from the straight and narrow, potentially we are in the wrong and pose some sort of threat to the future of mankind . . . That's very far from how I see it. People have only to look at us to see that we live in harmony, they have only to examine our track record to see that we are certainly not corrupting influences. I won't deny that we choose to keep ourselves to ourselves, a result perhaps of years of being scrutinised which has driven us back into our shells. Or it may be just in our nature. It might well be that our need for privacy contributes to their suspicion – what are they up to? It's hard to tell. With regard to where we fit in when it comes to the society of which we are a part, I can't speak for myself, but I know Trevor to be totally selfless, by which I mean that he cares more for others than he does for himself. The way he has supported me – this spoilt, cantankerous old fraud – throughout the crisis of my illness is living proof of that, if proof were needed. Of course it's reciprocal. I should be doing the same were the positions reversed – though, I suspect, with considerably less efficiency.

King George III, if we are to believe all we're told, had just such a relationship with Charlotte, his wife, who bore him fifteen children (extraordinary that an actor known by most to be homosexual should be entrusted with a role encompassing such irrefutable heterosexual attributes). One of the most moving aspects of Alan Bennett's play, *The Madness Of George III*, was the tenderness between the King and the Queen, how she stuck by him even though physically they were ripped apart and forced to live separately from one another. 'Mr King', she liked to call him. As I've recently discovered, doctors are a law unto themselves, and this particular patient, even though he was their monarch, was torn away from his prop and stay, the love of his life, so that he could act as their guinea-pig. The issues at stake weren't insignificant. Were they to be successful in their experiments with the royal patient, it would make their fortunes, and besides the word 'revolution' was on everyone's lips. At the back of the King's mind he knew that Charlotte wasn't far away, metaphorically holding his hand. The image is a sentimental one, but no less pertinent because of it. Theirs was a partnership of a rare kind.

Seven years earlier in my life there had been another George, though known as 'Georgie', and in referring to him at the head of this chapter, I've not found it difficult to be deprecating about him, calling him 'the Queen'. Because he was a fictional character, I suppose I felt I had more licence to generalise, and there's no doubt that, were you to see him coming towards you down the street, you would be left in no doubt that he wasn't the captain of the local rugby club. What prevented his being sad was his capacity for affection. What he thought about in the solitude of his home, his toupee (which deceived no one) safely secreted in its cardboard box ready for him to 'dress' before his next social outing – away from all the larks with Lucia, Diva, Quaint Irene and the rest of that tea and buttered scone circle of scandalised gossip-mongers – can be imagined with little difficulty. But the naughtiness he served up with so little effort, the fun generated by this unmanly, insecure but delightful peacock butterfly of a person, introduced a welcome air of anarchy to the starchy parish of Tilling – its trembling net curtains barely concealing prying eyes – which more than compensated for the embarrassment of being in his company while crossing one of the narrow, cobbled streets between a gang of sweaty labourers digging the road and spewing up their own particular brand of judgment. Georgie Pilson was, as always, whisked into the protective stockade formed by his friends, who surrounded him with as much ferocity as if he'd been head of the Mafia.

Yes, Georgie Pilson was an old queen, of course he was. If one were looking for a stereotype, he would slot in with all the ease of the final piece of a jigsaw puzzle. It wasn't, I'm sure, that he yearned to be a woman that made him what he was – or even that he preferred to dress as one, and as far as I know he didn't, he just sought their company. Women made him feel safe. And Lucia, for all her treachery, her silliness and pretensions, even her cruelty, topped the list as far as he was concerned. Together they conspired, gossiped – though not really in a malicious way – he giggled and grumbled with her, pandered to her whims, indulged her, argued with her, accompanied her on the piano, comforted and stuck by her however wrong he knew her to be and however selfishly and inconsiderately she was behaving. In fact, they were inseparable. It was, in its own peculiar way, if not a marriage at least a sort of love.

E.F. Benson, who wrote the *Mapp And Lucia* books, lived in Rye and from his home had just such a vantage point where he could sit and observe the very little, inconsequential world of the town going by, and wrote a series of books in which the petty rivalry between Lucia and the portly Miss Mapp formed the main theme.

Trevor, for a long while, had it in mind to secure the rights of the books so that he could adapt them into a television series, but to our disappointment someone had pipped him to the post. To add insult to injury, London Weekend Television who had bought the option offered me the part of Georgie Pilson. Was this, I wondered, how the rest of the world saw me? Refusing to be daunted, such was my affection for both the text and the character that I accepted on the spot. An added incentive was knowing that Geraldine McEwan was to be Lucia and Prunella Scales, Mapp. The hugely inventive Frances Tempest was designing the clothes, and the Thirties was a treasure trove to her – what a field day she had. The series, apart from being huge fun to make – the director, Donald McWhinnie, enjoying himself as much as anyone – proved successful and subsequently attracted something of a cult following in the United States.

All projects attract their quota of anecdotes. The whole nature of our piece being silly, and of very little consequence, this tale was bound to follow suit.

It was shortly after we'd finished shooting the 'pageant', an event masterminded by Lucia herself, imposingly be-ruffed and be-jewelled as Queen Elizabeth I. The skies had been playing up all day, and frequently we were herded in the direction of shelter as the raindrops spattered the camera lens, only to stop when we were within arm's length of sanctuary. Finally the heavens opened. We hurtled into the minibus at breakneck speed, scooping up our finery, ready to be taken back to base, the fields and tracks around us already a quagmire, the windscreen wipers throwing themselves to left and right like demented pendulums. Then we stuck. Round and round roared the wheels but we didn't budge. By now the rain had eased off so it seemed sensible to me, despite the fact that I was rather foolishly got up as Sir Walter Raleigh – mostly white and raspberry pink with a large cockaded hat and a sword – to get out and push (my white shoes with their perilously high heels being early victims). Some bright spark took himself off to find something to pack under the wheels, but ahead I noticed that the five-barred gate had slammed to in the wind so, delicately negotiating the puddles, I went over to open it, which proved more difficult than expected. It seemed to be jammed. I pushed and prodded and wrestled with it, eventually turning to the minivan for moral support. I couldn't help noticing that the vehicle seemed to be shuddering, and screams of laughter were issuing from within. Glancing to my right, I realised why.

Presumably attracted by my finery, standing ominously close behind was a large, wet billy goat, its head lowered, pointing threateningly in my direction. I had no idea of how to cope with the situation, particularly as, by that time, I was laughing as much as the others in the minivan. I backed up against the gate and unsheathed my sword ready to do battle. Faces at the windows of the minivan appeared and disappeared from view as members of the cast and crew kept diving for their cameras. Not that the goat felt in any way intimidated, as suddenly, with one mighty leap, plainly illustrating its disdain, it hurdled the five-barred gate and disappeared into the trees.

Needless to say, I didn't hear the end of it – though I had sweet revenge when none of the photographs came out. They'd all been laughing so much they hadn't been able to hold their cameras steady. The incident was trivial in the extreme, but I wouldn't have missed the idiocy of that afternoon for the world.

'Georgie' Pilson was a far cry from George III. Some years separated their lives as indeed some years stood between my connection with each, but I developed a deep affection for both characters and hugely enjoyed working on both the *Mapp And Lucia* series and the stage play and subsequent film which surrounded the illness of the poor, abused monarch.

Alan Bennett seemed to have assembled his script rather than written it. Appearing to work on an assortment of antique typewriters, he would compile a sequence (using either factual quotations or inventing his own dialogue), snip it out and paste it with other extracts on to a sheet of A4 before photocopying the completed page, saving it in a file and pressing on to the next. Having written on one side of the page only, the manuscript was so bulky it resembled Gray's *Anatomy*, yet I just couldn't put it down. It bore all the hallmarks of Alan's distinctive style – his gently mocking wit, his uncanny power of observation, his love of detail and his keen sense of the absurd. In a record of this tragic period in George's life, he managed to find fun and pageantry, even though for dramatic reasons he had to encapsulate events, infuriating the purists. With its formidably large cast and the need for opulent settings and costumes, only one of the major subsidised companies could afford to stage it (and even that was with actors doubling and trebling). Nick Hytner had taken on a handful, but the National Theatre, then run by Richard Eyre, swallowed hard and we were in business.

It began with a gentle reading at the National's studio along the road from the Old Vic in Waterloo, and an impressive number of actors, some of whom I knew, had been dragooned – even though I was the only one cast at that stage – to help out by reading in the other parts. I was so nervous, I could barely speak, see, think, breathe – but off we went. I took it at breakneck speed with as much energy as I could summon, not knowing what was expected, hoping I could bluff it out. After all, I barely knew Nick and, even including the embarrassing encounter at the Fortune Theatre during the *Beyond The Fringe* run, the same might be said for Alan Bennett. It read nearly four hours that first time through, then I staggered towards the Underground with a great weight of feelings – excitement, panic, anticipation but, above all, filled with the conviction that I'd blown it and that, on my arrival home, there would be a message from Nick to say that they'd had second thoughts and did I know where they could contact Anthony Hopkins?

In due course, the rewrites came. Nick and Alan, as a result of the reading, had tightened the whole text, pared down the narrative line, superfluous characters had been excised, so that what previously had been exciting was on the verge of becoming thrilling. As rehearsals began, Nick and I worked out the best way for me to set about tackling the many facets of the mammoth role. Eventually, the clothes and properties settled it. I arranged for an assortment of nightgowns, sashes, robes, a crown or two, bedroom slippers, white stockings which might hang either snugly or flop around the ankles, a wig for throwing at offenders and another for more controlled occasions, a chamber pot for interested medics to peruse, bandages and something which would do for a restraining chair with chains and straps to restrict movement – and these bits and pieces helped us chronicle the King's state of mind throughout the course of his illness. They were scattered at vantage points around the rehearsal room to be accessible if and when required. This seemed to work well as a basic scheme of things.

Alan used to drop by most days wearing his by now familiar sand-coloured sports jacket and trousers, sometimes with duffle coat to match, having bicycled in from his home in Regent's Park, always unassuming and willing to change things if persuaded. The only altercation we had was with the epilogue. He wanted the audience to go along with the theory upon which he'd based the play, which was that the King was suffering from porphyria, a theory researched by doctors McAlpine and Hunter from the intricate medical records of the time, which chronicled almost every second of the King's illness. As theirs was a twentieth-century conclusion, it had to be performed in modern dress, which, as an observer as well as participant, I found uncomfortable and anachronistic. It was fine on the screen when later we made the film as subtitles were used, but not on the stage. For more than a year I stubbornly pursued my objections but Alan was equally stubborn and stuck to his guns. It was only in the last months of the run that finally he succumbed. I could hardly believe I was hearing it. 'I don't know why I didn't cut the scene before,' he said to me. 'It's so much better without it.'

Clearly, the play was going to be massively demanding for me – even the term 'interval' seemed not to apply. There was always a change of costume, sores to be applied, blistering cups to be attached. I came to look upon it as a long evening with a rest period right at the end – when we all went home. When the play opened, the production was not without its technical hitches – the vast golden silk traverse curtain was forever getting fouled up – but the response from the audience and most of the critics was thrilling, and each night we received an ovation. It proved to be the greatest stage success I'd ever had.

Bruce's health, like the King's, was deteriorating. He'd lost a quantity of weight and his energy level was disturbingly low. His legs were so spindly, it was almost as though someone had applied a pump to them and sucked out everything from within, leaving him with sagging folds where once there'd been solid flesh. He was persuaded to move house twice in quick succession, each time going where there were fewer stairs, and was on the lookout for a flat which would spare him too much maintenance as he was really too frail to cope. Much of the time he was in and out of hospital, the Mildmay Hospice, or staying with us in the country, and we were to find nursing him increasingly difficult. It was, in fact, during one of these enforced absences from his flat in Islington that it was burgled and some precious items were looted – oddments of antique porcelain or pottery he'd had for years or memorabilia – which would have meant nothing to a thief but a great deal to him. He took the news unexpectedly well, but he must have been hard pushed at times not to think that the whole world was against him. The last few months of his life were becoming more and more difficult for him to endure and distressing for his friends – we felt so powerless to help. He had shrunk to a shadow barely recognisable as the Bruce we once had known.

A short tour of *The Madness Of George III* around England was set up, taking me away from home, but, as Bruce was nearing the end, Trevor stepped into the breach to make sure all was well. The company was in Bradford but, not finding the hotels very congenial, I drove out into the beautiful countryside and rented a place on the outskirts of Ilkley, which proved ideal even though there was a lengthy haul to and from the theatre. One morning Trevor telephoned as usual (we've maintained this lifeline through the years wherever we've been in the world). Bruce had been unconscious when he'd arrived at the hospice, but after a quarter of an hour or so, Trevor looked up to find him staring at him very intently. He didn't appear to be threatened by this visitor, whoever he might be, but wasn't quite able to focus. When the mists had cleared Bruce suddenly said quite loudly but with a welcoming smile, 'Oh, hello. What are you doing here?' Trevor took his hand and held it for a short while – and that was how he died. It was ironic that Trevor should have been the last person to see him alive. I put down the phone and went for an aimless wander across the moors, not feeling very emotional but needing to be alone with my thoughts, feeling a huge relief for Bruce's sake that it was all over.

I'd spent over twenty-five years with him as my partner, most of which hadn't been what you might call easy. That he should have succumbed to HIV and spent the last section of his life so wretchedly I found heartbreaking, though, in a strange, perverse way – and Bruce was nothing if not perverse – the disease seemed to give him status. It established him as a member of a brotherhood, ended his feeling that he was out there on his own. He spoke with pride of the other patients, their stamina and their determination not to give in. His change of attitude was admirable and made me look at him with new eyes. The longer he'd suffered from HIV the higher up the ladder it lifted him. Horrible and degrading though it undoubtedly was, it finally gave Bruce a place in the sort of society into which he'd never before believed he was totally accepted. To begin with, he felt he was a pioneer in this scourge which was so afflicting the world, but, most particularly, he was now, really for the first time, one of the frontline troops in what was predominantly a 'gay' cause, he'd been over the top, and that made him feel prouder than he'd felt for a very long time . . .

It will be years I'm sure before I'll be able to shift all the images to the back of my mind. They're like polaroids which capture a moment and then, once the picture is established, there are no reassuring variations – that's it. Yet, with Bruce no longer around, however callous it may sound, Trevor and I, for the very first time, had been given our freedom. No longer would we be haunted by his reproof, no longer suffer that persistent guilty feeling that we hadn't seen enough of him, hadn't picked up the phone to speak to him for three days. Aware of my long association with the Christian Brothers, Bruce was expert at invoking this guilt. Yet even knowing the trap as we did, where it was and how it operated, we never failed to plonk ourselves down right in the middle of it and, once Bruce activated it, we'd disappear through it like a couple of floundering Demon Kings. But now it was time to put all that aside as best we could, and get on with our lives.

It was beginning to look as though we were going to have to move. I couldn't bear to think about it. We loved our home, had built up the garden from scratch, yet the prospect of a motorway service area within something like three hundred yards from where we lived was impossible to envisage. A monstrous cuckoo had chosen to dump itself in our nest and nothing was going to make it budge. Unfortunately for us, we were contesting one of the largest oil companies in the world which had big bucks in their sights. They were going to pull out all the stops. The obligatory public inquiry in the village hall ran its course like some absurd Ealing comedy. Tempers flared, key witnesses slept and the local headmaster, a jazz enthusiast, arrived with his colleagues to drum up attention, until rebuked by the Inspector for turning a serious matter into a circus. The opposition fielded a QC but we couldn't afford one so theirs walked all over our equivalent.

Christmas came and went . . . While we were awaiting the verdict, to our astonishment it was announced in the national press that our particular project had been sanctioned. In a fury, I telephoned the local Tory MP for an explanation. How could there be a decision when the results of the public inquiry wouldn't be known for another month? He went into a dither and eventually an adjournment debate was called at the House of Commons, which I and about four other people including a Deputy Speaker attended. A junior transport minister waffled on with grovelling reassurances to 'Sir Humphrey' that no decision had yet been reached. The press had jumped the gun, et cetera, et cetera. So, all in all, it cost Trevor and me in the region of £32,000 in legal fees, which we could ill afford, and we were going to have to look around for somewhere else to live, as well as losing on the sale of the house. I wonder what gave them the impression that we'd be voting Conservative at the next election?

For some weeks there had been rumours floating around that a film was to be made of *The Madness Of George III* so I encouraged my splendid and kindly agent of some thirty years' standing, Ken McReddie, to keep his ear to the ground as I didn't want another role I'd created going, like *Shadowlands*, to someone else without a struggle. Joel Silver, the Hollywood producer best known for his 'action' films, then approached him as to my availability for *Demolition Man*, due to star Sylvester Stallone and Wesley Snipes, offering me the bad guy. The film was a load of old hokum but quite promising with some witty lines. The futuristic theme was brilliantly realised and the characters quirky and out of the ordinary, so I accepted. The money was okay, though it wouldn't make me rich, but it was pointed out to me that it was virtually my first American movie and it was Stallone and Snipes who put bums on seats. Above all, I realised that, having no credibility in American films, doing this one might well swing the balance in my favour when the British producers were casting the part of 'George'.

As it turned out, it was a miserable experience. The egos of the two stars were irrepressible. I'd heard stories of what went on in the big studio films, but to see it on a daily basis was something new. Neither of them appeared interested in me or my background, and would keep everybody waiting on the set as a matter of course. Stallone, in particular, liked to parade around, with a large cigar jammed between his lips, cheerfully wisecracking, until dragged forcibly away by the ever-indulgent Joel Silver, who dressed in what appeared to be brown silk pyjamas.

Silver lived on junk food and had an obsession with Frank Lloyd Wright, the architect. In fact he owned one of his houses. He'd contrive to have as many as six arguments running at the same time, mobile phone to his ear, forefinger angrily stabbing the air. They wanted Sandra Bullock for the girl but, as she was busy on another film, they gave the job instead to Lori Petty, kept her on standby for six weeks, gave her costume fittings and make-up tests and then fired her. They had to pay her off, of course, but the story gives an indication of the ruthlessness attendant on those big-budget films. It didn't do to get on the wrong side of Joel Silver. In addition to these internal problems, the script was changing out of recognition, but I was powerless to do anything about it – a cipher. I counted the days to my return home to find there were rather more than I would have wished. I longed for the world I knew and understood. All I could do was keep reminding myself of the reason I was there. I wanted to play 'George III' in the film.

It so happened that I needn't have bothered. Alan Bennett let it be known that he wouldn't allow the film to be made unless I played the King and Nick Hytner directed. It would be his first film. If one film had been a grisly experience the next more than made up for it. There was, undoubtedly, a huge amount we had to achieve on a pretty small budget. It seemed so unfair. *Demolition Man* had a massive budget and precious little to justify it apart from some moderately funny lines, many of which were impossible to understand because of Stallone's delivery. (I used to keep my eyes on his lips. When they stopped moving, I knew it was my turn to speak.) Now, it was time to write off the Hollywood experience and look afresh at the future.

Alan Bennett's talent is prodigious and he is so intrinsically modest and original that were I to be given the opportunity of working with him every day for the rest of my life, I should think myself a very lucky man. When success is in the wind everything slips effortlessly into place. Which of us can boast total success? It would take a brave man or a foolish one to admit to being successful. If you're lucky, it's there for a while and then it goes. Sometimes precipitously, sometimes gradually – but it's inclined not to hang around. There had been no pattern to my career. It began slowly and inched forward in an encouraging way, then disconcertingly – for no apparent reason – it began to falter almost as though I were clinging to a greasy pole and kept slipping out of reach. And this seemed to be the norm until I was nearly fifty when things started to improve. Could I equate this change of direction in any way with the change in my emotional life? It almost exactly coincided with Trevor coming into my world, as though the happiness he brought me was the catalyst. People could see I was happy. They noticed the change in me. I like to think it was this that somehow pulled everything together.

I look back over what I've written, reflect on my first sniff of greasepaint as a schoolboy doing Gilbert and Sullivan, hear again (as I consistently do) Brother McEvoy's devastatingly negative appraisal of my future, wander through the years of bewilderment and despondency – my 'wilderness years' – and then become aware of something special happening to me when Trevor came along. And so to 'George'. Was this, I couldn't help wondering, as good as it would get? If so, I was content. If there was life after George that was fine. If not, that was fine by me too. My life seemed to have settled, and not before time, into something approaching contentment. It's just that my hope – and it's pure greed, I know – is that everything shouldn't just stop dead, even though it is buspass time and beyond; that it should go on a bit, just a little bit longer.

They'd extended the play's run yet again at the National and there was a tour planned to the States, Israel and Greece. In Boston, I gave a King George tea party at one of the hotels which I was assured was expert at English tea. Not the day we were there. It was a curious concept. They served the tea in pots, which was correct, though having the labels belonging to the teabags dangling over the side was less correct. It was English Breakfast, if I remember. Then they cleared it all away and brought on pots of Earl Grey. Then followed Lapsang Souchong, and so on down the line until they reached the herbals – pronounced without the 'h' in the American way – mint, jasmine, camomile and the rest, each with its identification label. Not that I'm telling the story out of malice or in an attempt to mock our American friends. It was just a novel way of doing things. In any case, I have no interest in the niceties of serving tea. As long as it's hot and quite strong I have no feelings about it. A cup of tea is a cup of tea.

That evening, despite the connotations of wicked King George and his treatment of the Colonies, we were given a standing ovation, which was to be the pattern in the weeks to come. Trevor had joined me and together we flew to Baltimore, while the rest of the company went to New York where we were playing a sometime opera house, the vast Brooklyn Academy of Arts. In Baltimore, they needed me to do some interviews as bookings were slow due to a shuffle-round of the theatre's management. Our flight was terrifying. It was the only one allowed out of Stamford, Connecticut that day. A cyclone was all around us and, as we pancaked down in Baltimore, it rained so heavily we couldn't get off the plane until people with umbrellas were sent across the tarmac, which was virtually a river, to rescue us. After the interview session, we were advised to go by train to New York because of the appalling weather conditions. On board the train, it was announced that the electricity supply had broken down due to the storm, so there was no heating or air conditioning and the train crawled along at a snail's pace. After a short while the lavatories began to smell. The atmosphere became insufferable. Every lady in the compartment reached into her handbag and the air was filled with the hiss of atomisers. It was with the greatest relief that we arrived safely at our destination and gulped down the invigoratingly clean, fresh air of Penn Central Station.

Israel I'd visited twice in the past, though it was always exciting to go back. We ventured into the Arab quarter where a small cave-like theatre was mounting a production considered very daring at the time. The play was *Romeo And Juliet* and an Israeli had fallen in love with an Arab. I had to make a speech wishing the production well, and knowing how volatile the situation was out there, that young couple certainly needed all the good will we could muster. Our coach driver, for example, wouldn't wait for us outside the theatre; we had to give him a time and he'd come back to fetch us. We played *The Madness Of George III* in Jerusalem where the reception was as enthusiastic as it was turning out to be wherever we went. On a day off, we were taken on a trip to Lake Tiberias, the Sea of Galilee, which was both evocative and moving. It was as though nothing had changed, and the easiest thing in the world was to put the time machine back two thousand years and imagine the same boats bobbing about on the water netting the so-called St Peter's fish with which, to this day, the lake abounds.

The making of the film *The Madness Of King George* turned out to be one of the happiest experiences of my life, much of it due to director Nick Hytner, whose flexibility and invention made his inexperience behind the camera of very little consequence. His first assistant, Mary Kenney, was a great help guiding him in the direction of the options open to him. Nick's willingness to be helped by others without being embarrassed or resentful endeared him to the crew, while his fondness for actors meant that approaching him with a problem, however small, meant that, whatever the pressures of the day, you had his undivided attention. Helen Mirren had been cast as the Queen and her choice proved an inspiration though, to be truthful, she was far too beautiful to play such a little dump who, judging by portraits of the time, looked more like a Pekinese. Ian Holm, my dear old friend from *Uncle Vanya* days at Hampstead, was wonderfully generous to me and really good as the manipulative Dr Willis, and we had the pleasure of Julian Wadham's company again, being in superb control as the younger Mr Pitt. Ken Adam, who was to win an Academy Award, was the designer and Mark Thompson, who had done the costumes in London, added his sure touch to the sumptuous visual effect. I could add to this list again and again – in fact, I shouldn't have begun it in the first place, as in such a powerful ensemble it's unfair to single anyone out, so let me stop there.

On the first day of the shoot, we were on location at Windsor Great Park where I was to do some riding. I'd ridden as a youngster in Cape Town but needed three or four refresher lessons, as the King was known to have been a brilliant horseman, riding on a regular basis from Windsor to Kew and back. It had been a very dry summer and the ground was like concrete but I was really looking forward to it. For some mysterious reason, we weren't allowed by the Crown to have a shot of the Castle, even in the background, so we had to add it in at a later date, which amounted to more or less the same thing. As it was, we could have filmed the sequences in any park in the world. I had to canter into shot and approach some farm buildings, one of which was a piggery. Time and again my horse refused. It being Nick's first day as well, he was understandably nervous and hissed at me through gritted teeth, 'I thought you said you could ride!' We did it again. And again. It was only on the following day that we were told that horses had a natural antipathy to pigs and that, in fact, we were extremely lucky to get the shot in at all. It was also pointed out that it was probably unwise to have scheduled the scene at the piggery (and another scene where I had a race with one of the equerries) on the very first day, as no protective headgear was possible because of my wig. The miracle was that we survived and even the look of panic on my face as my horse suddenly swerved is there on film to add a touch of authenticity.

Filming near Arundel, and the weather being particularly balmy, a group of us decided to go skinny-dipping one night after we'd 'wrapped' – though an extended visit to the pub beforehand proved to be not such a good idea. I remember swimming out to one of the groynes and the water being wonderfully warm, so much so that I lay back on the pebbles under the stars and drifted off to sleep. I'm unclear as to how I got back to the hotel and into bed, but the next morning, on passing Reception, I was told that there was a package for me. There was only one item in the envelope – my underpants.

Altogether it was a very happy shoot. Sam Goldwyn Junior, who was our chief producer, flew over from Hollywood to see how it was all going and began a friendship which I value enormously. Now he and his wife Peggy come to visit when they're in England, and always entertain me lavishly when I'm in Los Angeles. But, like all good things, the film had to end, and I was left with a sackload of memories, and the strong feeling that if I could do the whole thing again from the beginning I'd be a very happy man.

Our lighting man on the theatre tour was Brian Ridley and, on our return, he was to die suddenly and tragically from cancer. He was a gentle man, excellent at his job, and his death shocked us all. I went to a memorial gathering at the National Theatre, a day when something unexpected happened to me which was to have a number of startling repercussions. Barely was the ceremony finished than someone rushed over, taking me to one side. It transpired that I'd been nominated for an Academy Award for *The Madness Of King George*, as the film was now called, due to the fact that Americans reading 'George III' might feel they'd missed out on the previous editions (rather like 'Rocky II' and 'Rambo IV'). It was my suggestion that the new title might be proposed to Alan Bennett, who was perfectly all right about it, while the Americans were equally satisfied, as they could be certain that the story was about a King rather than Stallone.

In no time at all there was someone from the press, and attention was rather cruelly diverted from Brian's memorial to the nomination. The furore kept up for a while, and when the itinerary was being planned, it was decreed that Trevor would be with me, and an old friend, Loretta Swit – 'Hot-Lips' in *M.A.S.H.* – decided she wanted to join us. Unfortunately, only two seats were allotted to each nominee. Trevor very generously said that we couldn't expect her to sit at the back of the Shrine Auditorium, which is vast. He would go to the back and she could sit next to me in the seats allotted to nominees – usually aisle seats so that you're accessible if required. I flatly refused and wrote to Loretta explaining the situation and asking her whether she'd mind sitting at the back. She replied equally generously that of course I should sit beside Trevor. It all worked out in the end as they managed to find an extra seat at the front, so that's where we ended up, with Loretta in the middle. I was exhausted before it had even begun.

The time for travelling to the Oscars was drawing near. I was as nervous as a kitten but interviews still had to be done and the Goldwyn publicity people rang, as they were doing almost on a daily basis. I was asked whether I'd do an interview with an American journal called *The Advocate*. I said I didn't know the publication and they told me it was for the gay community. I said I was interviewed out and would it be all right if I refused? They answered that it had only a small circulation and that the interview wouldn't therefore be important. After several more attempts, the magazine rang me a couple of days later at home. I don't know where they got my number. The young lady was very persuasive. I asked whether she'd mind if I put some questions to her, the first being, 'Have you got a relationship yourself?' She said she had. She told me it was with another woman. I then told her that Trevor and I had been together for nearly twenty years and that, were I to agree to the interview, I hoped she'd respect that fact. She told me she would. That was just over a week before the Oscar ceremony, which took place on a Monday. On the Wednesday prior to our departure – we went on the Friday – the shit hit the fan.

On the Tuesday evening, a journalist had arrived at the house, having read the *Advocate* interview, and spoke to Trevor. I was staying in London that night as on the Wednesday I had interviews right through the day. I woke up in the hotel to realise that Trevor and I were all over the papers. And not just the tabloids, either – and some of the headlines were cheap, not to say disgraceful. I phoned Trevor in alarm to be told by him that there was a huge queue of press cars lined up our drive, that the journalists had been hammering on the door and shouting through the letterbox since daybreak. I had to hang up as I was being summoned to my first interview, but there was more to come. Even with such a smattering of information about what was being said about us, I was careful to request each of the interviewers throughout the day not to ask questions about my private life, but without exception each of them did. I fielded the probes with as much sense of humour as I could and, on conferring at a much later date with Trevor, found that he'd done the same. But there were cameramen and journalists everywhere, scampering about the garden, rattling the windows, refusing to leave until Trevor gave them a story.

'There IS no story!' he kept yelling. 'Go away!' To this day I haven't been able to work out what the fuss was all about.

We had always treated the press with great courtesy, always made a point of going together to public functions. They had cabinets full of pictures of the two of us arriving at BAFTA, the Olivier and Evening Standard awards, which we've done through the years. They knew perfectly well that there wasn't a story. This wasn't a sudden revelation. In any case, why should the fact that two men in their late middle age – I was pushing seventy and Trevor fourteen years my junior, neither exactly love's young dream – be a news item in that connotation unless the papers were particularly bereft of something to fill up the columns? It was simply to do with the Oscar nominations, though what possible connection my private life should have was beyond me.

It was a long, tiring and frightening day. My last interview was at London Weekend Television and going out 'live'. Pretending to take the barrage of questions about my private life seriously, I suddenly said, 'There is something that I've never told anyone. That's because it's so private. But, in view of the personal slant the interview has taken, I feel it would be in order for me to mention it. Would that be all right?' The interviewer, whose blushes I'll spare by not naming, looked uneasy. 'What sort of thing is it?' she wanted to know. 'Well, it's very personal, but your viewers would be the first to know. May I talk about it?' After a good deal of shuffling about, looking uncertain and embarrassed, she agreed. Dropping my voice to the merest whisper, I leaned forward and confided in her, 'I've got a hole in my right sock.' She threw back her head and, in the relief of the moment, let out a great whoop of laughter. The atmosphere had lost its tension. It was time to go home.

Trevor had calmed down considerably since the last time we'd managed to speak, but there were stories to tell by the hundred. Four hefty security guards had been hired by Ken McReddie to ward off intruders, and by early evening there wasn't a journalist to be seen. The whirlwind events of the day had left us totally shattered. The evening paper followed the pattern of the rest and there were dozens of messages from well-wishers and friends, sympathetic, outraged on our behalf and angry. In a short while, it was time to set all that aside and get ready to go to the Oscars.

We were trailed all the way to Heathrow by our heavy mob, checked in at the back of the car park and smuggled in through a side door. It was all very cloak and dagger, but once the plane took off for Los Angeles we felt a great weight had been lifted from our shoulders. It was very disheartening to have all this happen on the eve of what should have been one of the most exciting moments of my life. After all, it's not every day you get an Oscar nomination. At least, in America, these issues don't carry the same weight they do in England, so Trevor and I could settle back in our business class seats and look forward to a few nights at the Peninsula Hotel in Beverly Hills.

The 'Junior' suite set aside for us was a little on the cramped side, but it would do for the short time we were there. I hung up my brand new Versace dinner jacket which had been presented to me for the occasion, hoping that the rather naff tie I'd brought wouldn't let it down too badly, and we started to meet up with all the Goldwyn publicity people and, of course, Trevor's and my wonderful agent, Ken, who had flown out especially for the occasion. We had allowed ourselves a couple of days to get acclimatised so, nervous as I was, I settled down with the rest of our party to get rid of jet lag and have a good time.

And what an evening the Oscar ceremony proved to be. I think it occurred to a number of us as we took our seats and star spotted that Tom Hanks was a likely winner, not just because of the enormous popularity of his film *Forrest Gump*, but because his seat was ideally placed for easy access to the stage. Whereas the rest of us were spread across the first half dozen rows, his seat was plumb in the middle. All he had to do when the winner was announced was get up, climb three or four low steps, extended his hand, kiss the presenter, wait for silence and then start to blub. Trevor made my favourite comment of the evening. As Hanks's name was announced he leaned across Loretta to say to me, 'What a relief!' I think Loretta was quite shocked, but I knew exactly what he meant. Knowing that several million people would be watching, apart from the six thousand which the Shrine Auditorium held, and the fact that every star you'd ever seen or read about seemed to be there, was a nerve-racking experience to say the least.

One of the mistakes it is possible to make during the length of an extremely long evening is to go to the loo – especially if the time you pick is within forty minutes or so of your particular category being called. A call of nature at this particular juncture is understandable – this is when the bladder is at its most unreliable, when you're very nervous. I decided to risk it, and in no time at all relief was provided, sandwiched between the likes of Steve Martin and Arnold Schwarzenegger (not a lot of room). So far so good.

What you don't know is that there is a battalion of 'seat fillers' ready to deputise for you, and that the moment you go, one of them will slip effortlessly into the seat you've vacated so that at no time would the Auditorium look less than crammed to the rafters. The 'seat fillers' are well dressed and well paid and, of course, get a free ticket for the show. When you return from the loo it all goes wrong. Regardless of whether or not your nomination is imminent, nobody is allowed to move until the commercial break. You stand in the aisle and wait. As the programme slips effortlessly into the break, you race down to where you think you were sitting. The man (or woman) in your chair will be wearing a necklace with a label identifying him or her. The label will be swung round to the back for easy reading. It then takes only a few seconds to regain your seat, at the end of which you are both exhausted and bursting for another pee.

After the ceremony, when we were desperate for something to eat and drink, a disembodied voice advised us to remain in our seats until we were called through to the Governor's Ball in an adjacent building. After about half an hour, we noticed a group of people gathering on the low stage, just standing round chattering. Assuming these to be guests for the Governor's Ball, we joined them. For nearly an hour, our queue began to snake around the huge stage. We'd obviously picked the right thing to do. After a while we went through a rather grubby pass door plastered with playbills, only to find we had travelled in a complete circle, and that we were back where we had started.

There were the endless parties to latch on to if you found the Governor's Ball too noisy – which we did. The room was bristling with stars and not only did I get the chance to meet some of them but quite a few said 'You was robbed', which was reassuring. I was so fascinated to be talking to Jodie Foster that I stupidly overlooked the fact that in order for food to be served to you, you first had to sit in your allotted seat. So, by the time we decided to leave, which was in the early hours of the morning, none of us had eaten and our eardrums were near to bursting. Shuffling through my pockets which were crammed with invitations, we decided to go to the Vanity Fair party, having first of all to get past the line of journalists lined up outside. ITN, the only English company represented, having sworn blind that they wouldn't refer to my private life, used that as their second question. Fortunately, I'd learnt a trick. If you're asked a question, the camera won't be on the interviewer but on you, so that you can answer however you like. I thanked the man for his congratulations and warm thoughts about the film, smiled graciously to all the people back home, and moved on down the line. They could only screen what they saw. Once inside the building, we managed to find a waiter and asked for some food. It was then 2.30 a.m. He shook his head sadly. It had all gone. Loretta, Trevor and

I wound up in the kitchens, picking cold bits of pizza off used plates. So much for glamour.

If the 'outing' had done anything, it had established the fact in both Trevor's and my mind that nothing had really changed. We were the same people as we were a week before, and in fact a lot of the gay community seemed to look up to us. It was apparently unusual for a nominee to invite his 'boyfriend'. I hadn't done it in any spirit of bravado but because it's what we always did. We always went to functions together. The gay community apparently thought this was something special, and I must confess to feeling proud that our contribution, however innocent, had the seal of approval.

Back in London, still apprehensive about how we would be accepted now that everybody knew what they had already known, I had to present an Olivier Award at the Shaftesbury Theatre. I needn't have lost any sleep over it, the audience roared its welcome. There were still press chasing us through the streets, and a few days later at the Cannes Film Festival, where we were in competition, the same old faces turned up. Helen Mirren couldn't be there to collect her Best Actress award so, in a difficult moment, I collected it for her, immediately following Jonathan Pryce's acceptance speech (he won for *Carrington*, pipping me at the post). Once the Cannes Festival was over, peace was restored and, award-less but proud of our achievement, we flew back across the Channel, eager to pick up the threads and see our dogs, walk round the garden, phone some friends and, generally speaking, get back to the land of the living.

15

Secret Marriage

In one of her more reckless moods, my old friend Thelma Holt suggested I direct a play for her in the West End. I had relished directing in the past as I enjoy exploring a text and finding alternative ways of doing things. Design and composition fascinate me too and I like it when actors are cast against type and can be encouraged to give something which to them is uncharacteristic – besides, acting is generally so uncreative. In addition, I had a play up my sleeve called *The Clandestine Marriage*, which hadn't been done for some time and was a cheerful, sometimes hilarious and often poignant story of New Money trying to marry into the aristocracy. There were no particular contemporary angles or social messages which would throw new light on this particular neck of the late eighteenth century woods, just a 'feel-good' comedy written by George Coleman the Elder and the famous actor, David Garrick, with some rattling good parts and amusing situations. I baulked, however, at the suggestion that I should direct as well as playing Lord Ogleby, a raddled octogenarian half-buried in cosmetics and at saturation point with his daily intake of restorative tonics – in other words a crumbling ruin of aches and pains. Unfortunately, the directors we went after were all busy and, because time refused to be on our side, I found myself agreeing to being a one-man-band – though with a number of misgivings.

With the help of Thelma's team of wily conspirators, I assembled a splendid cast headed by Christopher Benjamin as Mr Sterling, and Susan Engel as his wealthy sister, constantly threatening to withdraw her substantial share of the money.

Tim O'Brien designed models of the frivolous sets very much as he wanted rather than as I had envisaged, playing up the side which would most happily show off his costumes but curiously giving the vulgar angle (vital to the play) a wide berth – and however deviously I tried to manipulate him he was intractable. I realised later that I should have laid down the law more firmly, but he was a reputable designer and I couldn't help hoping that if I gave him his head he'd come up with something good, even though it might not tally with my own concept. And so, to a certain extent, it turned out. His costumes were ablaze with colour and greatly enhanced by the simplicity around them. If I had a criticism it would be that by opting for good taste he missed out on a lot of the fun he could have had. I took one of the interior scenes in which the glories of the garden are extolled and set it outdoors, dressing some members of the cast as figures of topiary, which I don't think they enjoyed very much, and asking them to carry about light, oblong frames closely interwoven with greenery to simulate hedging. It meant that, once on the stage, I could move them about at will, suggesting alternative sections of the garden – and also add to the fun. My hero for many years, the artist Ronald Searle, designed a superbly witty poster for us of Lord Ogleby at his most decrepit, and soon this was to leer down at the crowds in Shaftesbury Avenue.

But first, our pre-London dates. In Bath, the show was a triumph and, as we ticked off the touring dates in the approach to our opening at the Queen's Theatre, it was looking increasingly likely that we had a hit on our hands. Enter the critics. Apparently they objected to my stepping out of line. I was either an actor or a director, I couldn't be both. Having their censure cast a bit of a blight on the run, although audiences had a really good night out and at each performance the reaction was very much what we had hoped. We ran our allotted 'season' and even made some money – not the cast, I hasten to add, but the investors – yet I would always be disappointed at the critics' reaction and aware that it was coming up to my turn for them to 'have a go'. After the success of *The Madness Of George III* they wanted me to go one better. This trivial comedy, mounted on a shoestring, didn't fit the bill. Yet, I shan't bury my head in my hands in remorse at having let everybody down. I was sure we had delivered the goods, provided an evening both comic and poignant, and been truthful to the play. But there was a warning note reverberating in the air which I found distinctly unsettling.

A director who had seen the play on tour contacted me wanting to turn it into a film. I warned him that, despite the success of *George*, plays very seldom made the transition into another medium, but he persisted. Trevor volunteered to write the screenplay. The two got along famously, and the director was most enthusiastic about the draft Trevor presented him. They were both experienced in their field. Trevor's previous film adaptation (made for Miramax) had been *A Month By The Lake* from a short story by H.E. Bates which had starred Vanessa Redgrave, Edward Fox and Uma Thurman. Although both of us had reservations about the way the film turned out, it had some excellent reviews and was also considerably admired in America. The director-to-be of our picture, *The Clandestine Marriage*, had made a couple of films of international repute which we liked very much, and, with a producer in tow holding tightly to the strings of a modest purse, everything looked very much as though it might be going ahead.

I did a bit of commuting over to America and back to make a handful of independent films, also one in South Africa directed by Arthur Penn of *Bonny And Clyde* fame, which unfortunately weren't picked up by the distributors and ended up on television. Actors have often said that if you get a major award, or even a nomination (as I had), you're quite likely never to work again. Mercifully, in my case this hasn't happened, but the work I was being offered fell short of the top bracket . . . The money was just adequate, but the scripts, despite the very best of intentions all round, lacked popular appeal, chasing instead after the 'worthy'. This doesn't mean they weren't enjoyable to make – independent films are usually more fun than the studio films – but you have to have the gods smiling on you if you want a success.

We began to think more seriously about *The Clandestine Marriage*, even though the money wasn't in place. The director knew a mutual friend of ours, Joan Collins, and offered her the very showy part of Mrs Heidelberg, and she and her boyfriend, Robin, went with us to dinner at the Ivy to celebrate. We were both very fond of Joan and Robin, surprising friends, as we led such very different lives. Our friendship began when I was doing *The Madness Of George III* on the stage and they invited me to dinner after the performance. They asked if the National ever gave me time off, and when I said they did, they invited me to spend a few days at their magnificent home near St Tropez. Jumping in at the deep end, I asked whether I could bring Trevor. Without hesitation, never having met him, they agreed . . .

A date was arranged and Robin picked us up at Nice airport. It's a long journey, but by the time we got to their house nestling in the hills among the pine trees with its incomparable views and superbly tasteful décor, we had become friends. It was of the greatest possible disappointment to us when some years later Joan left Robin. In so many ways he was ideal for her. He seemed to be there for life, except that it didn't work out that way. But all was happiness when we dined that evening at the Ivy – though something odd did occur.

The manager of the Ivy, full of apologies, came over with a note for me from one of the patrons. It was just somebody being complimentary so I asked who it was in order that I could thank them. Joan very sensibly said, 'Don't get involved – just leave it.' I ignored the advice, saying, 'You never know. He may invest in movies.' When I returned to the table, I said,

'You'll never believe this – he invests in movies!' The next morning, we posted Trevor's adaptation to him, and less than a week later he responded, saying he was jubilant about the script, and offered to invest three point five million pounds. Seldom can so handsome a deal have been reached over so casual a dinner.

On the strength of this windfall, the smile on our producer's face broadened considerably, the strain left his eyes and wheels were set in motion. I wish I could report that there was a happy ending to all this, however. Enough money arrived for the costumes to be made, so the cast was shunted down to Stanway House in Gloucestershire to begin the shoot. But the rest of the money – the other three million – mysteriously did not arrive. For four weeks we kept going while to the left and right of us the cheques were bungee jumping like mad.

Late one Friday afternoon, the cast and crew convened in Stanway's great hall in the presence of the BECTU official, the union representative. It was unanimously agreed by the crew that, as the film was half-finished, people would have a far better chance of getting at least some of their money if they carried on and completed the job. I felt hugely proud of them. After that, my admiration for film crews leapt ahead. Despite the filthy weather, the mud and the total absence of money – the hotels were threatening to throw people out into the streets unless they paid up (including Miss Collins, which didn't go down well at all) – they were prepared to stick it out. Never before had I known a crew show such loyalty. Without this and a willingness to carry on regardless, we certainly would never have finished.

A week later, again on a Friday evening, our producer telephoned to say that a further batch of cheques had bounced and that unless I personally could invest £50,000 by lunchtime on Monday he would withdraw the film. Taking a very deep breath, I phoned the bank manager first thing and found him to be affable, extremely sympathetic and helpful. Late that morning, leaving me with a fat overdraft, a car was winging its way down to Gloucestershire with the loot. The caterers were able to pay for the vegetables, petrol for the courtesy cars, and a number of the hotel bills. Sighs of relief all round. But before very long the well was on its last drip before running dry. Joan Collins came over in her high wig, her frills and her furbelows to say 'well done' to Trevor and me and, to our astonishment and delight, added to the donation with a considerably larger one of her own, then her agent put in a hefty sum and so, by some miracle, we finished the film (and – surprise, surprise – even got back our money).

We were invited to see a rough cut. It was quite frankly awful. Slow, unfunny – visually quite splendid – but too many non-sequiturs and a stack of unfunny sight gags which seemed to have no foundation. We had our say and were invited to see another cut, a third and a fourth, and there seemed, despite the suggestions we all made, no perceptible change from one cut to the next. They were all so lifeless. Because we had invested in the film, Trevor and I were now considered part of the production team so that our opinions were sought on what improvements, if any, should be made. The director was about to go to Africa where he was beginning another picture, so I had a deputation from the management knocking at my door proposing that I should take over the editing of *The Clandestine Marriage*.

I was both flattered and terrified. I had some ideas about how to make certain scenes work better than they were, but I'd never edited before in my life. However, they seemed to think I had a good grasp of what was required so, finally, I was let loose. Every day, Trevor and I drove out to Twickenham Studios, trawled through the miles of film we had shot and began to recut and reshape it. It proved to be the most riveting experience and I relished every second of it. But the massive stumbling block of not having enough coverage hit us again and again. 'There must be some more footage!' I'd yell. 'Well, there isn't.' We did the best we could, stealing from other scenes, trying to cover with music and sound effects but, quite simply, not enough had been shot, and that was that. The film wasn't a write-off, but it was both frustrating and heartbreaking. However, if the material isn't there, you can't conjure it out of thin air, and as the coffers had run dry there was no more money to reshoot stuff that was clearly needed.

We were due to be screened at the Cannes Film Festival, though not in competition. Having completed the edit, it was with great trepidation that we flew out for the viewing. The cinema was packed, and there was friendly applause at the end. We filed out into the street, heading for the statutory producer's party. Suddenly a man we had never seen before began whistling the theme song from the film. It's a particularly haunting tune and we all stopped in our tracks to listen, the streets with their tall buildings acting as an echo-chamber. Seeing he'd engaged our attention, he smiled and went on whistling. As he got to the end, we applauded and waved at him. He waved back before turning a corner and disappearing from sight. This fleeting moment of contact between film-makers and audience lifted our spirits. To each of us who had invested so much time, hope and invention into the picture, it was an incident we would never forget.

It would seem as though I'd run into the doldrums. Nothing I'd touched lately had a good feel about it. Were the good times also the times when things didn't last? On top of everything, things at home were worrying. Trevor had been for a check-up and was told he had inherited a rare form of muscular dystrophy. His mother had died as a result of it, his sister, uncle and cousin all suffered from it. The specialist told him that there was no treatment and no cure. Nor had we any idea how it would manifest itself. His eyelids were becoming so droopy it was as though they weren't strong enough to keep his eyes open. A shiver passed through our house on receipt of the news, and we both believed for a while that it was the end of the world. What was it we had done to turn the gods against us? In moments of crisis, fortunately our resilience stands us in good stead though we knew we'd have a fight on our hands should the condition advance with any alacrity.

After an emotional week, things settled down again. Trevor discussed with the specialist the idea of the eyelids being lifted. Perfectly possible with minor surgery, involving strings attached to the eyelids being passed through the forehead. It all sounded pretty grisly, but Trevor was prepared to go through with it and, in due course, it was done, was not unsightly and helped immeasurably. We discussed each step of the way honestly and sensibly – nothing was withheld. We knew that we had one another and that the support we gave could only strengthen us through whatever troubles or crises should present themselves. It wouldn't be long before that strength would be called upon to steer us through a catalogue of shockwaves, the like of which neither of us had ever encountered before.

David Mamet asked me to play Arthur Winslow in his film of *The Winslow Boy*. When I had recovered my breath I accepted, but I could hardly believe what I'd heard. Mamet and Rattigan! I was intrigued that so modern and abrasive a writer and director should want to adapt and direct a Terence Rattigan play, but my apprehensions were without foundation. He did it beautifully with full respect to Rattigan – not a word out of place – as well as creating a loving evocation of the period with its Edwardian standards of social behaviour and passionate feelings towards women's suffrage. I was fortunate to have Gemma Jones playing my wife, David's enchanting wife Rebecca Pigeon as my militant daughter, and playing the silky-smooth barrister was that fine actor Jeremy Northam, who stepped in neatly to steal the film.

After *The Madness Of George III* and all its associations with

King Lear a number of people had tried to push Shakespeare's great tragedy in my direction as a future project, and I'd managed to fend them off as gently as I could. I said it was too near *George*, that I wasn't sure I wanted to undertake anything quite as strenuous, that theatre and I had rather fallen out anyway, and I had decided that I enjoyed film-making. Besides, the exertion of playing that massive role for a long period – it's never just a short spurt – was too daunting even to think about. In addition, the play had problems, particularly in the first scene where the King's relationship with his favourite daughter takes a nose-dive for no discernible reason. In any case (I had considered the cons as I had weighed the pros), I've never quite been convinced that the old boy was a tyrant. Every time I've seen the play there's a lot of ranting and raving which hasn't persuaded me. I can't find a reference to it in the text. Isn't it more interesting when a normally reasonable man begins to behave uncharacteristically? But, before I allowed myself to be talked into it, which I could feel was happening, I had to be sensible – no. The answer was no. I didn't think *King Lear* was a good idea for me. Too many inconsistencies, too many problems – yes, that was it. Too many problems, but thanks all the same.

That highly eminent theatre and occasional film director, Peter Brook, now stationed in Paris, where he operates one of the most beautiful theatres I've ever seen in my life, telephoned out of the blue. We'd bumped into each other through the years, though I'd never worked for him. 'I'm about to offer you,' he announced in his precise voice, the words carefully chosen, 'the most exciting job of your life.' My reply was, I hoped, similarly in control. 'May I ask what it is?' 'No, you may not. I'll tell you when the time is right,' he replied mysteriously and not a little brusquely, the schoolmaster with the pupil.

A few days later he elucidated. It was a film to be called *I Am A Phenomenon* about a Russian Jew who had a phenomenal memory – in fact he employed mnemonics, a system I've used myself on occasion, particularly during the *Yes, (Prime) Minister* series when I had one of my complex speeches. I would use images to conjure up the phrase for which I was searching. Shereshevsky, the phenomenon in question, could remember huge passages even though he'd learnt them once perhaps as long as fifteen years previously. He also suffered from synesthesia, a heightening of the senses, which exaggerates sound and light to a degree which would be unbearable to most people. They put him on the halls as a turn for a while, but then he and his family decided to emigrate to America where he was taken up by the renowned neuro-psychologist, A.R. Luria, who was much intrigued by this naïve but unique man.

Once while I was in New York, Peter, armed with his camcorder and wearing his research baseball cap, took me down to Brighton Beach to observe the Russians who live there. We strolled along the promenade, ate in a Russian restaurant, took lots of pictures of me mingling with Russians ambling along the seafront, and I did my best in a short space of time to immerse myself in their way of life, without giving the impression of staring. Back in London Peter, his collaborator Marie-Helene and I frequently met and there were numerous occasions when we would research the scientific explanations for Shereshevsky's problems. Then Peter talked to me about casting. He began looking around for someone to play the neuro-psychologist – Paul Scofield, who turned it down, being first choice. He then jumped to the South African playwright, Athol Fugard, who was brought over to New York for discussions – but that didn't work out either, so there was an even more eccentric leap to Woody Allen. Unfortunately, the evening chosen for our meeting (and the only one possible) was the night Woody Allen played jazz, so that fell through. And so we went on, though I have to confess that some of the suggestions bordered on the absurd.

Then the money fell through as money does, and the film

had to be cancelled. However, Peter had no intention of giving up and persuaded Trevor Nunn to run it as a stage play in the Cottesloe Theatre at the National. I wasn't too happy about this, but Peter dangled the carrot of turning it into a film at a later stage in front of my nose, so I found myself agreeing.

One morning, I was working away in my office when the phone rang. It was Peter. Would I meet him at two o'clock at the Round House in Camden Town as there was something he wanted me to see? I was under the impression that the Round House had been out of commission for some time. Besides, I lived in the country so it was highly inconvenient for me to come into London at such short notice. But, because it was Peter, I went.

I was first there and waited outside where there were some Portakabins used, I think, as the box office and for various other administrative purposes. Peter arrived and, having introduced me to a young man he described as the director, led the way from the light into the dark . . . Occupying the entire central section of the Round House was a huge, white plastic bouncy castle. The young director led us to the 'drawbridge' and we were invited to remove our shoes and, in our stockinged feet, Peter and I solemnly climbed the ramp. Music, quite loud music, filled the whole area. Peter Brook and I stood alone in our socks on the base of the bouncy castle. I watched him carefully as I wasn't sure what was expected of me. Suddenly, Peter started to jump. Well, it was more of a self-conscious spring than a jump. He was very stiff, arms by his side, his face betraying no emotion at all. Still watching him, I followed suit. Every so often, Peter threw himself with some caution and the minimum of abandon against the white, plastic battlements and then back to base with a meticulous hop. Not a word was spoken. He just fastened his ice-blue eyes on mine as together we solemnly bounced up and down. I was fairly certain that he expected some kind of reaction from me but decided to play it safe by staring back, confidently radiating an inner assurance.

Finally, with the merest suggestion of an oriental bow, Peter indicated that he'd had enough. Together we returned down the ramp of the 'drawbridge' and replaced our shoes. As we left the Round House, our eyes screwed up against the bright light outside, Peter turned to me to say, 'That was interesting, wasn't it?' 'Yes,' I replied. 'Very.' And I meant it. Then I made my way home to East Hertfordshire. To this day, no further reference to our experience on the white, plastic bouncy castle at the Round House has ever been made.

I remember, some years ago, the first reading of a repertory production of Pinter's *The Caretaker* in which I was cast as 'Aston'. As we turned back the first few pages of notes, including Pinter's CV, the director announced to a startled cast, 'Now, as you all know, this is a play about Jesus Christ.' The silence which followed was every bit as full of meaning as one of Harold's own. Yet, under such circumstances, you have only two options – get up and go home, or be patient and hope the director will return to his senses. In fifty years as an actor, I have come up against many moments of this kind, each of which I've dealt with in the way I thought appropriate, but as long as a sense of humour is not far away, you're in with a chance. Otherwise you're in for a wretched time. Besides, for all I knew, Pinter may well have written the role with the Son of God in mind.

As Peter's film had capsized, I accepted a job on a film in Paris. It was the children's story, *Madeline*, and, being immediately before Christmas, Paris was looking at its most enchanting. Huge branches painted white and covered with tiny lights were dotted everywhere. I invited Peter and Marie-Helene round to my hotel for some champagne, then took them to dinner. He asked whether I'd care to see *L'homme Qui*, his current production. Shamefully, I arrived at the theatre only just in time as I'd got on the wrong train, and felt very embarrassed seeing the two of them standing in the vestibule nervously awaiting my arrival, and itching to go home. The beauty of the theatre took my breath away, though Peter's production lacked his old theatrical flair. It was sparse and functional – a modern office block lifted up and lowered into the Sistine Chapel. The scenes were short, meticulously handled and, in order to move on to the following scenes, the actors had to pick up their chairs and rearrange them to give the impression of a change of location. It was a technique very much in vogue during the latter part of the Sixties at the Royal Court and had the effect of making the play seem interminable and dated.

Afterwards, I went backstage to pay my respects to the cast. They asked me what I was up to, the question every actor asks another. I told them about *Madeline* and then mentioned that I was to do Peter's project, *I Am A Phenomenon*. To my amazement, I was told they had already begun rehearsals on that in French and it would be performed in the very theatre in which we were then standing. I was flabbergasted. The reason I had wanted to do *I Am A Phenomenon* was because I was excited by the prospect of creating a major role alongside him, a director with whom I'd always wanted to work. I wasn't happy about just being slotted in to do the English translation in London. I wanted to be in at the beginning – the exchange of ideas, the intrigue of all the technical effects, the welding of the research with the text. To say that I was bitterly disappointed is an understatement, and I withdrew from the project.

One day, I was writing some letters in my office back in England when the phone rang. It was the artistic director of the Royal Shakespeare Company, Adrian Noble, telephoning from New York. Would I play Lear for the RSC, its millennium production, to run over a six-month period, opening in Japan, playing a month at the Barbican in London and then up to Stratford to finish in February? It was all a bit much to absorb, but in my head I ran it over and over and over again. Arguably Shakespeare's greatest play, over the millennium, my first time at Stratford, I wasn't far off the right age, strong enough to carry the heftiest of Cordelias and, if I was thinking of retiring from the theatre after fifty years' service, what better vehicle to choose for an exit? With these thoughts and a million others racing through my head, I'd forgotten to ask the name of the director!

It turned out to be Ninagawa, Japan's most celebrated interpreter of Shakespeare. As I'd suspected, my old sparring partner Thelma Holt, a Japan-enthusiast, was in there somewhere plotting and conniving. Trevor and I discussed the offer in detail and it seemed as though the opportunity was too good to miss so I accepted. I had a whole year to prepare, so I jumped into my car and eliminated from every bookshop within miles anything remotely to do with *King Lear*. Each day, whenever I was, whatever I was doing, I worked on *King Lear*, gradually learning it, trying to unravel some of the conundrums which had so often beset me. One thing I simply couldn't get out of my mind was a little woodcut left me by my beloved grandmother which I have in my spare room. Like a photograph left in the sun, I don't even know whether the colours are accurate any longer. I've owned it for fifty years and heaven knows how long my grandmother had it before then. Since she'd been a student, I supposed. It is a storm scene by Hiroshige, the great Japanese artist. Lashing rain. People with umbrellas struggling to force their way through diagonal lengths of string, or so they seem, representing the atrocious weather.

Ninagawa came over to London and, through an interpreter, we discussed some of the ideas he had for the production. He let me have his drawing of the set. It didn't mean very much at that stage, apart from the fact that there were small circular objects littering the ground which he identified as rocks. I asked their function, but as yet he was undecided and deflected the question with a good deal of smiling and bowing. He was an extremely likeable man and I thought there was a good chance that we'd work well together. Later, my mentor Joan Littlewood was to reprimand me for what she thought was my folly in choosing a director whose first language was not English. But at the time I felt that it was essential simply to have a bottomless pit of ideas, an open mind and a wealth of imagination. After all, the days before directors came on the scene are not all that distant. Our predecessors were perfectly happy to work out their interpretations for themselves, in fact they wouldn't have had it any other way, would have thought it impertinent if anyone had tried to advise them. The actors helped one another. Nowadays we are blessed with a tremendous variety of textual guidance from the vast number of editions and books of reference there are of every Shakespearean play in the canon. If Ninagawa had a poor grasp of English, well, mine of Japanese wasn't any better, and if anything went disastrously wrong, we'd have the paternal, richly experienced, solid and dependable shoulder of the RSC upon which to lean – or so we thought.

The months seemed to skid by. It would be totally correct to say that I was very nervous. My director, after all, was in Tokyo and I wasn't. Should I need to communicate, I had to do so by letter or fax. Long pages of suggestions and theorising carefully written so that a child could understand passed between our home in Hertfordshire and the Saitama Arts Centre where we were to perform. One theory I came up with for explaining the King's mood in the first scene was the death of the Queen – Queen Lear. Not a character who normally features. There must have been one. Perhaps her coffin could dominate the stage, everyone in mourning, then the rows between the King and Kent and the King and Cordelia would take place across this omnipresent symbol of grief, which would better explain the emotional and irrational behaviour of the King. No, thought David Hunt, the young assistant from the RSC, the scene was celebratory. It concerned the betrothal of the King's favourite daughter. He was adamant, so the idea was scrapped, although I must confess to having had a secret liking for it. Besides, the theory might have been helpful in our struggle to find a way through the first scene in particular. I don't suppose Ninagawa would have minded either way. I was starting to edge closer to the suspicion that the King's madness was some form of senile dementia, which began to manifest itself at the beginning and then gradually took hold.

The first day of rehearsal was upon us. The RSC had granted us a room at the Barbican for three days before we went to Japan so that the cast could get to know each other a bit, we could read the play together, talk though some of the problems and generally speaking get ourselves in a tizz before we set off into the unknown. In the absence of our director, David Hunt would be in the chair, and a visit from Cicely Berry, the official voice coach (and the lady whose flat I used to clean when I was out of work), was promised. She had done a studio production of the play, I think, for the RSC and saw herself as something of an authority. Some actors had done a lot of preparation, others surprisingly, if not shockingly, very little. David wanted to discuss the Christian message of *Lear*, tied up in a pagan theme. I kept out of the discussion as I was sure that Ninagawa would have his own ideas.

Cicely Berry must have got wind that we were to read through the play on our second day so, armed with a great sheath of papers which turned out to be photocopies of a Shakespearean sonnet, she marched in, scattering them about the floor like a farmer distributing seed. Used to this kind of procedure, the actors obediently scooped them up and she invited us to read through the sonnet, each actor entrusted with one line. That achieved, we sat down to read the play. Miss Berry sat next to me, which was a bit unnerving to say the least. David Hunt made a short introductory speech during which Miss Berry turned to me and announced with authority in a loud stage whisper, 'Lear is a Marxist play.' At the end of the reading all she said was, 'There's too much to be done before I can make any comment,' gathered up her paraphernalia and was consumed by the labyrinth we all know as the Barbican. We didn't see her again.

The flight to Japan is a long one, and I have since suspected that my enforced sedentary position over such a lengthy period was the harbinger of the deep-vein thrombosis which clotted my arteries and later led to so many of my health problems.

Japan looked to the newcomer like a large number of cities seamlessly joined together. There seemed to be no demarcation. The sub-tropical temperatures we'd been alerted to seemed to have slackened a bit although we had a lot of steamy rain, but I loved the area of Ikibukuro where we were staying. The girls were as pretty as dolls, and in their anxiety to avoid looking identical they dressed themselves in skimpy frocks, wore massive, clumpy moon-boots, painted their faces, dyed their hair orange, and remained as alike as peas in a pod. The streets were spotless, the food rather hard to identify, even though large glass cases of brightly-coloured plaster replicas of the dishes you could order (with the prices attached) were on display to entice you as you entered the restaurant. My not eating meat proved less difficult than I had feared; besides, there were vast supermarkets – reputedly the largest in the world – within a short walking distance, where you could buy virtually anything you wanted. Counter after counter of pre-cooked delicacies beautifully presented were on display, and there could be no arguments about lack of variety. I'm ashamed to say I was provided with a limousine (and it would have been very insulting had I ignored this courtesy). We all gathered on the first day in one of the vast rehearsals rooms for the first of many receptions.

The Japanese are fond of making protracted speeches, which take twice as long when they have to be repeated in another language. It seemed that everyone had to put in a word. Jokes, if they were in Japanese, lost a bit in translation, but there was a huge turnout. The entire crew, the assistants and representatives of the various departments, wigs, make-up, publicity, sound, music. Everybody, without exception, was dressed in black. Then, the speeches over, Ninagawa, our director, invited us all to come and look at the theatre. The massive procession – rather more Japanese than British – followed him down a very long linoleum corridor at the end of which were some doors which, with a proud flourish, he flung open.

I don't think I've ever been more shocked in my life. The monumental set with its sharply raked floor was already in place fully painted, while a team of black-uniformed experts were busy focusing the lights. The crew, resembling a swarm of insects for they, too, were all wearing black, scrambled across the ramp on to the stage, showing us all what a huge space we had in which to work. Backstage there were racks of practice clothes, swords, bows and arrows, spears, carcases of wild animals for the hunting scene, various items of furniture including a throne, cloaks for disguises – in fact it was almost as if the Japanese were saying, 'All right. You are members of the Royal Shakespeare Company over here to perform *King Lear*. We have invested one and a half million pounds in the venture. You're standing on the set, our crew is here to provide you with everything you could possibly need for the performance. Off you go! And good luck!' There's no doubt about it – it was daunting.

Ninagawa wasn't a great one for giving direction; in fact for the whole time I worked on the play he gave me not one single note. Having trained as an artist, he enjoyed tinkering with the sets, the props and the lights. He was like an opera director. My finished performance as the King was supposed to have travelled with me from London in my luggage. He was only there to make it look good. One word came instantly to mind – 'HELP!'

But the help that I sought wasn't forthcoming. David Hunt, the extremely likeable assistant from the RSC, had a good mind and was well informed over textual matters, yet less clued up when it came to interpretation. Every time I went to him with a problem about the King's emotional state he couldn't enlighten me, all he could do was explain the meaning of the text. There was no doubt about it, from this moment on I was on my own and I'd just have to get used to it. The first problem was with the company and I could understand why. Because I was playing Lear I was being given special treatment, like the courtesy car and a dressing room on my own. I spoke to Thelma about it, saying I'd far rather muck in, go with the others by train, but she knew the Japanese and that they would be offended. I don't really know whether I was popular or unpopular with the company at this stage. I suspect the latter. I knew a few of them, like my old friend Christopher Benjamin who was playing Kent and who had been with me in the stage version of *The Clandestine Marriage*, Michael Maloney who was Edgar and John Carlisle who was playing Gloucester, but that was all.

The difficult first scene was upon us. One of the daughters refused point blank to curtsey when I entered as the King. She said she had no intention of being 'subservient', so a lot of time was wasted in argument and indecision as there was no one in charge, and I was aware of whispering in corners. My problems, instead of easing, were becoming more acute. In an effort to follow through my reasoning for the King's behaviour towards Cordelia, I had not only the other actors to persuade, but the director, who seemed perfectly satisfied with whatever I put before him. It was as though he'd been told, 'Just keep the King happy and everything will be fine.' However, any suggestion I made about the approach to a scene was viewed with suspicion by my fellow actors, for they believed the ideas should be coming not from me but from the director. But I could see very clearly that if we didn't make some sort of start on our own, we were never going to get anywhere.

For the King to behave in an uncharacteristic way, signalling the approach of Alzheimer's as we now know it, the cast would have to respond accordingly – it was essential to me that they cooperate by looking disconcerted. If I was going to follow through my plan, I needed help. It's an old tradition of the theatre. I could protest that I was playing the King until I was blue in the face, but until someone bowed to me (or curtsied) nobody would believe me. And so it went on. I had learnt the part before coming so never had to worry about the lines, which meant that if there was time to spare, I could spend it on how I was hoping to carry through my theory on the King. I don't believe that I've ever worked so hard or under such stressful conditions in my life.

By the end of the second week, the ice was beginning to thaw, although there would remain pockets of resistance some of which would never be breached. I expect the company thought me stand-offish when I didn't go with them to the Kabuki, take excursions or go out to dinner, but the responsibility of the situation had got to me, and I spent all my free time working in my room. I had no option. There was so much at stake. Sanada, the Japanese actor who was cast as the Fool, was doing sterling work, but he too needed help. His English was poor and sometimes it was difficult to follow what he was saying. He was quite the nicest, most generous actor I'd ever worked with and the company liked and respected him enormously. He was working as hard as anybody; indeed his whole attitude was inspiring.

The RSC sent one of the casting department to come and see a preview. To my horror she had a journalist in tow, who not only checked in to the same hotel as the actors but appeared in our Green Room the following morning, and was then allowed to watch a rehearsal. I was extremely angry about this as, not only had I not been consulted, but discontented actors are quite happy to unburden their souls, and I was worried that any bad pre-publicity in the London papers wouldn't be much help to us. Happily, he was an extremely nice man and wrote with sympathy about his flying visit to Japan. But it could have gone the other way.

We were sent a voice coach who was a delight and very helpful, though her stay was all too brief. Also one of the RSC producers, who shall be nameless, flew in and came to a performance. Whether she liked what she saw or not, she should have had the courtesy to come and see me afterwards, it's accepted theatre practice – although I noticed her hovering in the backstage area before she went out to dinner. Courtesy is constantly used by the Japanese, but we English seem to find the need for it less and less. Things were getting tense. The opening night was upon us. We needed all the support we could get. On her return to the hotel later, the nameless producer would find a curt note from me in her key box saying simply, 'Are you naturally bad-mannered, or is this just RSC policy?' I had become angered by the lack of support we were getting from them – we were, after all, appearing under their banner – and this anxiety was adding to my problems rather than easing them.

The play opened to an ecstatic reception, but I wasn't allowing myself to be fooled that it would be the same in London. We were floundering about rather like a ship without a rudder, and there was still a great deal of work to be done. There was no time to be sitting back on our heels. I was passionate in my determination that we would get it right in the end.

The artistic director of the RSC, Adrian Noble, whom I have known for some years, flew in for two days. On the evening of his second day, he came to see the show, gave me three wonderful notes for which I was immensely grateful, but as a source of guidance he was less useful than I had hoped, as the length of his stay was so limited. The notes he gave me were unspecific, but very much in tune with the way I had conceived the role. They were very simple. 'In the first scene,' he told me, 'don't move around. Show your authority. Make them do what you want them to do.' In the scene on Dover beach, 'Don't stand over Gloucester, go and sit next to him. Don't be afraid to put your arm round him.' It's such a simple adjustment but it turned the scene into one of the best in the play. He was in my dressing room for less than five minutes but I felt heartened and invigorated. Suddenly, he too was gone. It was beginning to look as though the RSC had no time to hang around, and that what we were doing wasn't of sufficient significance to persuade them to stay. We felt they were deserting a sinking ship.

Next, it was Trevor's turn. A thoughtful man at all times, he hadn't liked to come earlier for fear of being in the way. Never having been to Japan, he was very excited by the prospect of spending some time there seeing the sights, though his reaction to the show was alarming. Trevor has a wonderful instinct. I may complain sometimes that his criticism of things I do is undermining me, but he's usually right and through the years I've learnt to acknowledge this and listen to what he has to say. His comments on this occasion concerned me deeply.

He was worried about the lack of cohesion, feeling that some of the cast were doing their own thing instead of working as a team, felt that I was straining and shouting, probably through insecurity, trying too hard, and had to establish myself as the leading man, not just a good company member. In other words, play the King. I'm lucky in that I can change very quickly. When Trevor came to the play the following night, he was astonished at the difference. By taking the initiative in the first scene, the rest of the play seemed to slot into place and the other members of the company, for the first time, knew where they were. I had always suspected that the first scene would be my Waterloo, but once I had been told to take my time, to set myself apart, everything changed.

Also, it helped immeasurably with my concept of Alzheimer's. I found moments where I could legitimately pause, as though I'd forgotten what I was about to say, hesitate over people's names, have the sudden squally rages subside as quickly as they'd arrive. The way for me to play Lear was, as I'd suspected, not as a ranting old tyrant, but a perfectly likeable and respected though volatile old man who loved Cordelia and she him, whom Kent venerated and loved so much that, having been banished on pain of death, he would return in a dangerously penetrable disguise to continue to serve his master, and whose life would be saved by Gloucester, blinded for his pains. This was surely no despised tyrant and I could find nothing in the text to convince me that he was.

What about the storm scene, then? Given the terrifying image of huge rocks crashing to the stage all around us – hurling against the scenery, sometimes rolling into the audience – augmented by wind, rain, lightning and thunder effects as well as music, nobody could claim that Ninagawa had presented the actors with an easy ride. He was adamant that the falling rocks remain a feature and constantly resisted any appeal from the actors that they were dangerous and would land at irregular times, making it difficult to accommodate the lines. I even went so far as to suggest they be cut, but the only concession Ninagawa would make was to reduce the number. Feeling that we could lose another half dozen without missing them, I suggested it but to no avail. Fortunately, Shakespeare didn't want the actor playing Lear to drown out the storm. In fact, in the previous scene with Kent, as the storm clouds are gathering, he gives a line to 'A Gentleman', who reports that Lear 'Strives in his little world of man to outscorn / the to and fro conflicting wind and rain'. He's in his eighties. All he can do in his impotent frustration is to wave his pathetic old fists at the elements. 'Strives' – he doesn't succeed. That's what is so wonderful about the scene. Man's battles with the elements, with his health and the increasing restrictions imposed by his age, make it a scene not about power but the fact that, however hard we try, nature will always reign supreme. Man is insignificant by comparison.

Our Japanese visit had been enjoyable and we'd grown fond of Tokyo, but our season at Saitama was winding down. There were many more official speeches to endure but also happy memories of visits to the flea markets where second-hand kimonos could be bought for a song, the temples, to Kyoto on the amazing 'bullet' train, the warmth and generosity, the courtesy of the Japanese people – these we will never forget, but regretfully, it was time to pack.

My dressing room at the Barbican was, I believe, one of the few with a window. I looked out on to the steep ramp which led to the car park. It was noticeable how different attitudes were back in London. In Tokyo, nothing was too much trouble. Here, there was a take it or leave it feel to the place. The personal touch to which we had become accustomed belonged to the past and had been replaced by doing the job for the money, not because of any affection for it. We certainly knew we were back in London. On the stage the noise level was louder by several decibels and authority was low on the list of priorities. It was heartening to know that, although it was late autumn and we were playing every night, the theatre was sold out for the run and only standing room was available.

The opening night was a catastrophe, one of the most wretched of my life. It wasn't as though things had gone wrong technically, but there was a sinister feeling in the air that the critics hadn't liked it – to put it mildly. The next morning, at our home in the country, the bell on the gate kept ringing. It turned out to be a journalist wanting to know my reaction to the bad reviews. I don't ever read them. Trevor asked her if she was a sadist. She looked, he said, a little bewildered. But there was a feeling of despair at hearing that this had been the critical response, and it was heightened when, on arrival at the Barbican for the evening performance, I was smuggled in through a side entrance to avoid the journalists. The phone had been ringing all day, well-meaning friends rallying on my behalf and totally unaware that they were, in fact, making things worse, so I was left in no doubt that my time had indeed come and that, by all accounts, they had gone for the throat. It was heartbreaking after all that work to hear that I'd been ridiculed, and the production mauled. Friends were hugely angry on my behalf. The Sundays were more favourable, the *Sunday Times* ecstatic, but the reaction of the dailies still hurt like a deep knife wound, and I shall never be able to erase it from my mind. I fully understand that one of the hazards of the job is critical abuse. We stand up on that stage to be treated as they think fit and we have no redress. The press will always have the last word.

Adrian Noble had popped in on the second night to give moral support – 'Don't change anything' – but as far as the rest of the RSC was concerned, we were a write-off – a company of pariahs. I don't think I'd ever felt quite so lonely in my life. But there was no time for dwelling on how it might have been better, no time for self-pity. I had to rally the troops, and they were magnificent . . . Perhaps they had come to understand what I had been aiming for during the rehearsal period. It wasn't just I who went down with the ship, we all did, and yet, something quite astonishing was happening. With the sort of reviews which I'd had reported to me, you would have thought the theatre would have emptied and that there'd be queues of indignant patrons demanding their money back. Quite the reverse. You couldn't get a seat for love nor money, they were standing right across the back of the stalls, and, at the curtain calls, they were cheering themselves hoarse. Letters started to pour in. I've kept a lot of them because they said things I needed to hear: 'the first time I've understood the play', 'the first time I've been moved'. The packed houses and the deluge of 'the press got it wrong' letters were my reward.

Christmas and the millennium both came and went and suddenly I was playing Stratford for the first and last time in my life. Once again, that huge theatre was sold out every performance, once again they cheered, once again the letters poured in. Though this was wonderfully encouraging, still the memory of how we'd been treated in London refused to go away. On our opening night in Stratford, not a single representative from the RSC was present and, when the Japanese came over in force – all their technical experts, the director, the composer, the designers – the RSC announced a party in the rehearsal room. It was so humiliating to watch them being served warm sparkling wine and pretzels that the cast had a whip-round and took them all out to dinner the following evening. There was a great spirit of unity about the *Lear* company, and a lot of the credit must go to Thelma Holt, who knows more about how to maintain a company than the RSC will in a month of Sundays. To add to this catalogue of criticism, since my operation in June 2000, the front of house manager at the Barbican has been the only member of the administration thoughtful enough to send me a message of good will. It's as though I'd never worked for them.

I have been harsh about the RSC because I believe they deserve it. I know that currently they're having problems and that there's a lot of bad feeling, but one thing is clear. They don't know how to behave towards the people they employ. As an actor, I have been horrified by their arrogance and their lack of support. In our case, the Japanese had invested one and a half million pounds in *King Lear* – the RSC did very nicely, thank you, out of all our full houses. They chose to ignore how they came by the windfall and to treat our Japanese colleagues as something of an embarrassment, even a nuisance, much like their attitude to the actors. On our last performance, as the quantities of sweetly-smelling spring flowers were sprinkled from the flies, supplied not by the RSC but by Thelma Holt, and there was an air of celebration and achievement, I could feel only sadness. Fifty years as an actor and what should have been something special had been sullied. I was left with a nasty taste in my mouth and feeling grateful that, if theatre had disintegrated into this sort of heartlessness, I was no longer part of it.

I had no intention when I set out on this book to slam the press, the RSC or, indeed, arrive at the end of it with even the slightest trace of bitterness. When I embarked on it, it was with a spirit of fun, even if my intention was to sprinkle it with a few samples of straightforward honesty. I'm not by nature a bitter or vindictive person but I do get angry at injustice. Also, I try to see the other point of view. I might not have come up to expectations when I played King Lear, regardless of the enthusiastic reception from the public. Not having read what the press said when they slammed me, it's a little hard to argue with them, a little hard to make a case. One thing illness teaches you is what your priorities are. Ultimately, King Lear is only a part in a play. Though I have to confess, the critics' bile at the time was hurtful and I probably magnified it out of all proportion. That's because it was my job, about which I care very deeply, an important job too, playing King Lear in Shakespeare's home town over the millennium and the play in which I would retire from the theatre. All that. Yet, unlike my physical condition, it wasn't life-threatening. The pain it brought was wounded pride for which no pills are required.

If my interpretation was faulty to those first night scribblers, I can only say that the performance was carefully considered and I believed that even if the way I had chosen to see this old man may perhaps have been different to the norm, it was consistent and truthful and I knew what I was doing. There is nobody to blame because nothing wrong – nothing 'faulty' – was done. If Ninagawa was lacking in giving me the help I was craving, well – I've acted for over fifty years and if I couldn't cope with making a few decisions of my own, then perhaps I should have learnt to drive a car earlier than I did and stuck to motor insurance. It might have made my father a happier man.

But I'm a typical Aries, headstrong and impulsive, and I wouldn't have had my life any other way. Despite the setbacks, the loneliness, the unemployment and the instances of harsh, even unjustified criticism, I've had some glorious times, most of which took me completely by surprise, which have allowed Trevor and myself – we go together like brothers – a measure of independence and financial stability we wouldn't otherwise have had. We'll never be rich. Money never was a priority, but we have a watertight relationship which, in a squabbling world, is worth its weight in gold. I didn't ever believe I would have such happiness in my life. I imagined it would all be much of the same – swimming, gulping in the sunshine, climbing my beloved Table Mountain, finding work where I could until slowly but inevitably I disintegrated into senility – or whatever fate the gods had in store . . .

At the moment, and for the past eighteen months, it has been cancer. It came late and cast a blight on Trevor's and my life. Cancer's a great spoilsport. And it hasn't been easy because of the location of the tumour and the effect it has had on the rest of my body. So things aren't straightforward, they keep going wrong. Just when I think I'm starting to get better, put on a bit more weight, along comes an uninvited gremlin – jaundice, pneumonia, fluid on the lung – and everything is held up once again. A flip through the book will indicate that I am a fighter and fighting back is what I'm doing. With Trevor by me, I know I will be cared for and guided through every step of the frightening unknown.

Last November, I had one of my better periods. The treatment was working so I was encouraged to take a job. It was for television. The BBC were doing *Victoria and Albert*, a two part series, and I played Lord Melbourne. It was so enjoyable I was prepared to try it again. In the New Year, Whoopi Goldberg was producing a Christmas special called *Call Me Claus* –

would I play Santa? Certainly. Whoopi is a wonderful actress and two months' work in a TV studio while staying in Santa Monica would probably do me the world of good. I explained that I'd lost a lot of weight, but I was assured that I'd be padded and bearded, so off I went. And then the pain came back. I did the whole shoot with the only sort of painkillers I thought my doctors back in England would allow me, didn't miss a day's work, got on extremely well with my leading lady and the film broke all sorts of viewing records in the States this Christmas. Then I came back to face the chemotherapy.

So, whatever the future holds, I acknowledge that I've been very lucky. There was a black moment when we were 'outed' just before the Oscars back in 1994. We both believed the world would be looking at us with disgust and that our lives had been irrevocably changed. Things did change – but for the better. We no longer felt the need to pretend. The 'Straight Face' we'd worn through the years was no longer necessary. Everybody knew. We'd been liberated. Life would never be quite the same again, but then, if it were, what a very dull place the world would be.

Epilogue

by Trevor Bentham

Nigel died at home in Hertfordshire at 9.30 a.m. on Boxing Day 2001. Whilst I had rushed downstairs to phone the doctor, he had tried to make his way from the bathroom to the bed – and, unable to breathe, collapsed into a chair and simply ceased to live. The cancer that had plagued his pancreas for eighteen months had recently moved to his lungs and finished the job quickly – and, I am forced to admit, with the greatest dignity. No trace of panic; a quiet end in a shaft of winter sunlight.

When Rowena Webb of Hodder & Stoughton approached Nigel to write this autobiography he was about to embark on *King Lear*. That – combined with a galloping reluctance to talk about himself – kept him stalling for weeks. Only the onset of cancer provided the catalyst he needed to put pen to paper – or eventually type into laptop. Suddenly there was a purpose for writing; a fearful deadline he fought so hard to meet. Through major surgery, radiotherapy, chemotherapy, jaundice, pneumonia and septicaemia, he wrote on, clinging to the best lifeline that he could have been thrown under the circumstances. He finished the last chapter in hospital the week before Christmas, checked it through when he got home, and sent it off to Rowena on Christmas Eve – two days before he died.

We had agreed before he started to write that I would have no part in the process. This was to be utterly his story, without help or hindrance from anyone. I was not to read a word until the book was finished in case any misplaced criticism should dent his enthusiasm. Of course then I had no idea that the first time I should set eyes on these pages would be after his death. In the circumstances, this could have been traumatic – but turned out to be enormously comforting. To travel through Nigel's life from the beginning, through old familiar and utterly new territory, brought him back in a way that nothing else could ever hope to match, a rare act of 'mediumship' for which I will always be grateful.

Living with Nigel was certainly not dull. He used to ask me anxiously, 'Am I eccentric?' and I would nod obediently as he knew I would. Nobody I ever met had such maverick energy. His head was constantly filled with ideas – sometimes wonderful, sometimes outlandish, frequently contradictory. In many ways his whole life was a paradox: he was a conservative socialist, an agnostic Christian, a heterosexual homosexual, a man with prodigious skills on stage and in front of the camera who would nonetheless spend half-an-hour assembling a deckchair to have it collapse beneath him when he sat on it. He hated being bored. Worse, he hated others being bored and would plague them into reluctant amusement. It was frankly easier to give in – as I discovered early in our relationship – and let him do the entertaining or the educating. He always said that he would have loved to have been a father, but I can't help wondering at the state of a child of his by the time he or she reached adulthood. They would have ignored his enthusiasm at their peril!

If this sounds carping, it's not meant to. In life I was the tortoise and he was the hare, always rushing back to check that I was still there, dragging a smile from my sighing lips. And humour – God bless that humour. He invented a shorthand – one word usually – that never failed to make me laugh. 'Bandy', he'd say as we walk behind a fat dog. 'Tiny', the length of a skirt or the height of a tall man. Not unkind, just a shared moment of mischief. He would protest a love of privacy and a dislike of parties, and would then appear astonished to find how entertaining people could be and how much he enjoyed their company. Fiercely loyal to those he liked and deeply wary of those he didn't, he would sometimes find the change from one emotion to another almost comically troubling. Bruce, his long-term 'companion' – for want of a better word – tied him up in knots of guilt, frustration, anger and a sort of love that lasted for decades until Bruce's death. His own father both frustrated and fascinated him, based, I think, on a longing to be liked and approved, a real need for affection.

We hardly ever rowed. We'd sulk for possibly twenty minutes, then start teasing each other back to a truce. But with others, occasional black moods would descend that no amount of diplomacy could shift. It made him sometimes difficult to work with. 'A bit of an old fusspot', Jane Lapotaire once described him with charming accuracy. His standards were unnervingly high and quite unpredictable, both at work and at home. You had to keep on your toes to second-guess his moods or his motives. But, oh boy, did he give back! Anyone who ever had his undivided attention – and so many did – will never forget the intensity of his interest, the warmth of his affection. Even people met only once while walking the dogs felt that they had found a lifelong friend in a few short pleasantries.

He enjoyed jokes against himself. Beneath the sure exterior beat the barmy heart of Monsieur Hulot. Listening to Nigel trying to open a container of Nurofen would produce tears of joy, as did the beach umbrella slowly closing around him without his noticing. He once caused havoc by disappearing on holiday. Search parties roamed the hotel complex until he was discovered hours later having a very pleasant sleep after raiding a minibar in someone else's identical room. In Egypt he attracted a large audience at the Luxor Museum, convincingly lecturing on hieroglyphics, based entirely on a pamphlet for children he'd found at the entrance. Wherever he went, anecdotes followed and a great deal of laughter.

Directors had a problem with him. His brain would work so prodigiously that he would come up with dozens of interpretations – each as valid as the next – leaving the poor person to resolve which one would work best. When he was rehearsing *The Madness Of George III* at the National Theatre for Nicholas Hytner, his catchphrase of 'Nick – I've got an idea . . .' even made it on to a T-shirt.

And yet he never short-changed an audience. They got the very best from him at each performance. In trying to analyse the astonishing loyalty of his colossal following, at least some of it came from an understanding by the public that they would get one hundred per cent commitment, an unwritten pledge that made them eager to watch him – a real feeling of event. It stood him in good stead during *King Lear* when, despite the vitriol heaped on him by some critics, the audiences quite simply understood something the reviewers didn't, which was that for many the play was made comprehensible for the first time.

Nigel's grandmother Mrs Rice was a fine painter, and really this is where his truly remarkable talent originated. He was fiercely intelligent, but gifted with a painterly skill rather than intellect. Instinct governed his latter years: he could 'smell' his way into a part and give it a living, breathing reality; unchoreographed, unpredictable and always dynamic.

To have known him was a joy. To have shared my life with him was exhilarating. I hope there is an afterlife so he will have been aware of the shock caused by his death and the massive love that came – still comes – to act as comfort for the sadly missing years.

Trevor Bentham
Hertfordshire, 2002

Index

Photographic Acknowledgements

© Alex Bailey: 13 above left, 14 below. © BBC: 9 below. Charles Bird, Durban: 5 above. Crossberg Studio, Johannesburg: 5 centre left. Srdja Djukanovic © Telegraph Group Ltd: 10 above. © Zoe Dominic: 7 below, 8 above right, 9 above. The Samuel Goldwyn Company © 1995: 13 above right. Havering Press Agency, Romford: 8 above left. Helmut Herz, Cape Town: 3 centre. Hank Kranzler: 7 above. Landseer, London: 3 below. © Gemma Levine: 11 above. Coen. C. Oosthuysen, Johannesburg: 5 below right. Personal Collection: 1, 2, 3 above left, 4, 5 below left, 6 above left and right, 8 below, 11 below, 12 above left and right, 13 below, 14 above, 15. Rafael, London: 6 below. © Ken Reynolds 1999: 16. © Eric Thompson: 10 below. Warner Brothers: 12 below.

Every reasonable effort has been made to contact the copyright holders, but should there be any errors or omissions, Hodder & Stoughton would be pleased to insert the appropriate acknowledgements in any subsequent printing of this publication.